An Insight into Mergers and Acquisitions

Vinod Kumar · Priti Sharma

An Insight into Mergers and Acquisitions

A Growth Perspective

Ane Books
Pvt. Ltd.

palgrave
macmillan

Vinod Kumar
SGND Khalsa College
University of Delhi
New Delhi, Delhi, India

Priti Sharma
Institute of Management Technology,
Centre for Distance Learning
Ghaziabad, Uttar Pradesh, India

ISBN 978-981-13-5828-9   ISBN 978-981-13-5829-6   (eBook)
https://doi.org/10.1007/978-981-13-5829-6

The print edition is not for sale in India, Pakistan, Sri Lanka, Bangladesh, Nepal and
Bhutan. Customers from India, Pakistan, Sri Lanka, Bangladesh, Nepal and Bhutan please
order the print book from: Athena Academic/Ane Books.

Cover credit: Image—fotyma/iStock/Getty Images Plus
Cover design by Tjaša Krivec

This Palgrave Macmillan imprint is published by the registered company Springer Nature
Singapore Pte Ltd.
The registered company address is: 152 Beach Road, #21-01/04 Gateway East, Singapore
189721, Singapore

PREFACE

This book provides an insight into the phenomenon of mergers and acquisitions inter alia, various other forms of corporate restructuring. It highlights the importance of M&A as a strategy for faster growth for corporate. The book provides detailed description of process, deal structuring and financing of mergers and acquisitions. Reader will gain an in-depth understanding of the art of valuation from M&A perspective. Book also provides the broader perspective of accounting and regulatory aspects of M&A.

Manuscript sufficiently covers the conceptual underpinnings of M&A and supplements it with substantial number of real-life examples on each sub-topic. Various numerical examples shall further help in assimilation of the knowledge of M&A activity. The judicious blend of theory and practical aspects through numerical as well as real-life case studies make the book an interesting reading. Hence, the book becomes a source of vast knowledge in the highly complicated and dynamic world of M&A.

Book will be useful for the students pursuing the management education, commerce graduates and postgraduates who are willing to make a career in the field of financial services, investment banking, and merger and acquisition consultancies. Book will also be helpful for the practicing managers in the field of corporate finance, strategy formulation, and implementation.

Book can serve as the corporate training module for the entry- and middle-level managers working in the field of corporate finance, management consultancies, and deal strategists in investment banking.

Following features make the book a unique read for the targeted audience:

(a) Detailed real-life valuation case studies.
(b) Inclusion of latest accounting and regulatory aspects more specifically INDAS (IFRS) for M&A and provisions of New Companies Act (2013) in India.
(c) Affluence of real-life examples at relevant places. For example, in case of deal structuring numerous examples are included to explain each structure in detail while regulatory insights are explained with suitable overview of M&A documentations of past few deals.
(d) Inclusion of reasonable numerical examples to strengthen the understanding of the subject.

New Delhi, India   Vinod Kumar
Ghaziabad, India   Priti Sharma

Acknowledgements

We express our sincere thanks to all those who have supported in the completion of the book and making it an insightful read for all those who have their interest in fascinating but complicated world of mergers and acquisitions. We are extremely grateful to Principal SGND KHALSA College, Delhi University and Dr. S. R. Musanna, Dean IMT CDL for their continuous support and encouragement.

We would like to acknowledge the contributions made by our student Mr. Santhana Gopalakrishnan—MBA (Financial Analysis). He has actively worked on case studies incorporated in the book. His serious involvement right from the very beginning to final typesetting of the book is highly commendable. The completion of the book without his contributions would have been a far cry.

We would like to express our sincere thanks to ICoFP, New Delhi, Mr. Sanjeev Bajaj and Ms. Jai Vani Bajaj for providing us the opportunity to work closely with the industry and aspiring financial analysts and investment banking professionals which helped us a lot while working on the book.

We are thankful to Dr. Mohd. Khalid Azam (Aligarh Muslim University) and Dr. Asif Akhtar (Aligarh Muslim University) for providing great motivation and support.

We are thankful to all the colleagues, friends, and students for their continuous support while working on the book.

Special thanks to Sh. T. D. Sethi (Law Faculty Delhi), Dr. K. K. Bajaj, Mr. Rajiv Bajaj, Sanjeev Bajaj and Mr. Anil Chopra (BAJAJ CAPITAL),

Dr. Vinay Dutta and Dr. Ambrish (Fore School of Management), Dr. Suresh Aggarwal (MBE, South Delhi Campus), Dr. Kavita Sharma (DSE), Dr. Madhu Vij (FMS), Dr. J. K. Goyal (JIMS), Dr. G. C. Sharma (NSE), Mr. Pullock Bhatacharjee (BSE), Dr. Ahindra Chakarborty (GREAT LAKE), Ruchi Arora (NDIM), Dr. Sanjay Jain (DSE), Dr. Rachna Jawa (SRCC), Prof. Y. P. Singh, Dr. Vanita Tripathi (DSE), Dr. Raj Nangia (Lakshmi Bai College), Ms. Suganda (JIMS), Dr. Mahesh Madan, Dr. G. S. Sood, Dr. Vineet Kapur, Dr. Neeta Dhingra, Ms. Silky Jain, Dr. Manmeet Kaur, Dr. D. S. Sharma and G. K. Arora (SGND), Dr. Mani Arul Nandi and Dr. Rekha Dayal (JMC), Dr. Naina Hasija and Ms. Sonia Kamboj (Kalindi), Dr. Alka Harneja, Dr. Purnima, Ms. Neelam, Ms. Neha Kashyap (LBC). Dr. K. L. Dahiya (SOL), Dr. Saklani, Dr. P. K. Khurana and Dr. Suneel Kumar (Bhagat Singh), Dr. Sushma Arora (DRC), Dr. Sarita Sachdeva (IP), Mr. Amit Gupta and Mr. Manish Gupta (JIMS), Mr. R. C. Garg (RDIMS), Anand Sharma (Haryana University), Ms. Bimal Deep Kaur (GGS), Dr. S. B. Rathore (Shyam Lal), Dr. Keshav Gupta, Dr. Prabhat Mittal and Dr. Bhuvnish Grover (Satyawati), Shri Mala Jain (KNC), Dr. Ravi Gupta, Ms. Ritika Ahuja, R. P. Rustagi and Dr. Ashok Sehgal (SRCC) and Dr. Amit Kumar Singh (DSE), Dr. Bharat Bhushan and Ritika Seth (Hansraj), Dr. Hemant Porwal and Dr. Kumar Bijoy (SSBS), Dr. Satish Bhatia (CVS), Dr. Vibha Jain (JDM).

The book could not have been completed and taken the present shape without the great support of Neena Arora who was kind enough to spare the time for editing the manuscripts with valuable comments. Kiran Negi helped me in typesetting and in proofreading the manuscripts. Girish Sardana, Sujata Sardana, Sunayna Kawatra, Girish Chander Chugh, Dinesh Arora, Kartik Arora, Rahul Chugh Astha Chugh, Kanika Chugh, and Varun Chugh were always available to support me in my present work.

We shall be failing in our duty if we don't express our sincere thanks to our family members Veena Kumar, Dr. Kanika Taneja, Abhishek Taneja, Dr. Surinder Taneja, Dr. Anurag Taneja, Ms. Garima Looned, Mr. Manoj Sharma, Ms. Riddhi Sharma, Mr. M. R. Sharma, Mr. K. K. Gupta, and Ms. Shashi Gupta for their continuous support in all forms while working on the book.

We are extremely grateful to the staff of SGND College and Rattan Tata library for making available necessary material and facilities. Last but not least, we are thankful to the publisher Palgrave Macmillan for bringing out the publication in time.

Dr. Vinod Kumar
Dr. Priti Sharma

CONTENTS

About the Authors

Dr. Vinod Kumar is M.Com. M.Phil., Ph.D. DBF (ICFAI), AFP (FPSB). He is NSE certified for capital markets' dealers, derivatives, mutual funds, and commodity market modules. He is merit scholarship holder and gold medalist from Delhi School of Economics, Delhi University for his postgraduation. He is an alumnus of Shri Ram College of Commerce. He has teaching experience of 40 years teaching graduate and postgraduate classes in Delhi University and many of the management institutes of repute. He was dean and director of International College of Financial Planning for a period of 2 years. He presented research papers at various national and international universities on financial markets, derivative markets, commodity markets, and financial planning, etc. He got an award of best paper in Chartered Accountant on reported earnings. He has been conducting workshops for FPSB, NSE, BSE, ICFP, BNP PARIBAS, and BAJAJ CAPITAL on various subjects of financial markets. He is the founder editor of the investors' India magazine of Bajaj Capital. He is also an associate of IIAS, Shimla. He was the coordinator for Ministry of HRD Project, EPG—Pathshala for financial markets and institutions. He was awarded a major project of UGC for commodity and currency markets interrelationships which were submitted in 2013. Dr. Vinod Kumar is the associate professor at SGND Khalsa College, Delhi University. He teaches at Faculty of Management Studies (FMS), Delhi University, National Stock Exchange (NSE), American Academy of Financial Management (AAFM), JIMS, and Bharti Vidhyapeeth and Great Lake Institute of Management as guest faculty.

Dr. Priti Sharma is an astute researcher, trainer, and academician. She is currently associated with IMT CDL Ghaziabad as Asst. Professor (Finance). She has more than two decades of experience in the field of financial teaching, training and practice. Since the year 2000, she has imparted financial education and training to several students and finance professionals. She has been associated with various educational institutes of repute like ICFAI, NSE Ltd., BSE Ltd., ICoFP New Delhi-A Bajaj Capital Group organization, etc. She has been actively involved in content development of MOOCs for Financial Institutions and Markets course under Ministry of HRD Project in India, EPG Pathshala. She has worked with Flex Industries Ltd., Noida in corporate finance division during the period 1997–2000.

She completed her doctorate in the area of mergers and acquisitions from Aligarh University (AMU). She is a UGC NET certified academician. Her financial research papers are published in UGC recognized journals. She has presented papers in National and International Conferences. Her paper won the Best Paper Award in National Research Conference organized by AIMA, New Delhi in the year 2009. She was awarded as Best Finance Faculty at ICoFP New Delhi in the year 2015.

LIST OF FIGURES

LIST OF TABLES

CHAPTER 1

Introduction to Merger, Acquisition, and Corporate Restructuring

1.1 INTRODUCTION

Growth is the objective of almost all the organizations, whether big or small. Organizations can grow by using a strategy of internal growth of expansion or diversification known as greenfield expansion. Organic growth is where a company builds its own infrastructure and sets up its own manufacturing, distribution, and selling networks or building an ecosystem, internally, without impacting the corporate structure or the business model of its own. For decades, this has been a major strategy followed by most of the corporate all over the world including India. M&A is a route to achieve exponential growth rather than a linear and slower growth. M&As have become an integral part of the Indian economy and daily business headlines.

When Relaxo Footwears sets up its own manufacturing plant and enhances its distribution network to expand its reach and cater to a wider customer base, it is greenfield expansion. But when Coca-Cola enhances its presence in a country by partnering with local manufacturers through franchising and by acquiring an established brand like "Thums Up", it is inorganic growth. So inorganic growth is a typical way to climb a ladder multi-foot, by way of strategic tie-ups, mergers and acquisitions, where an entity tries to expand its business with the help of the others.

Basically, the projects which have to be build up from scratch are called greenfield projects while the projects which are established by using an existing facility or upgrading or modifying it are called

© The Author(s) 2019
V. Kumar and P. Sharma, *An Insight into Mergers and Acquisitions*,
https://doi.org/10.1007/978-981-13-5829-6_1

brownfield projects. For example, in 2010, Fortis Hospitals acquired assets of Wockhardt Hospitals, which included eight operational hospitals and two semi-constructed hospitals. This is an example of one of the largest acquisitions/brownfield project in the Indian healthcare sector. The expansion of Reliance's exploration project in KG-D6 basin is an example of greenfield project. The route of organic expansion or growth is a time-consuming process and also involves the risk of a competitor taking the lead during the time of completion of expansion. Another risk of taking this route is that the economic momentum envisaged in the segment may slow down by the time the planned expansion is actually completed. The other route to growth is an inorganic one through mergers and acquisitions. This route of brownfield expansion has certain benefits in terms of expansion of capacity at a faster pace, an easy entry in the new industry, or a new geographical market. For example, Airtel's acquisition of Zen is an example of easy entry to South African telecom market, the inorganic route.

Another example would be the recent acquisition of Kesh King by Emami Ltd.

Emami Ltd., in June 2015, acquired the "Kesh King" a brand associated with hair and scalp products for Rs. 1651 crores. This was one of the largest deals in India's fast-growing hair oil market; the acquisition is an attempt by Emami to take advantage of the established brand image of Kesh King in the hair oil market.

Emami is aiming to capitalize on the brand image and the higher margins of Kesh King to boost its own bottom line. Emami management believes that Kesh King which has an EBITDA margin of 40% as against the normal FMCG margins of 25% will strengthen Emami's bottom-line post-acquisition.

Over the past few decades, mergers and acquisitions have been increasingly used for achieving rapid growth and increasing shareholder value. Achieving competitive advantage through consolidation and strategic alliances is another objective of mergers and acquisitions. According to an E&Y report on mergers and acquisitions in India, during the past 5 years, mergers and acquisition transactions have increased in absolute number from 825 in 2011 to 930 deals in 2015. The absolute value of all the deals was nearly about $26 billion in the year 2015 (Fig. 1.1).

Global M&As had a mixed first quarter with a dip in the number of deals but a rise in the overall value of deal activity, according to a merger market report.

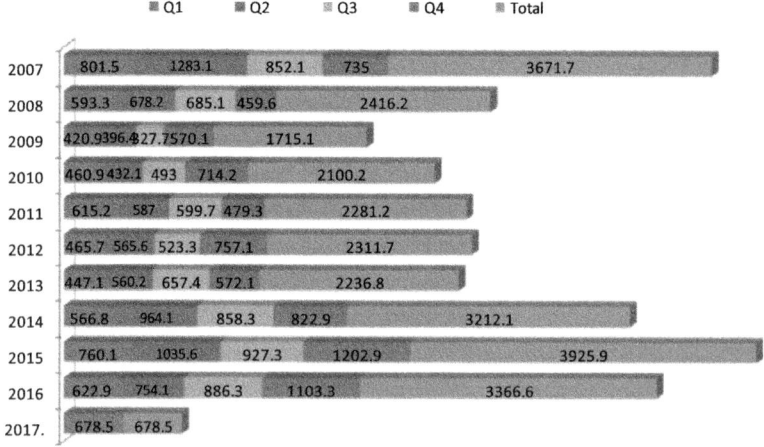

Fig. 1.1 Mergers and acquisitions (M&As) since 2007 (*Source* http://www.livemint.com/Companies/vQsq4BmZLIACFuMgDA9YNL/A-mixed-March-quarter-for-global-MAs.html)

While the total number of deals fell 17.9% compared with the first quarter of 2016, the overall deal value was up 8.9% to $678.5 billion. In the first quarter of 2015, the deal value was $760.1 billion, the highest since 2008.

During the first half of 2016, the Merger & Acquisition activity rose by nearly 12% to $15.7 billion in terms of value.

1.2 CORPORATE RESTRUCTURING

Corporate restructuring is referred to as a change in the business structure and/or financial structure of an organization via diversification, acquisition, change in management, spin-off, hive-off, etc., to meet the goals of an organization.

Change in corporate structure such as a change in business model, management team, and capital structure can be termed as corporate restructuring (Fig. 1.2).

Corporate restructuring takes place in several forms:

1.2.1 Amalgamation/Combination

Amalgamation or combination is an action, process, or result of combining or uniting two entities. In case of amalgamation, two separate

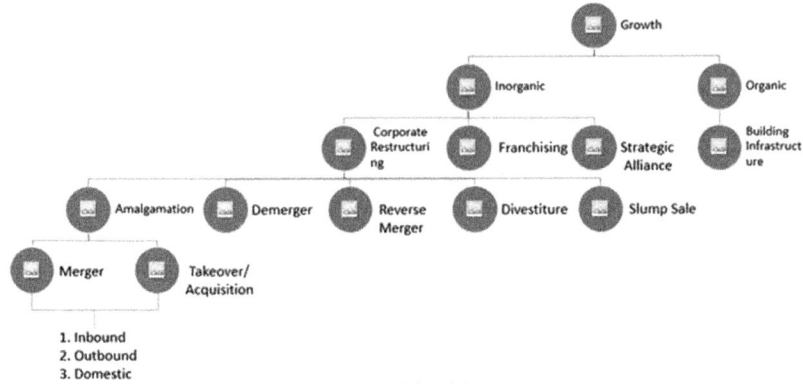

Fig. 1.2 Growth and corporate restructuring

entities come together to achieve a common goal, for fulfilling either financial or strategic objectives. Based on the type of amalgamation, an entity may combine its assets and liabilities with another entity. This can be:

1. Combination through merger(or)
2. Combination through acquisition/purchase

1.2.1.1 Combination Through Merger
In case of a merger, two companies or entities join together, in which one of the entities ceases to exist. The acquiring company would generally consolidate or add the assets and liabilities of the company acquired. The shareholders of the acquired company may be paid either cash or the shares of the acquirer company in exchange for the shares held in the target company. Post-merger, it is at the option of the acquirer company to decide whether the brand name of the acquired company would be used or not. A typical merger would involve combination of books of accounts in the stand-alone statements of the acquirer company.

For example, in the year 2015, Ranbaxy Laboratory got merged into Sun Pharma, where Sun Pharma acquired all the assets and assumed all the liabilities of Ranbaxy in an all-stock deal. However, Sun Pharma chose to use the brand name of "Ranbaxy" for all the products of Ranbaxy. This is a typical strategy, which might be used by the acquirer company to take advantage of the brand image of the acquired company.

1.2.1.2 Combination Through Acquisition/Purchase

In case of an acquisition/purchase/takeover, one entity purchases the stakes of the other entity resulting in taking over the management control of the acquired entity. The principle of substance over form applies here, that is, even if the acquiring entity purchases, say, 20 or 30% of the target entity resulting in higher individual shareholding to take control over the management, the acquired entity would be called as the subsidiary of the acquired entity. The mode of payment may be cash or combination of cash and stock.

For example, in the year 2007, one of the world's largest telecom company Vodafone purchased 52% stakes in Hutch Essar Ltd. The identity of the Hutch has been subsumed by Vodafone.

1.3   Types of Mergers and Acquisitions

Mergers and acquisitions can take various forms:

1.3.1   Horizontal Merger

In this type of merger, two companies operating in a similar line of industry come together. A company may either opt to take control of a competing company or a potential competitor so as to retain its market share. Horizontal mergers, generally, increase the concentration level in the industry.

For example, the cement division of L&T was acquired by Grasim Industries, which operates in the cement industry with brands such as Birla Plus and Birla Super. ICICI bank's acquisition of Bank of Rajasthan for about 3000 crores was a great move to enhance market access across the northern and western regions of the country. TATA power acquired Welspun Energy's assets in 2016 for Rs. 9000 crore to consolidate its renewable energy business.

Some of the other examples of horizontal mergers and acquisitions in consumer electronics industry include acquisition of Electrolux by Videocon and Spectramind by Wipro. Banking industry saw few of its consolidation activities, namely Times Bank's acquisition by HDFC Bank, Bank of Madura merging its operations with ICICI Bank, etc.

Horizontal mergers help companies achieve economies of scale, increase market share by reduction in competition, etc.

1.3.2   Vertical Merger

It is a type of merger in which a company merges with either the supplier of raw materials or the retailing/distribution network to save time and costs. Merger of a company with its raw material manufacturer/supplier is known as **Backward Integration,** whereas a merger with the distributor or retailer is termed as **Forward Integration**.

- **Reliance Industries Ltd. slew of activities from foraying into refinery and exploration from textiles, polyester to petrochemical is a classic example of backward integration where the downstream companies got merged with their upstream companies.**

1.3.3   Co-generic Merger

In this type of merger, companies operating in a similar line of industries but offering different products, generally, complementary in nature, tend to merge as a strategic measure to increase the profitability of both the companies.

For example, merger of Procter & Gamble and Gillette in 2005 is a co-generic merger. P&G is largely a consumer goods company, and Gillette was operating in men's personal care market. The product portfolios of two companies were complimentary. The merger created one of the world's biggest consumer product companies.

1.3.4   Conglomerate Merger

In this type of merger, companies which are not related to each other and are operating in different segments decide to merge.

For example, merger between L&T and Voltas, operating in different line of businesses, is a conglomerate merger.

1.3.5   Domestic Merger

These horizontal, vertical, or conglomerate mergers or acquisitions may take place on the domestic turf known as domestic merger.

The acquisition of Air Sahara by Jet Airways in 2007 is the perfect example of a domestic merger.

1.3.6   Inbound Merger

An inbound merger can take place when companies of foreign origin merge or acquire the companies of domestic origin. Daiichi Sankyo Co. Ltd. acquiring the entire stake of Ranbaxy Laboratories Ltd. is an example of inbound merger. With the opening up of Indian economy and initiatives like Digital India and Make in India, inbound activity shall further get the fillip.

1.3.7   Outbound Merger

An outbound merger can take place when a domestic company merges with companies of different origins, globally. For example, Hindalco's acquisition of Novelis (Canada), TATA Tea's acquisition of Tetley, TATA Steel's purchase of Corus, Lupin's acquisition of Gavis, Motherson Sumi's acquisition of Finnish truck wire maker PKC group can all be classified as an outbound deal. Similarly, GHCL acquired Dan River, an American textile company, and the same can be categorized as an outbound merger.

Takeover or acquisitions can be classified as:

1.3.8   Friendly Takeover

In this case, the acquirer company buys a controlling stake in the target company with the consent and will of the target company's board and its management. The acquisition of Myntra by Flipkart can be categorized as a friendly takeover. Myntra is a leading entity in the fashion apparel e-commerce market. In contrast, Flipkart is largely absent in the fashion apparel segment despite it being the largest e-commerce player in India. To augment its product line and to grab a higher share of the e-commerce market, it acquired Myntra in 2014.

1.3.9   Hostile Takeover

In case of a hostile takeover, the target company shows resistance to acquisition. In such a case, the acquirer approaches the shareholders directly. Acquisition of Zandu Pharmaceuticals Ltd. by Emami Ltd. in 2008 can be categorized as India's first hostile takeover. Similarly, **Tata's** acquisition of Corus was also resisted initially by Corus management.

1.3.10   Leveraged Buyout

In case of an leveraged buyout (LBO), the acquirer goes for borrowing to fund the acquisition. In most cases, the debt is backed by the collateral of the acquired company's assets. Several large-sized acquisitions have been carried out in recent decades with this method of LBO.

1.3.11   Management Buyout

When the management of a company buys overall or majority stakes of the company or buys the assets of the same, it is termed as a management buyout. If the management of a company tries to take controlling stake in the other company, it is referred to as **"Management Buy-In".** **Glaxo India Ltd.** (now GlaxoSmithKline) was a classic example of management buyout. ICICI ventures buyouts of Ranbaxy Fine Chemicals Ltd., Tebma Shipyard can be attributed to **Management Buy-In.**

1.4   OTHER FORMS OF CORPORATE RESTRUCTURING

1.4.1   Demerger

This is a category of corporate restructuring in which a company is segregated into different division or components. In other words, demerger takes place when one company splits into two or more companies. This is usually done with an objective to concentrate more on a specific segment. For example, in the year 2012, Wipro Ltd. demerged its business into two different operational units. Wipro Consumer Care & Lighting and Wipro Infrastructure Engineering and Medical Diagnostic Products & Services were hived off from Wipro's IT business, to form a new entity known as Wipro Enterprises. The demerger allowed the company to focus on its core business activities.

1.4.2   Reverse Merger

Reverse merger is typically equivalent to that of a merger, but in case of a reverse merger a large entity or a parent entity merges with a small entity or a subsidiary entity. Through a reverse merger, a private company may aim to get listed on stock exchanges (without having to go through the entire process of listing). By merging with a smaller public ltd. company whose shares are already listed. However, as per Companies Act 2013, a private limited company will not become a listed company simply by merging with a public ltd. listed entity. Rather, they have to follow the proper laid down procedure in the act and the SEBI guidelines in order to get it listed.

A reverse merger might also be undertaken to avail of taxation benefits. The merging entity might be a loss-making company and when it is merged with a profit-making company, the taxes of the combined entity go down.

For example, in 2002, ICICI parent company merged itself with ICICI Bank (Subsidiary). But the group retained ICICI Bank as the brand for the combined entity. Similarly, IDBI Bank which was the subsidiary of IDBI got IDBI merged with itself to be known as IDBI Bank.

1.4.3   Divestiture

Divestiture happens when an entity liquidates either the assets or a part of its business, usually, subsidiary, to concentrate on the core operations. It may be undertaken to hive off loss-making units or to cut down leverage of an entity, etc. It is also known as **disinvestment** or **Spin-off**. In case of divestiture, some division of business is sold to outsiders, while in case of spin-off a separate company is created from the parent company with the same shareholding pattern.

For example, in July 2016, Thomson Reuters sold one of its business divisions operating in Intellectual Property and Science (IP&S). This transaction helped Thomson Reuters in bringing down its debt burden besides allowing the company to concentrate on its mass media and information business and improve profitability.

Another example of divestiture is Coromandel Fertilizers Limited selling its cement division to India Cements Limited. Consequently, the size of Coromandel Fertilizers Limited contracted while the size of India Cements Limited expanded. But the deal allowed Coromandel to focus on its core competency of manufacturing fertilizers.

Usually, the motive behind divestitures would most likely be to concentrate on one particular business line and ease up the liquidity by unlocking the capital through selling non-core or non-performing businesses. CEAT sale of its Nylon Tyre plant to SRF helped CEAT raise

Rs. 3250 Crores which was used for the purpose of settling its payment obligations.

About ten years ago, in 2007, Reliance had entered the field of fuel retailing in Africa through a 76% equity stake in Gapco to expand its footprint in the continent. Last year, it announced plans to sell the stake in Gapco and use the funds to concentrate on fuel retailing in India.

1.4.4   Spin-Off

A spin-off does not result in an infusion of cash to the parent company. Instead, it allows a company to focus more on the spun-off entity which was becoming too large to be managed as a division in the parent company A separate business structure and management approach helps the company to realize the full potential of the spun-off unit. In case of a spin-off, the proportionate stake of the existing shareholders is same in both the entities, that is, parent as well as the newly formed legal subsidiary because the parent company distributes its shareholding in the subsidiary to its own shareholders on pro rata basis. This entails the creation of new entity with its new own management operating independently.

For example, Kotak Mahindra Capital Corporation was an investment division unit spun-off from its parent entity Kotak Mahindra Capital Finance Ltd.

1.4.5   Split-Off

Split-off is similar to that of spin-off where a new entity is formed to take over the operations of the parent company's one business division/unit. However, in case of a split-off, the existing shareholders (of a parent company) are given stocks in new entity in exchange of shares held in the parent entity. This would result in reducing the equity base of the parent entity as the shareholders are ceased of their claims from parent entity. As in case of spin-off, split-off also does not result in any inflow of cash.

1.4.6   Split-Up

This is an extended version of a spin-off where a parent company is broken down (or spun-off) into various business units and new entities are formed for those spun-off units. As the parent company is spun off in multiple units, the parent entity gets dissolved eventually forming new subsidiaries with new class of stocks. The shareholders of the parent entity have the option to exchange their shareholding to various spun-off units as according to their shareholding.

For example, power sector reform in the year 1999 led to a major split-off of Andhra Pradesh State Electricity Board (APSEB) where the parent company is dissolved by separating its operations into two different units. Two new entities APGENCO and APTRANSCO were created wherein the former was a spun-off division taking care of power generation business and the latter being the spun-off unit taking care of transmission and distribution business.

1.4.7 Equity Carve Out

In case of an equity carve out, a business unit or a division is separated from the parent company and it is been sold by way of equity to the outsiders. The key concern here is to whom the equity stakes are offered. In our above cases, it is the existing shareholders who get to exchange their shares from parent company to new entity. In this case, it is the outsiders and not necessarily the existing shareholders who become the shareholders of the newly formed (or carved out) entity.

1.4.8 Assets Sale

In case of an asset sale, a company liquidates all or part of its assets to another company in exchange for cash or securities. Usually, the intention of asset sale is to strengthen its cash position/balance sheet by way of liquidating long-term assets and generating cash or liquid assets. The asset can be anything, be it tangible or intangible. A company may sell its loss-making manufacturing plant or a legal brand or an existing patent it owns to generate cash. In September 2016, JSW Energy entered into a deal along with Jaiprakash Power Ventures to buy its (MW) Bina power plant (500 megawatts). The deal was locked at an attractive valuation of INR 2700 Crore enterprise value, which is considered quite less than its project cost of more than 3000 crore. The deal was struck to help Jaiprakash Power, which had a debt of Rs. 22,414.94 crore (as on 31 March '16) to reduce its interest payments via the reduction in its debt.

1.4.9   *Slump Sale*

According to Sec 2 (42C) of the Income Tax Act (1961), "Slump sale" means the transfer of one or more undertakings as a result of the sale for a lump sum consideration without values being assigned to the individual assets and liabilities. In simple terms, when a business or a part of business is sold off as a whole or a going concern, and the sale price is generic in nature, that is, without allocating specified amount for specified assets or liabilities (sale on lump sum basis), it is classified as slump sale.

1.4.10   *Joint Ventures*

Joint venture is an agreement between two parties to come together for a specific business venture. A joint venture is a contractual agreement with specific, time-bound objectives, and a unique identity of the entity, to have an ownership interest/common objectives/profit/loss sharing and common management.

The entities forming joint venture will continue to exist separately and will come together for the specific venture only. For example, Birla Sun Life Insurance is a joint venture between Aditya Birla Group and Sun Life Financial of Canada

There are no specific laws for joint ventures in India, and it can be formed as company, LLP or through contract, etc., and is governed by various regulations like Companies Act, Partnership Act, FEMA, etc.

Another example could be the Hero-Honda joint venture between, Hero Motors Ltd of India and Honda Corporation, Japan for the manufacturing of two-wheelers in India. However, the JV came to an end in **2013** and the business is now owned by Hero Motors Ltd.

1.4.11   *Franchising*

Franchising is where one party allows the other party to use its brand name or the trade name. It either allows them to use the business system, process, manufacturing and marketing methods of the franchiser company (the one who allows for franchise of its brand name) or outlines certain specifications regarding the process, manufacturing, and marketing methods to be followed. Typically, a fixed amount of royalty has to be paid for using the brand name. For example, Varun Beverages is a franchisee of PepsiCo Ltd. As directed by PepsiCo, Varun Beverages can manufacture and sell cool drinks under the brand name of Pepsi.

McDonald's is considered as one of the most successful franchisee models across the world. The local MC franchisee owners have to pay a royalty and in return are allowed to adopt the business model and the brand name of McDonald's. Thus franchising is a form of inorganic growth, as it allows a company to expand its reach across the globe.

1.4.12   Strategic Alliance

An agreement between two parties who come together to achieve a certain objective or to take up a certain task benefitting both of them is referred to as a strategic alliance. The two parties decide at the initial stage itself, the amount of capital to be invested by each entity, the profit shares of both, the nature of their control of the newly agreed entity, etc. The alliance may last for a specified time period or till the completion of the agreed objective.

1.4.12.1 Delhi Aviation Fuel Facility Pvt. Ltd

It is a strategic alliance between BPCL and DIAL, established during the year 2010 formed for the purpose of maintenance, designing, etc.

Mergers, Acquisitions and Corporate restructuring may take several forms as discussed above. They are considered as one of the most complicated business decisions. Involved business entities have to be quite careful during the entire process of decision making and implementation; else, the entire exercise may become a bane for them.

1.5   Historical Developments of Mergers and Acquisitions

1.5.1   M&A in US Economy: Merger Waves

See Table 1.1.

Number of countries have had high levels of M&A activity in the past but USA has the longest history of takeover activity going back to 1890s.

Table 1.1   Different merger waves in the USA

Period	Name	Types of M&A
1895–1904	First wave	Horizontal mergers
1916–1929	Second wave	Vertical mergers
1965–1969	Third wave	Diversified conglomerate mergers
1981–1989	Fourth wave	Concentric merger: hostile takeovers, divestitures
1990–2000	Fifth wave	Cross-border mergers
2003–Present	Sixth wave	Private equity, LBO

Source http://shodhganga.inflibnet.ac.in/bitstream/10603/45734/9/09_chapter%201.pdf

Since the beginning of the 1900s, merger & acquisition activity gathered pace in the USA. Rest of the world too experienced merger activity; the intensity was not as high as that of the USA. This activity, however, gathered pace in other countries too thereafter and is likely to continue indefinitely.

M&A activity can be divided into five major "waves" of mergers, with the first four taking place mainly in the USA. The fifth and sixth waves have been described as international merger waves. A common feature of all these waves of M&A activity has been that they typically arise in strong "bull" markets and fade when the market goes to bear phase. Each wave permanently reshapes one or more particular industries forever. These generally prompt regulators to react to subside merger activity. For instance, in the USA, the fourth merger wave prompted legislatures to enact law to prevent hostile takeovers even golden parachutes invited tax penalties.

1.5.2   The First Wave Turn of the Last Century (1895–1904)

The first of mergers wave consisted mainly of horizontal mergers resulting in monopolistic market structure. During this wave, which is sometimes called the "merging for monopoly" wave, the major horizontal mergers in the basic manufacturing and transportation industries took place. This merger wave was dominated by large steel and railroad mergers that led to a number of enormous trust monopolies (e.g., US Steel, Bethlehem Steel). Huge entities were created in the telephone, oil, and mining industries. This wave was largely spearheaded by men who are still considered icons—J. P. Morgan, John D. Rockefeller, and Andrew Carnegie.

This era of mergers for monopolies wave peaked between 1898 and 1902 and gradually died out due to the Panics of 1904 and the outbreak of World War I. New state laws that allowed the formation of holding companies facilitated this consolidation. In fact, the process that J. P. Morgan used to consolidate the railroads, after nearly 200 of them had become insolvent, is known as "Morganization." This process involved having stockholders of an insolvent railroad place their shares in a voting trust that he controlled until the railroad's debt was repaid—an essentially risk-free proposition for him.

A landmark consolidation during this first wave was Andrew Carnegie's $1.4 billion combinations of 10 companies to form US Steel. The monopolies created in the first merger wave were possible because the companies were not constrained by any government regulations. The US Congress acted to limit this consolidation with the adoption of the Sherman Antitrust act and nineteenth-century Interstate Commerce Act, the first antitrust laws.

First merger wave ended because of the financial factors. Fraudulent financing and the crash of stock market in 1904 followed by the 1907s banking panic led to the end of this wave of mergers and acquisitions. The era of easy availability of finance ended resulting in the halting of the first wave. Antitrust legislations became very stringent, and a crackdown on large monopolies was initiated. For example, Standard Oil was divided into 30 companies such as Standard Oil of New Jersey (subsequently called Exxon), Standard Oil of New York (rechristened Mobil), Standard Oil of California (called Chevron later) and Standard Oil of Indiana (subsequently renamed Amoco).

1.5.3 Second Wave (1916–1929)

With an upturn in business activity, the second wave of merger movement was initiated. Several industries were consolidated during this second merger wave. The result was an oligopolistic industry structure rather than monopolies. The consolidation pattern of the first merger wave continued in the second merger wave also. The mergers in this period occurred outside the previously consolidated heavy manufacturing industries. The most active were the banking and the public utilities industries. Mergers occurred in industries like primary metals/petroleum products/food products/chemicals and transportation equipment. After World War I, consolidation in the industries that were the highlights of the first wave continued. This observed consolidation is sometimes referred to as the "merging for oligopoly" wave. For example, more than 8000 mining and manufacturing companies disappeared through mergers or acquisitions during this period. With the growth of monopolies and oligopolies, the vertical integration became common.

General Motors, a huge company, got its start during the second wave. Founder William Durant started a merger binge by forming a holding company and broadening the product line by merging and buying many of the components suppliers of automobiles.

The second merger wave came to an end when the stock market crashed again on October 29, 1929. The crash resulted in a dramatic drop in the business and investment confidence. After the crash, the number of corporate mergers declined dramatically. This era is largely known as an era of vertical mergers where forward or backward integration was the main feature of mergers.

1.5.4   Third Wave (1965–1969)

The merger activity reached its zenith during this period of booming economy. This period is known as a conglomerate merger period. Small and medium-sized firms adopted a diversification strategy into businesses that were outside their traditional areas of interest. During this period, relatively smaller firms targeted larger firms for acquisition. 80% of the mergers that took place were diversification of the product lines. For example, ITT acquired such diversified businesses like car rental firms, bakeries, consumer credit agencies, luxury hotels, airport parking firms, construction firms, etc. In the post-World War II prosperity, a prolonged merger wave ensued.

A number of established US companies took to the diversified conglomerate paradigm. Entirely new conglomerates were also built from the ground, such as International Telephone & Telegraph Ling-Temco-Vought and Litton Industries. Diversification became widely accepted because management skills were assumed to be easily transferable among industries. Managers who believed in this philosophy sought to build the largest companies they could.

Faced with growing antitrust scrutiny of both horizontal and vertical mergers, companies sought merger partners in other industries to maintain steady growth, which further fueled diversification. With the wide acceptance of management principles, managers believed that they had the broad-based skills to manage a wide range of organizational structures. The belief that conglomerate mergers could be manageable became a reality. ITT merged with nearly 250 companies in the span of a decade, many of them in unrelated businesses.

During this third wave, some companies grew into "multinationals" as they expanded beyond their domestic borders. The merger wave gradually ended in the early 1970s as the Dow Jones Industrial Average fell by more than a third (e.g., the largest conglomerates fell 86%, and computer and technology stocks fell 77%) and a worldwide energy crisis began. This led to a reduction in the availability of funds for merger activity and a devaluation of the US dollar. Many of the acquisitions that took place during this period were followed by poor financial performance. Many of the mergers failed as managers of the diverse enterprises had little knowledge of the specific industries that were under their control. For example, Revlon, a company that has an immense success in the cosmetic industry, saw its core cosmetic industry business suffer when it expanded into unrelated areas such as health care.

1.5.5 Fourth Wave (1981–1989)

After the recession in 1974–1975, the US economy entered a long period of expansion during which the merger and acquisition trend moved upward again. Hostile mergers were significant part of the fourth wave. Takeovers were considered healthy or hostile based on the reaction of the target entity's board of directors. If the board agreed to the takeover, it was considered friendly and if it opposed it, it was deemed to be hostile.

The 1980s merger wave was known as a "takeover" wave. As the number of hostile takeovers proliferated, they were recognized gradually as an acceptable tool for growing companies.

Morgan Stanley on behalf of INCO initiated the first hostile takeover in 1974 by seeking to take over ESB. This bid was the starting point for the major investment banks to make hostile takeover bids on behalf of raiders. Corporate raiders, such as Carl Icahn, T. Boone Pickens, and Ronald Perelman, profited handsomely by putting companies into play (i.e., forced them into being a target), sometimes accepting "greenmail" to sell back equity to management, and sometimes taking over a company to break it up and sell its assets. These corporate raiders leveraged limited resources to make millions of dollars for themselves and never really built anything.

Junk bond financing and leveraged buyouts (LBOs) became commonplace and were sources of quick financing. Investment banker Drexel Burnham Lambert led the charge in using new and controversial financing techniques to facilitate the takeover of companies. Increasingly, US companies used mergers or acquisitions as a response to global competition. For example, Amoco and Exxon bought Canadian oil companies. Also, non-American companies increasingly bought US entities and other cross-border entities as many of the largest companies in the world came into existence in countries outside the USA. The best example of this was the US$16 billion acquisition of SmithKline Beecham Corporation by UK's Beecham Group plc's for.

In the mid-1980s, the pace of takeovers was at slow down due to the introduction and usage of various defensive techniques like the poison pill and their eventual judicial acceptance. However, even after the stock market crash of October 1987, merger activity continued, and by 1988, there were more than 200 buyout firms with aggregate assets of $30 billion to facilitate takeovers.

With the collapse of the junk bond market, this wave also ended. Subsequent to this wave, the market was marred by the insider trading scandals and excesses that became evident. The lawsuits were brought by the US government against some of the best-known names in the market such as Ivan Boesky and Michael Milken, the mastermind behind Drexel Burnham Lambert's novel financing techniques.

During the fourth wave, the signature takeover battle was the bidding war for RJR Nabisco in 1988. This battle involved a proposed management buyout led by CEO F. Ross Johnson opposed by Kohlberg Kravis Roberts (KKR), a takeover specialist. During the battle, RJR Nabisco's board faced immense pressure and conflicting facts from its own management team, as each detail was widely reported in the media. The result was a $25 billion LBO by KKR.

During this era, the corporate raiders earned handsome profits without taking control over the management of the target company. They attempted to take over a target and later sell the target shares at a price higher than that which was paid originally. Investment bankers played an aggressive role during this time. M&A advisory services became a lucrative source of income for investment banks. The merger specialists at investment banks and law firms developed many techniques to facilitate and prevent hostile takeovers.

The increased use of debt to finance acquisitions was the major characteristic of this era. The yield on junk bonds was significantly higher than that of investment grade bonds. Hence, the ready availability of finance helped even small firms to acquire far bigger and well-established firms. LBO emerged in a big way as method of financing during this period. This merger wave also featured innovations in acquisition techniques and investment vehicles. The investment bank Drexel Burnham Lambert pioneered the junk bond instrument. This further helped a full-scale growth and development of junk bond markets in the USA.

1.5.6   Fifth Wave (1990–2000)

Mega mergers as in the fourth wave began to take place in the fifth wave too. The number of hostile deals was less than strategic mergers. With the recovery of the economy in 1992, companies sought to expand and mergers were seen as a quick and efficient way to grow fast. Unlike the deals of 1980s, the transactions of the fifth wave emphasized more on strategy rather than quick financial gains. Most of the deals were financed through the increased use of equity.

The fifth wave is considered to be an international one, as majority of the notable mergers have been either entirely outside the USA or involved a non-US party. Overall, the worldwide volume of transactions rose from US$322 billion in 1992 to US$3.2 trillion in 2000. The glaring reflection of this trend is the $180 billion Vodafone AirTouch-Mannesmann AG combination, the largest in the history of M&A. This 2000 transaction was a hostile takeover by the British giant for the second largest German telecommunications company.

Major mergers and acquisitions turned to be cross-border transactions as real growth for many of the companies required global-scale operations. Technological improvements in the form of linking of many of the major stock markets helped in this globalized M&A activity.

Worldwide consolidation in many industries, such as the automobile, telecommunications, airlines, and metal industries, have been an outcome of this wave. In the highly regulated industries, such as banking, the merger activity remained mostly domestic, but even this domestic consolidation is often a response to international competition.

In particular, this may be a primary factor for the increased level of activity in Europe, from the adoption of a single currency (i.e., the euro) and an increasingly linked market to the widespread privatization of government-controlled entities. Many European governments significantly shattered long-standing restrictions that had prevented many cross-border deals. Even in the USA, some major impediments to mergers and acquisitions activity were removed. For example, the Telecommunications Act of 1996 and the partial repeal of the Glass–Steagall Act had directly caused consolidation in the telecommunications and financial services industries.

In addition to the global nature of this wave, the pace of the fifth wave has been boosted by the communications and technology revolution brought primarily by the Internet toward the end of the twentieth century. The incredibly high valuations of many of these technology companies enabled them to buy other technology companies to allow them to grow—or to fill in their product line. The biggest technology companies, such as Microsoft and Cisco, regularly bought 10 or more companies every year. Other companies, like AOL, bought "old-economy" companies, like Time-Warner, to create the conglomerate "clicks and bricks" media company.

While European companies were willing to use hostile takeovers, such activity did not find much favor in the USA. During this merger wave, the considerable appetite for initial public offerings (IPOs) diminished the need for LBOs. Even when the number of hostile transactions was relatively small, the fear of hostile activity undoubtedly fostered the "buy or be bought" sentiments. Since the collapse of the stock prices of Internet companies at the beginning of 2000, the merger wave slowed down considerably.

1.5.7   Sixth Wave (2003–Till Present)

The sixth and the ongoing wave of M&A started in the year 2003 is still going on. This wave is characterized by mergers in which corporate governance and shareholder activism have become areas of prime importance. Deals have now reached such humongous proportions that LBOs again became the dominant method for acquisitions.

The growing footprint of private equity firms on the merger and acquisition space cannot be overemphasized. The rise of private equity

Table 1.2 Latest prominent M&A deals

Top deals

Deal value ($ bn)	Bidder company	Bidder country	Target company	Target country	Target sector
60.7	British American Tobacco Plc.	UK	Reynolds American (57.83% stake)	US	Consumer
29.6	Johnson and Johnson	US	Actelion Pharmaceuticals	Switzerland	Pharma, medical and biotech
25.4	Essilor International SA	France	Luxottica Group SpA	Italy	Consumer
17.8	Reckitt Benckiser Group Plc.	UK	Mead Johnson and Company	US	Consumer
17.2	ONEOK Inc.	US	ONEOK Partners Lp (60% Stake)	US	Energy, mining and utilities

Source http://www.livemint.com/Companies/vQsq4BmZLIACFuMgDA9YNL/A-mixed-March-quarter-for-global-MAs.html

has changed the face of M&A on a global scale. Flush with cash from institutional investors for supernormal returns, buyout funds have an edge while hunting for assets. As per a Reuters report, "Pvt Equity firms or financial sponsors accounted for 11% of Asian M&A Activity in the first half of 2007. Since then private equity firms have played a pivotal role in the M&A scenario (Table 1.2).

1.6   Merger and Acquisition Trends in India

In Indian perspective, mergers and acquisitions came into limelight after liberalization and it started picking up only from the mid-1990s. That is mostly attributable to the liberalized economic policies since 1991. Therefore, M&A phases in India can be categorized as pre-liberalization phase and post-liberalization phase. Undoubtedly, the post-liberalization phase was more supportive for M&A with many of the policy decision in favor of mergers and acquisitions.

1.6.1   Pre-Liberalization Era

Various studies have been conducted on the mergers and acquisition activities in India to ascertain the trend. Studies of Rao, 1998, and Venkateswaran, 1993, suggested that the pre-liberalization era (especially post-1970) was devoid of action for mergers and acquisition activities in India. Few common reasons for such a dull scenario were as follows:

The tight regulatory environment (MRTPA, FERA, and other regulations);

Higher licensing and clearance resulting in higher entry and exit barriers; and

Ownership pattern—predominantly corporate ownerships with the financial institutions.

These among several other regulatory factors were not conducive for M&A activity. The Monopolies and Restrictive Trade Policy (MRTPA) was concerned with the regulations restraining the consolidation of market power resulting largely from horizontal merger. The FERA was relating to inbound and outbound deal restrictions. Consequently, mergers of conglomerate nature were not influenced by these stringent regulations, and there were stray cases of conglomerate M&A in India.

During the post-independence period and before the promulgations of stringent regulations, large number of M&As were executed in industries like jute, cotton textiles, sugar, insurance, banking, electricity, and tea plantation.

One of the very important amalgamations was the merger of over 200 insurance companies and provident societies to form Life Insurance Corporation (LIC) of India in 1956. The National Textiles Corporation (NTC) took over a large number of sick textiles units. In the year 1950, the Goenka Group acquired two British trading houses, namely the Duncan Brothers and Octavius Steel. They also had some successful acquisitions in the areas of tea, automobiles, tyres, jute, electric cables, and cotton textiles. The government had, in fact, encouraged M&A to help revive the sick units.

M&As as strategies were employed by several corporate groups like R. P. Goenka, Vijay Mallya and Manu Chhabria for growth and expansion of their empires in India during the 1980s. Some of the companies taken over by RPG group included Dunlop, CEAT, Phillips Carbon Black, and Gramophone Company of India. The first of the acquisitions was CEAT Tyres of India in the year 1981. The group then went on to acquire KEC (1982); Searle India (RPG Life Sciences 1983);

Dunlop (1984); Gramophone Company of India Ltd (now Saregama India 1986); and finally CESC, Harrisons Malayalam, Spencer & Co. and ICIL, all in 1989. Vijay Mallya's United Breweries (UB) group was created out of various mergers and acquisitions; in 1988, there was an unfriendly takeover bid by Swaraj Paul which however could not succeed.

1.6.2   Post-liberalization Phase

The economic liberalization in the year 1991 drastically changed the dynamism of the business within the Indian economy. Deregulations of the market to make the economy market-oriented, the changes which allowed greater foreign direct investment, tax changes to expand the role of private and foreign players has helped industries within the economy to pursue growth strategies. M&A being one of the easiest strategies in terms of effort was considered the mantra for growth among various industries.

The post-liberalization phase can be further subdivided into three phases of growth:

- Slow growth Period;
- Rapid growth period;
- Recovery period.

1.6.2.1 Slow Growth Period (1991–2000)
Notwithstanding its meager size compared to global M&As, the growth trajectory in India started picking up. The period from 1991 to 2000 was a period of growth through M&A among different industries which clearly reveals the start of the M&A activities in India (Table 1.3).

A major impetus to the M&A activity in the corporate sector post-liberalization speeded up the restructuring activities. However, as we observe from the table above, it is the latter half of the decade, that is, post-1995, the M&A activity intensified.

The major factors contributing to the increase in M&A activities in 1996 were:

- The industrial slowdown in 1996 made many corporates to lose on their profitability. Corporates, therefore, started using mergers and acquisitions to boost their profits and competitiveness in the market.

Table 1.3 Distribution of M&A activities across industry from 1990 to 2000

Industry/years	1990–1991	1991–1992	1992–1993	1993–1994	1994–1995	1995–1996	1996–1997	1997–1998	1998–1999	1999–2000	Total
Pharma				2	0	5	27	47	29	57	167
Petrochemical						4	11	5	11	13	44
Energy, gas, and power				1	0	3	6	13	15	16	54
Nonmetallic minerals					2	3	2	11	11	19	48
Tourism/travels						2	4	7	6	13	32
Paper products						1		9	4	1	15
Food products			3	1	2	8	8	10	9	20	61
Textiles/wearings	1	0	0	0	1	0	4	4	12	6	28
Finance/banking			1	0	1	0	7	24	35	51	119
IT & Telecom				3	0	0	11	20	31	45	110
Electricals/electronics				2	0	0	7	11	13	11	44
Basic metal, alloy				1	3	4	9	13	15	15	60
Equipment/machinery				4	3	2	12	26	25	30	102
Transport equipment						1	4	13	13	24	55
Tobacco/beverages				2	2	0	0	4	3	5	16
Others							12	31	37	61	141
Total	1	0	4	16	14	33	124	248	269	387	1096

Source http://www.igidr.ac.in/conf/money1/MERGERS%20AND%20ACQUISITIONS%20IN%20INDIA.pdf

- The industrial slowdown during 1997–1998 and the declining agricultural outputs coupled with cautious loans from banks led the existing companies buying sick units at a bargain price for tax benefits as well as growth.
- East Asian crisis in 1997 fueled further the restructuring activities to retain competitiveness in the market.
- The biggest boost for the M&A activity came in 1999–2000 from the union budget which gave relaxation to norms relating to taxes on mergers and acquisitions. The benefits of setoff, carry forward of accumulated loss, and unabsorbed depreciation were defined precisely to facilitate mergers and acquisition activities.

Deregulation, globalization, and improvement in technology in financial services led to higher M&A activities in the financial services industry. Technological changes led tech companies to involve in restructuring to constantly stay its competitive environment by acquiring companies with new technologies. The pharma industry is popularly known for its mergers and acquisition activities as many regulatory requirements including patents licensing supported them to do so.

1.6.2.2 Rapid Growth Period (2000–2007)

This period of M&A saw a tremendous involvement by the corporate world in M&A activities. Perhaps, it is the 2000s which saw the real boost in mergers and acquisitions in terms of numbers and the value. The period of 2000–2007 saw an exponential growth of nearly about 65% in terms of value from $999.43 million worth of deals within the select deals to $32,984.27 million. The number of deals also saw an exponential growth of 25% from 55 to 264. Average deal value also increased remarkably during this period (Fig. 1.3).

The value of deals started picking up steeply from 2005 with 2007 as the best year in the history of Indian M&A activities. There were a total of 661 deals in the year with a total value of $51.17 billion which was stupendously higher than that of the previous year of 480 deals valued at $20.3 billion.

There were a total of 348 cross-border deals worth $48.34 billion compared to 313 domestic deals worth just $2.83 billion. Few of the major deals were Tata Corus, Vodafone's stake purchase in Hutch Essar, and Hindalco's acquisition of Novelis. In May 2007, Suzlon Energy acquired German turbine producer RE power for $1.7 billion.

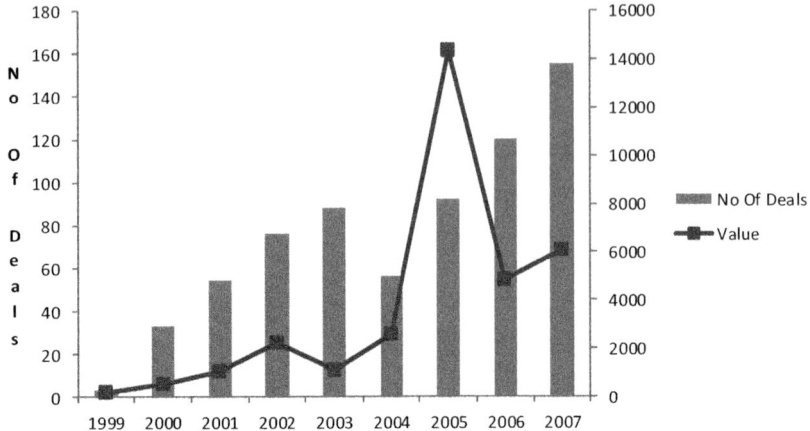

Fig. 1.3 M&A during the period 2000–2007 (*Source* Author's compilation from ET Intelligence data. *Note* The data contain only information relating to acquisitions of more than 50% equity stake and is restricted to domestic deals)

These mega deals accounted for more than 60% of the total value of the outbound deals during 2007.

In terms of industry, steel accounted for the maximum value of the deals with 29% of the total value during the year, followed by telecom industry with 22% and power and energy with 7%. IT and ITES sector saw the most number of deals followed by pharma, banking, media and entertainment, etc., with the number of deals 154, 62, 58, and 33, respectively.

1.6.2.3 Global Recession and Recovery

In 2008, NTT DOCOMO Japanese telecom firm acquired 26% stake in Tata Teleservices for $ 2.7 billion. Indian pharma industry registered the first biggest M&A deal in 2008 when Daiichi Sankyo acquired Ranbaxy for $4.5 billion. ONGC purchased imperial energy in 2009 for $ 2.9 billion and was considered as one of the biggest takeover. HDFC Bank and Centurion Bank merged in 2008. The deal was worth $2.4 billion. Sterlite industries, a part of Vedanta group in the year 2008, acquired copper mining company Asarco for $2.6 billion.

The subprime crisis of 2008 suddenly brought M&A activities to a screeching halt as shown in Fig 1.4.

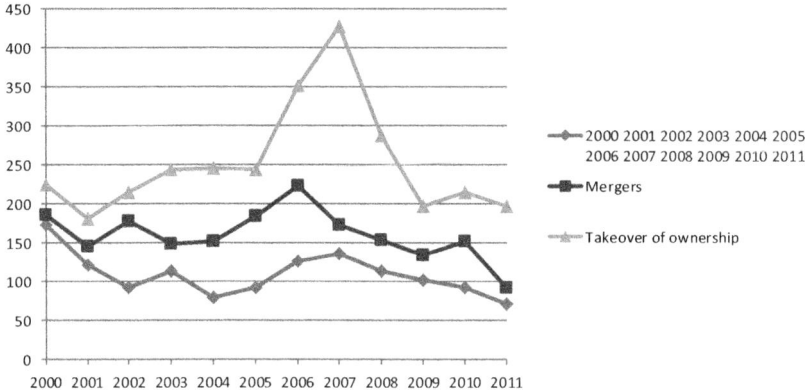

Fig. 1.4 M&A during the period 2000–2011 (*Source* http://shodhganga. inflibnet.ac.in/bitstream/10603/45734/9/09_chapter%201.pdf)

The year 2010 started signaling a recovery with not only the domestic deals but also the higher involvement or increase in the cross-border deals. However, 2011 went into stagnation in the aftermath of the global financial crisis. Few prominent deals in the year 2010 are Zain and Bharti Airtel, Piramal and Abbott, Reliance natural, Reliance power, etc. These three deals alone contributed nearly about $25.4 billion in terms of value. One of the most successful deals of 2010 is that of Tata chemicals taking over British Salt based in UK FOR $13 BILLION.

1.6.2.4 Ongoing Phase (2011 Onwards)

M&A activity took a surge again with the improved global economy and onset of new era of several reforms initiated by the government. After the 2014 elections in which BJP won with an overwhelming majority resulting from the positive response from general public and increased confidence of global and domestic investors, M&A activity has again picked up in India. It received a major boost from the various reforms initiated by new NDA government and India's image as one of the fastest growing economies in the world (Table 1.4).

The number of deals in the year 2011 was 642 with a total deal value of nearly about $46.4 billion. In the years 2012 and 2013, M&A activity

Table 1.4   M&A deals during the period 2011–2014

Deal summary	Volume				Value (in $ Mn)			
Year	2011	2012	2013	2014	2011	2012	2013	2014
Domestic	216	233	219	252	5627	6088	5646	16,192
Cross-borders	286	263	223	280	40,845	14,537	17,995	16,871
Mergers and internal restructuring	140	100	58	37	–	14,789	4541	3989
Total M&A	642	596	500	569	46,472	35,414	28,182	37,052

Source https://www.ibef.org/Grant-Thornton-India

slowed down because of softening of the equity markets. The year 2014 saw a recovery in both the number of deals and the value of M&A deals.

The year 2014 was of consolidation, with key players in the pharma, banking, and power assets consolidating their market positions. Domestic deal activities contributed to nearly $16 billion which is up to 189% over 2013 values. This is the highest ever domestic value of deals in the decade. The domestic and inbound deal contributed nearly 80% of the deal volume during the year. Some of the prominent deals during this era were Sun Pharma and Ranbaxy merger, Kotak Mahindra with ING Vysya, JSW Energy with JP ventures, Flipkart with Myntra, etc.

The year 2015 saw a total of 581 deals in volume and $30.42 billion worth deals in value. Domestic deals were the highest in the year with more than 300 transactions wherein majority of the transactions were done during the latter half of the year majorly subjected to ease FDI norms among sectors like defense, banking, construction, aviation, etc.

Top deals during 2015 include Vedanta Ltd and Cairn India's merger of $2300 million. Energy and natural resources sector saw the highest value amounting to $5.6 billion across 265 deals. IT and ITES, Pharma, health care, and biotechnology saw a good amount of deals but were stagnated. However, post-2013, there is a consistency in the deal volume and value with 2015 being one of the best years in terms of domestic and inbound deals, attributable to internal factors. The trend for the M&A is expected to continue in India as it is believed that India has now emerged as one of the top countries entering into mergers and acquisitions. The congenial environment for merger and acquisition has been primarily created during the past few years on account of the positive impetus from Confederation of Indian industry, Reserve Bank of India, and SEBI—the three main regulators of mergers and acquisitions activities in India.

CHAPTER 2

Motives of M&A and Deal Synergies

Corporate restructuring by way of mergers, acquisitions, demerges, spin-offs, hive-offs, and disinvestments is done in order to achieve certain objectives of the management. However, the major objective of every corporate restructuring program is to increase the profitability of the business thereby leading to increased shareholders wealth. The means of reaching the goals depends upon the various factors like deal value, industry life cycle, method of funding the deal, liquidity, tax benefits, prior deal experience of the parties, the extent of due diligence transaction costs, and business prospects.

Though there might be several theories which try to explain the possible outcome of a corporate action (be it a merger or an acquisition), three theories, namely Synergy or efficiency theory, market for corporate control theory, and the free cash flow theory, are considered somewhat efficient as these theories predict the performance of a corporate action using best sorts which are discussed below.

2.1   THEORIES OF M&A

2.1.1   *Value Creating Theories*

2.1.1.1 *The Synergy Theory*

Synergies are by far the most compelling factors to motivate mergers and acquisitions and the premium paid to avail of the synergistic benefits.

© The Author(s) 2019
V. Kumar and P. Sharma, *An Insight into Mergers and Acquisitions*,
https://doi.org/10.1007/978-981-13-5829-6_2

Synergies emanate through cost reductions and revenue enhancement. Synergies arise as a result of increase in the size or scale of operation, which provides economies of scale/scope. Vertical integration leads to complimentary benefits from forward or backward integration. Monopoly gains sprout from the increase in market share in a horizontal merger when size grows up. Efficiency gains are realized out of superior managerial performance and effectiveness if the post-acquisition managerial skills improve remarkably.

Value creation or efficiency in acquisition is a combination of improved financial and operating performance post-acquisition.

The above said value creation or increase in value arrives by way of "Synergy." The free markets have suggested that the acquisitions are majorly value increasing which are reaped by increasing combined performance and realizing synergies by way of efficient resource allocation, achieving cost-efficiency together, etc., which, otherwise, would not be feasible, if run individually. This efficiency in resource allocation is what leads to combined economic gains. Economies of scale, economies of scope, and market power are the major synergetic benefits sprouting out of M&A.

Economies of Scale

When the corporations/companies are able to generate efficiency through its size, it is referred to as economies of scale. This might take various prospects. For example, an individual entity might be having a highly leveraged balance sheet and raising capital through accessing capital markets or taking further debt would just not be feasible or would come at a higher cost. If the same company is acquired by another company with a healthy or a clean balance sheet (with low leverage), the combined entity can easily access markets for capital requirements and would be able to raise capital at a lower cost as the overall risk is reduced as a result of increase in size.

Another way with which efficiency can be achieved is through higher bargaining capacity in the entire value chain process, that is, production/manufacturing, transportation, distribution, etc. For example, a combined entity may be able to buy raw materials at a cheaper cost if the combination helps in increased market share. They might also be able to sell their goods at a higher price than the price they were able to fetch individually. This helps achieve higher economies of scale by way of lower operating and financing expenses, increasing margins thereby increasing efficiency leading to the creation of value.

Economies of Scope
These are typically found, however, not confined to non-conglomerate acquisitions. Economies of scope are a critical way of accessing synergy by using the complementary skills of each other companies. For example, in case of production, a company might be skillful in technology where the other company might have skilled workforce. When these companies come together, the cost of production for the combined entity will reduce with efficiency in production achieved through better use of technology in totality. This is popularly known as sharing of production know-how. This would help in lowering the cost and increasing the profitability.

Market Power
When the combination achieved by way of acquisition helps in increasing the size, the entity might be able to achieve higher market power. This is one possible source of synergy which helps the company increase its shareholders value by increased profitability. Higher market power can be exerted by two means, monopoly and monopsony. In case of monopoly, the firm might be able to fetch higher prices for its products (increased pricing power) as the competition would have lessened. In case of monopsony, the combined entity might exert power in purchasing raw materials or inputs for production at a lower cost from its suppliers as they would buy in bulk. Let's say, Firm X acquires Firm Y which are operating in the similar lines of business with 40 and 45% market share. The combined entity would now be having 85% market share wherein the entity can literally force its suppliers and distributors to accept a lower price and give a higher price. By this way, this enhances the margins of the combined entity.

2.1.1.2 The Market for Corporate Control Theory
This theory argues that the acquisition would help achieve/increase economic benefit by way of improved operating performance achieved through efficient and effective management of the company's assets. Usually, it is believed that, the acquiree company's asset would not have been efficiently managed. This acts as a stimulant for different

managers/company's to acquire those companies or the assets at a lower price and manage it themselves efficiently to increase its market value later upon. This would naturally, theoretically, draw attention from various managers or the companies to acquire those assets. This competition would make sure the assets are purchased by that management which would manage it efficiently. Glaring example of that corporate control is in the Indian corporate sector when the government insists a sick unit be run and managed by an efficient management after its takeover.

Free Cash Flows and Cash Consideration for M&A

According to studies, the free cash flow theory suggests that the post-acquisition performance would improve if the acquisition is effected through debt or cash and not equity. Acquisitions effected through debt limit the controlling management's ability to use the free cash flows generated in the business as they have a debt burden lying in the balance sheet. Unless the balance sheet gets stabilized, the misuse of free cash flows generated by the company would be minimal as the intention would mostly be tilted toward investing the free cash in its own business to generate higher returns and pay off the debt. The interest burden would also help the management to be more focused and achieve efficiency in cost/production/management, etc.

The crux of all these theories has been that corporate acquisitions result in value creation or value enhancement. There are contrary theories based on certain findings which advocate the opposite view that acquisitions may lead to value destruction.

2.2   VALUE REDUCING THEORIES

2.2.1   *Agency Costs of Free Cash Flow*

This theory suggests that free cash flows would lead to the creation of principal-agent problem. This is in contrast to the above discussed "Free cash flow and cash consideration theory." The above theory suggested that the acquisition being funded by debt would reduce mismanagement of free cash flows. This theory suggests that if acquisitions/mergers funded by equity and not debt would lead to mismanagement of free cash flows which would just lead to reduction in shareholders wealth. A substantially higher/big company having positive free cash flows (internal accruals higher than the cost of capital) would most likely lead the management to invest those free cash flows in negative NPV projects as the management remuneration is based on the asset it manages. Once the internal investment potential ceases, the management would start using the free cash flows generated in other projects which might not be profitable in the long run.

2.2.1.1 Managerial Entrenchment

"Agency problem" in the corporate world is well renowned. It is reflected in the phenomenon of manager's reluctance to distribute cash to shareholders but managers may be willing to make investments in the form of acquisitions where managers overpay but reduce likelihood of their own replacement. These are known as "agency-problem driven mergers."

2.3   Value Neutral Theory

2.3.1   The Hubris Hypothesis of "Corporate Takeovers"

Majority of the managers are afflicted by the behavioral bias known as managerial hubris or excessive overconfidence. The winner's curse theory suggests that the wealth is a mere transfer between the bidding firm and the target shareholders leading to no value creation. This is because the winner or the highest bidder entity would most likely end up paying higher to win the bidding process. This overpaying is a derivative of over-valuing the target firm's potential through optimistic forecast of target's business prospects. Thus, the value would most likely get netted out.

As seen above, different theories put forth different prospects toward a merger and an acquisition as some transaction might result in increased value or growth, some might result in reducing value and some might lead to neutral effects, which is purely detrimental to companies involved in the process.

2.4   Motives Behind Mergers/Acquisition

The first and foremost motive of any merger/acquisition transaction is to create synergy through several factors. However, there are certain dubious reasons for combining entities through mergers and acquisitions. Sometimes this might hamper the potential of both the individual entities if the operational integration post-merger doesn't turn out well.

Few such dubious reasons are:

2.4.1   Financial Nature

Sometimes, management's remuneration might be linked with the amount of assets they are managing or the profits they were able to generate rather than the profitability or the efficiency of the organization. This might incentivize managers to enter into deals to just increase the amount of assets they manage and in turn the pay package of these managers.

2.4.2   Management Intention

Managers of a company might be interested in a particular business and would be willing to offer crazy valuations for acquiring such business despite being against the interest of the shareholders. They may go for even hostile takeovers if the intention of the managers in acquiring those businesses goes high.

For example, Reliance acquisition of Pipavav Defense and Offshore Engineering Company Ltd. was purely an acquisition of choice. Anil Ambani eyed entering in defense industry for a long time and Pipavav Defense was one among the largest infrastructure manufacturer for Indian defense. Through the acquisition, Reliance was able to enter the segment making it the first private sector company in India to get license in building warships.

2.4.3   Fear of Loss of Market Share

Management, at times, might have a fear of losing its market share to a competitor or an upcoming market player. They might in order to not lose the market share merge or acquire those entities.

For example, WhatsApp was taking away the market share of Facebook within just a span of two years. This led Facebook to acquire WhatsApp at hefty valuations.

The above are commonly seen factors which, though not necessarily in the best interests of shareholders, but still the major motives triggering the M&A activity, though some might turn up positive for the company at a later stage. The key to analyze the motive or the success of merger/acquisition is by looking at the individual factors associated with the entities involved and the impact it could possibly exert in the industry.

From the above theories, we can understand synergy is something every entity is attempting to achieve. These are various forms of synergies.

2.5   Evaluation of Deal Synergy

The psychological aspect of humans suggests that when two intellectual joins together, they would be able to produce results higher than what they could have achieved individually. This drives or becomes the rationale for **"Mergers and Acquisitions."** Thus, it is clear that the motive behind a corporate being involved in "mergers and acquisitions" is to attain certain synergies which would help in boosting topline growth as well as bottom-line growth of profits.

Synergy can arise from operations and could be of any form like cost savings, topline expansions through pricing power, or it may be financial in nature like cheaper credit, tax benefits, etc. It varies vastly from entity to entity and time to time. One must have a deep understanding of a particular deal to analyze whether a probable synergy can be attained and in what form the synergy would be achieved.

2.5.1   Some Common Forms of Synergies

2.5.1.1   Economies of Scale

Economies of scales are achieved through the efficiency of the combined entity. Economically, a firm is said to attain economies of scale if it can lower down it's per unit cost. This would happen if the amount of production increases and the fixed cost does not change. For example, assume XYZ Ltd. produce 1000 units of watches for which it is incurring a total cost of 100,000 out of which variable cost is 70,000 and fixed cost is 30,000. However, XYZ Ltd. machine is able to produce additional 500 units without incurring extra fixed cost. So XYZ can produce 1500 units at a cost of 135,000 ($70 \times 1500 + 30,000$). Thus, per unit fixed cost would be 20 (30,000/1500) compared to 30 when production was less.

Economies of scale lead to efficiency in cost structure. When a company merges with/or acquires the other entity, the combined entity might be able to cut down cost by combining operations. This would help in achieving economies of scale and leading to increased profitability.

For example, the acquisition of cement division of L&T by Grasim in the year 2003 helped Grasim by cutting down its production costs by nearly Rs. 1 billion. This became possible because L&T was operating with relatively new plants compared to others, and it had low power and fuel consumption. The integration also helped in reducing transportation costs of cement to the dealers nationwide.

Cost savings are possible through avoiding the duplicity of some of the other functions. For example, marketing/branch offices of two companies at same locations can be shut down, double functional teams can be reduced to single teams, etc. This shall get translated into reduced overall cost of operation of the merged entity.

2.5.1.2 Access to Cheaper Credit

Generally, a company might be able to fetch loans at a cheaper rate only till a certain limit. Beyond a point, the lending institutions may consider the risk involved because of the existing debt burden and may not be willing to offer the loan at a lower rate of interest. Through merger/acquisition, the acquiring company may acquire companies with little to virtually no debt. This would help in bringing down the debt-to-equity ratio of the combined entity and, thereby, leading to cheaper and better accessibility of credit.

2.5.1.3 Increased Market Share

An industry with large number of players usually tends to have its market share scattered. Integration of companies would help in industry consolidation thereby increasing the customer base of the combined entity and gaining higher market share. This might also help companies achieving stronger pricing power since some companies might merge/acquire competitor companies and combined entity becoming a major market leader.

For example, the takeover of Bank of Rajasthan by ICICI enhanced the market share of the combined entity post-merger. Similarly, integration of State Bank of India with State Bank of Mysore, State Bank of Patiala, and State Bank of Bikaner would help not only achieving economies of scale, but also help State Bank of India in consolidating its customer base with a wider reach of its subsidiaries. As banks integrate, the customers of all the integrating banks would be combined into one entity of SBI.

The acquisition of Loop Telecom by Airtel in India and Zain in South Africa has helped Airtel increasing its market share domestically as well as internationally. Loop Telecom had strong presence and large subscriber base in Maharashtra circle, and Zain had a stronghold in South Africa. This acquisition helped Airtel to grab large market share and increase the subscriber base.

2.5.1.4 Diversification

By way of merger or acquisition, the acquirer entity might be able to diversify its product line or its product reach. When the acquirer acquires companies present in different product line, it is set to diversify its operations. If the acquirer entity acquires companies present in same industry but in different locations (where the acquirer may have little to no presence), it is said to be geographical diversification.

For example, the acquisition of Myntra by Flipkart in the year 2014 helped Flipkart strengthen its presence in e-retailing (fashion). Flipkart was one of the top market leaders in India in e-retailing (electronics). Through the acquisition of Myntra, Flipkart was able to diversify its presence within e-retailing industry.

Similarly, Lactalis SA Group, French-based diary player, acquired Hyderabad-based Tirumala Milk Products private limited in the year 2014. Tirumala was having significant market share in south Indian dairy industry and acquisition of Tirumala marks the presence of Lactalis in India. This acquisition helped the Lactalis group in diversifying its geographical presence. Tata Steel acquiring Corus is also an example of geographical diversification.

2.5.1.5 Tax Savings

If a profit-making entity acquires a loss-making entity at low valuations, then the accumulated losses of acquired entity can be carried forwarded to set off against the profits of the combined entity and can result into tax savings for the combined entity.

Similarly, if the acquired entity has received some investment allowances in the form of tax exemptions for initial years of operations. These benefits may be readily available to the combined entity which helps the company to improve its profitability.

2.5.1.6 Acquisition of Crucial Resource

Sometimes the acquirer may acquire some target because the target company may be in possession of some crucial resource which may be of great value to acquirer entity. For example, when Vijay Mallya-owned Kingfisher Airlines acquired Gopinath-owned LCC Air Deccan, it immediately became eligible for international flights. Because as per the regulations prevailing at that time, minimum 5-year presence of an aviation firm was required in domestic market, in order to become eligible to start international flights. Air Deccan already had that license and its acquisition by Kingfisher automatically enabled Kingfisher to go international.

2.5.1.7 Vertical Integration

Vertical integration though is a type of merger, in itself is a source of synergy. A company integrates with either the supplier of its raw materials (backward integration) or the distribution network of its products offerings (forward integration) or both. This would help in better accessibility to raw materials even in times of limited availability. This also helps in better reach of the product offerings to the target customers. Since the entire network is captured through such kind of mergers or acquisition, the overall efficiency in the operations tends to increase along with lower cost.

For example, Zara, a flagship brand of Inditex based out of Spain, achieved its position of one of the world's largest women apparel brand through vertical integration. It secured its competitive advantage by means of integrating with supply chain and distribution which helped them produce apparels internally, rather than outsourcing, which is been the case of many top clothing brand.

There are lots of other reasons through which a synergy flow can be generated. Few such reasons are cross-selling, transfer of expertise, and effectiveness through strengthened distribution networks.

2.6   Valuation of Synergy

Generally, experts call the math behind synergy as "$1 + 1 > 2$" or "$2 + 2 > 4$" rather than the actual of 2 and 4. To understand this, let us consider the case of Grasim and L&T in the cement industry. Before the merger, Grasim was having market share of 9.93% of the total cement capacity and L&T was having a market share of 12.22%. Post-merger, the combined entity would have nearly about 22.2% of the total cement manufacturing capacity making the combined entity the market leader in terms of market capacity. If both the entities operate separately, they might not be able to get market power since the capacity was scattered. By merger, they were able to get market power through consolidation in the industry.

This helps us in determining the value of the synergy generated as well.

The amount of synergy would be the value of the combined entity less the aggregate of values of the individual entities.

To put this in equation,

$$v = \Delta V = V_{AT} - (V_A + V_T)$$

Where

ΔV—Value of synergy created
$V_{A\text{-}T}$—Value of the combined entity (post-merger entity)
V_A—Pre-merger value of acquiring firm
V_T—Pre-merger value of target firm

Example 1

If the fair value of Company A is 250 Crore and of Company B is 300 Crore and it is believed that the value of combined entity will be 600 Crore then expected synergy out of this deal can be calculated with the help of above equation:

Solution

$$\Delta V = V_{AT} - (V_A + V_T)$$
$$= 600 \text{ Crore} - (250 \text{ Cr} + 300 \text{ Cr})$$
$$= \text{Rs. } 50 \text{ Crore}$$

Example 2

If the fair value of Company A is 250 Crore and of Company B is 300 Crore and it is believed that the value of combined entity will be 600 Crore. However, Company B is able to buy Company A at Rs. 225 Crore. In this case, also the value of synergy will remain same Rs. 50 Crore.

Solution

$$v = \Delta V = V_{AT} - (V_A + V_T)$$
$$= 600 \text{ Crore} - (250 \text{ Cr} + 300 \text{ Cr}) = \text{Rs. } 50 \text{ Crore}$$

This is so because synergy is value creation in addition to sum of fair value of combining entities irrespective of deal price.

2.6.1   Discounting Benefit Method

The alternate method of calculating synergy goes in line with the common understanding of synergy. That, synergy, as noted earlier, is the value of increase in the benefit or reduction in the cost which would be obtained by the combined entity which otherwise is not possible for separate entities. To put it in simple terms, the combination of both the companies should create value either through increase in revenue or reduction in expenses. This can be noted as synergy.

Though the realized difference in cost or revenue arising out of merger or acquisition would be felt, it would be realized only in the future years. Thus, it needs to be discounted with the appropriate rate, usually cost of capital, to get the present value of the synergy.

To put this in equation,

Value of synergy = Annual increase in sales in the future years/Cost of capital

(Or)

Value of synergy = Annual reduction in cost/Cost of capital

Example 3

If Earth Ltd. buys Moon Ltd. and the cost saving from this deal is expected to be 1% of current operating cost, perpetually. Calculate the expected value of synergy, if the current operating cost is 1000 Crore and cost of capital of combined entity (Ko) is 12%.

Solution

Annual cost saving from the deal = 1% of Rs. 1000 Cr = 10 Crore
Value of this perpetual cost saving = Annual cost saving/Ko
= 10 Crore/.12 = Rs. 83.33 Crore.

Since it is perpetuity, the mathematical equation for finding the present value, that is,

(Cash flow/rate) is used for calculation.

Example 4

Calculate the value of synergy, if the acquisition will result in 2% increase in pricing power and 7% growth in sales volume for next three years, which otherwise would have been no increase in pricing power and a growth of 5%. Current sales volume of acquirer is 1000 units, for target it is 500 units. Current market price is Rs. 50 per unit. Market capitalization rate is 10%. Given that there will be no change in cost figures in pre- and post-acquisition period.

Solution

However, the synergy obtained by the difference in revenue of merged entities and combined revenue of both the individual entities without merger stands in the future year 1, 2, and 3. Present value of these cash flows has to be calculated at the market capitalization rate of 10% in order to find out the value of synergy at present.

Calculation of Synergy :

Growth Forecasting of Combined Entity

Years	0	1	2	3	Forecasting Rates
Price	50	51	52.02	53.0604	(2% growth)
Volume	1500	1605	1717.35	1837.565	(7% growth)
(A) Revenue of merged entity (=Price *Volume)	81855		89336.55	97501.91	

Growth Forecasting of Individual Entities

	Years	1	2	3	Forecasting Rates
Price	50	50	50	50	
Volume (Acquirer)	1000	1050	1102.5	1157.625	(5% growth)
Volume (Target)	500	525	551.25	578.8125	(5% growth)
Revenue (Acquirer)		52500	55125	57881.25	
Revenue (Target)		26250	27562.5	28940.63	
(B) Combined Revenue without merger		78750	82687.5	86821.88	
In the absence of cost changes, this entire difference in the revenue of merged entities and combined revenue of two entities without merger will be treated as value addition or synergy caused by merger.					
Synergy (A-B)		3105	6649.05	10680.03	

To calculate the present value, we have to discount future synergy benefits as follows:

$$\text{Pesent Value of Synergy} = \text{Cash Flow}1.\frac{1}{(1+r)^1} + \text{Cash Flow}2.\frac{1}{(1+r)^2}$$
$$+ \text{Cash Flow}3.\frac{1}{(1+r)^3}$$

$$\text{Pesent Value of Synergy} = \frac{3105}{(1+10\%)^1} + \frac{6649.05}{(1+10\%)^2} + \frac{1}{(1+10\%)^3}$$

$$= 2822.73 + 5495.08 + 8024.06$$
$$= \text{Rs. } 16{,}341.87$$

CHAPTER 3

M&A Process and Defensive Strategies

When a firm decides to grow through inorganic route, then it is quite important that each element of merger/acquisition process is meticulously planned and cautiously executed to make the M&A successful. The deal process begins with laying out the correct strategic plan for merger/acquisition in line with the overall plan of the acquiring firm. It must culminate into the successful integration of merging entity realizing the forecasted growth of earnings through synergistic benefits flowing in. The process of merger and acquisition is detailed below.

3.1 M&A Process

Mergers and acquisition process involves the following steps:

1. Formulation of strategy and identification of target
2. Target evaluation and analysis
3. Reaching out to target and entering into deal negotiations
4. Due diligence
5. Closing the deal.

© The Author(s) 2019
V. Kumar and P. Sharma, *An Insight into Mergers and Acquisitions*,
https://doi.org/10.1007/978-981-13-5829-6_3

3.1.1   Step 1: Formulation of Strategy for M&A and Identification of Target

This step includes the study of industry dynamics, current and forecasted industry growth rate, firm's current market share, and identification of gaps to be filled to pursue the overall organizational goals. These gaps may be in the form of required footprints in other markets known as geographical expansion, product line expansion, and technical know-how, key inputs for production process or requirement of forward integration or backward integration.

Acquirer company has to decide the acquisition strategy which has to be in line with overall corporate policy where acquisition may be a part of growth strategy or portfolio strategy. The acquirer has to finalize the preferred characteristics of a potential target in terms of the following:

- *Geographical preferences*: Acquirer team has to finalize whether they are looking for a domestic or cross-border acquisition and that too specific locations which are strategically preferred. For example, Airtel acquired Zain in South Africa to exploit the geographical opportunities in South Africa.
- *Size of target*: It is important to decide what should be the size of target, whether it should be relatively large to enhance the market share or position of acquirer in the industry. Should it be a small-sized acquisition for acquirer to enter into a new geographical market/product line/customer segment? Tata's acquisition of Corus offered them both the benefits of entering into European markets as well as it elevated the Tata's position to be the 6th largest steel manufacturer from 56th position at global level.
- *Product line offerings of target*: Acquirer has to decide whether they want to expand in the same product line just to add the capacity. Like in the case of sale of Jaypee Cement to Birla Group, the intention may be to enter specific product line within their industry through acquisition, like in the case of Flipkart acquiring Myntra to get into apparel segment.
- *Positioning of target*: The acquisition may be to grab a special product range for masses or a niche area. For example, Fortis acquired Escorts to enter into Heart Speciality Segment. Another similar example is the recent acquisition of online jewelry retailer Carat lane by Titan which will complement its off-line retail model and help it to tap young customers.

- *Availing of tax benefits*: At times, the acquisition is preferred for the target's tax benefits since the target might be a less/non-profitable entity. And therefore, helping acquiring company reduces its overall tax outgo.

After an in-depth analysis of the requirements and formulation of acquisition strategy, the acquirer will identify the prospective targets, which fit into the overall policy framework of acquirer. This list of targets will be further filtered after preliminary screening and discussion with experts, and the most suitable ones will be identified.

3.1.2   Step 2: Target Evaluation and Analysis

The next step is the financial and operational analysis of the target, based on the past and forecasted income statement, balance sheet, cash flow statements and market data like PE, price to book value, market share, industry growth prospects, etc. The financials of target will be analyzed and growth prospects will be forecasted. Based on the analysis, a preliminary valuation will be assigned. Acquirer may avail the services of an investment banker to assess the value of potential target entity. For valuation of target entity, any of the following method or combination of methods is used (covered in Chapter 5 on M&A valuation):

- Discounted cash flow method (DCF)
- Comparable company analysis
- Comparable acquisition-based valuation
- Assets-based valuation.

After careful analysis, weights are assigned to each method; the normally higher weight is assigned to absolute valuation methods like DCF in comparison with relative methods like comparable. These weights are applied to respective value of the target calculated by each method and then a tentative weighted average valuation is arrived at, which will be used for initial discussions with the target.

3.1.3   Step 3: Reaching Out to Target and Negotiations

After finding out the tentative valuation, the target entity will be contacted either directly or through some investment banker. After the initial discussions, it will be clear whether target entity is interested to go ahead with the deal or not. In case target promoters/management doesn't agree, then acquirer has to decide whether to go ahead for hostile acquisition or not.

If target also shows interest in the deal, then non-disclosure agreement (also known as confidentiality agreement) will be signed between two parties. This agreement states that the information shared between two entities will remain confidential and will not be shared with any other third party and will be returned whenever demanded. After these both, the entities will start the deal valuation process intensively. They will exchange operational and financial information with each other. Detailed valuation will be carried out based on the internal and important information exchanged between the two parties. This may lead to substantial revision in the initial valuation of target. Then, a letter of intent (also known as indication of interest) will be sent to target entity stating the deal price and terms and conditions of the offer like business/assets to be bought, valuation summary, mode of payment, etc. The involved entities may enter into exclusivity agreement which restricts both the party from entering into merger talks with any other third party for a specified period. If target entity broadly agrees to the letter of intent, then due diligence is initiated.

3.1.4   Step 4: Due Diligence

Due diligence means taking the reasonable care while entering into a transaction and checking every area minutely so that acquirer is sure what is being bought and there are no major problem areas in the target. It is an analysis of what could be potentially problematic areas too. After incorporating all these factors in the process, it becomes relatively easy to find out the reasonable deal price.

Due diligence process broadly covers the following areas:

3.1.4.1 Operational Due Diligence
In the operational due diligence process, the operational aspects like its agreements and relations with suppliers, customers, distributors, equipment suppliers, etc., are checked and it is ensured that all agreements are proper and don't have any hidden problem areas.

3.1.4.2 Financial Due Diligence

It is very important part of due diligence process and can have an impact on deal pricing. All the financials of target company like income statement, balance sheet, and cash flow statement are intensively analyzed. All the projections and growth rates are evaluated which have been used by the target to fix the deal price in order to ensure that all projections are reasonable and not overestimated. Industry growth rate and companies future earnings have been forecasted based on most reasonable projections. Bondholders, shareholder agreements, borrowing documents, bank accounts, etc., have to be properly checked and verified for any dues and disputes on the part of target entity.

3.1.4.3 Legal Due Diligence

It is another area where extreme caution has to be applied because any mistake in legal due diligence process may lead to tremendous trouble for the acquirer in future. It is checked whether the company has paid all the dues to its suppliers, equipment manufacturers. All the dues toward taxation, excise, and other authorities are duly paid and regulations are complied with. There are no pending litigations against the company. Target entity is not in violation of any law of land and all the IPR related to patents, copyrights, etc., duly secured. All the documents like income tax returns, VAT, central excise, sales tax returns, service tax returns, TDS, electricity and water bill payment receipts, etc., will be properly checked and verified, and also they will check whether there is any pending demand or contingent liability on the part of target toward these authorities. The objective of legal due diligence is to safeguard the acquirer from any future shocks caused by negligence or intentional wrongdoings on the part of target.

3.1.4.4 Organizational Due Diligence

Under organizational due diligence, every aspect of business will be checked like what is the strategy of the target firm, how strategically fit is this target within the framework of acquirer strategy of growth, what is the rationale for this acquisition? HR-related aspects also have to be scrutinized minutely like who are the key employees, what kind of agreement they have with the target entity, will acquisition give rise to any special compensation to be paid to certain officials, whether certain key officials

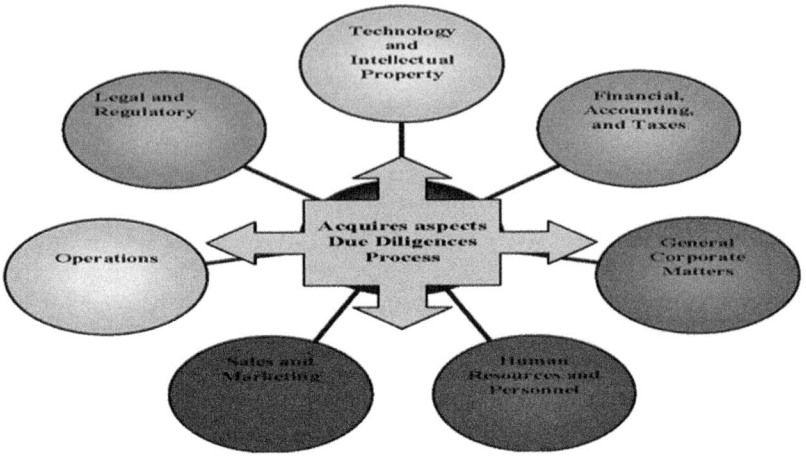

Fig. 3.1   Due diligence process

have to be retained, and whether target promoters have to be shared the seat on the board of combined entity are all important parameters to be looked into. The provident fund, gratuity, ESOPs, or any other liability toward employees will have to be checked. The agreement entered by company with key employees, bonds, etc., has to be verified. All these aspects have to be thoroughly checked as they will have an impact on deal negotiations and pricing.

For the conduct of due diligence, all the material information will be exchanged by two parties once LOI is signed. Acquirer will appoint the outside law and accounting firm in order to carry out the detailed due diligence and check every business aspect minutely (Fig. 3.1).

3.1.5   Step 5: Final Negotiations and Closing the Deal

Once both the parties have done their part of valuations and acquirer has conducted the due diligence, both the entities enter into final negotiation across the table. Based on the projections used by the investment banker of both side and information revealed during detailed scrutiny process of target, there is good probability that valuation of target arrived at by acquirer will not match; there will be differences of opinion on the continuation of past trends and forecasted industry and company growth rates. Problem areas found in target will heavily influence the offer price made by acquirer. Target will try to justify their projections and demand price while acquirer will try to discount many factors and finalize a lower price which will lead to a lower premium above the net asset value, to be paid by him. Target will try to extract the maximum value for its shareholders, especially, if they know that their company is a strategic fit for the acquirer. Based on the negotiations, mutual understanding and how strategically important this acquisition is for the acquirer they will reach a mutually decided price, mode of payment, etc., and deal will be closed. A definitive agreement will be signed between the two entities.

After this, acquirer has to arrange for the financing of the deal based on the payment mode decided between them. If they have decided on the cash deal, then acquirer may use internal accruals or may borrow from the market. If it is a stock deal, then acquirer has to make arrangements to issue company's share to target shareholders based on the decided swap ratio. In case of stock deal, they also have to agree on the role of target promoter/CEO in the combined entity and whether they will be offered seats on the board. They also have to mutually agree whether total consideration will be paid immediately by the acquirer or a part will be in the form of earn-outs in future. Earn-out is the part of acquisition consideration which is paid after a certain time period of acquisition, depending on the performance of merged entity. Earn-outs are to be paid by the acquirer, if the combined entity achieves the mutually pre-decided level of performance in the form of sales/earnings, etc., in the specified time period.

3.2   CONCENTRATION MEASURES

Concentration measures are used to check whether industry is dominated by one or few large players in the industry as they have large market shares and can dictate the pricing and other terms in the industry. A high concentration is undesirable as the few large firms control the market and use it for their benefit. This will pose problems for consumer at large as these monopoly or large firms will dictate the high prices and unfavorable terms for customers in the absence of better alternatives. Antitrust law in the USA and Competition Act in India don't allow the merger of two entities which will lead to higher concentration in the industry.

3.3   Hostile Acquisitions

Mergers and acquisitions is a shorter route for corporate seeking faster growth. The buyer acquires the target company for several reasons inter alia access to new distribution channels, customer base, brand name, or technology or access to financial resources. Many a time, the acquirer is serious about an acquisition whereas the acquiree is not willing itself to be acquired. One of the reasons may be that the members of management of the target company might fear the loss of their jobs after acquisition. The fear pervades among shareholders that the deal would reduce the market capitalization causing them pecuniary loss.

When the acquisition is not acceptable to acquiree and the acquirer forcefully goes for an acquisition through various means, it is known as hostile acquisition. A hostile takeover or acquisition occurs when a company gains control over the other company without the consent of the board of directors or the management of the target company. In such a scenario, the acquiree makes all-out efforts to ward off this unwanted invader by adopting various defensive strategies. Since the majority of publicly listed companies face the risk of being a target of a hostile takeover bid, they need to protect themselves by implementing various defensive strategies.

The most effective defensive methods are generally built-in measures that make it difficult for an un-intended invader to take over. These methods are collectively referred to as defensive strategies to avoid hostile takeovers.

3.3.1   Defensive Strategies in Case of Hostile Takeovers

The takeover defense mechanism or anti-takeover strategies based on the timing when they are exercised can be classified as

    a. Pre-offer or preventive defense strategies and
    b. Post-offer or reactive defense strategies.

Pre-bid defenses also called preventive or preemptive defenses are put in place to prevent a sudden or unexpected hostile attempt for control of the company. When preventive takeover defenses are not successful in fending off an unwanted bid or were not put in place in advance, the target implements post-bid or reactive defenses. These takeover defenses intend to avoid the takeover by bringing about a change in the corporate control position of the promoters and some of the other changes in the company.

3.3.1.1 Preventive/Preemptive Defense Strategies

These defensive techniques are put in place to ward off potential take-overs attempt before the event is initiated. A company can put in place any of these various types of preemptive defense strategies to avoid an attempted takeover.

Pre-offer takeover defense mechanisms can be classified into:

- *Right-based defense strategies:* This involves the issue of additional rights to shareholders which triggers, when a hostile takeover bid is initiated against the company. This makes the acquisition difficult to be executed for the hostile bidder.
- *Change in corporate charter (Shark Repellants)*: Many companies make the provisions in their charter which get triggered only when a hostile takeover bid is initiated. This makes target unattractive for the bidder.

3.3.1.2 Preventive Pre-offer Measures

Control Over the Register

Generally, when it comes to hostile takeover, the raider company does an exercise where it needs to know that who are the shareholders of the target company so that they could directly approach the shareholders and offer to buy their shares. All such data are contained in the share register of the company. Hence, it is important for the target company to control such register and keep its privacy. The share register provides the information about the shares held by shareholders which can be identified by them. Any persons who are not authorized should not have any access to the share register of the company. This can be achieved by choosing reputed and reliable share registrar to maintain the share register is the most important task for the target company. Every now and then, the company must keep track records of the share register, so that it is under strict surveillance. The target company must have a proper control over the registrar company.

Differential Voting Rights Shares (DVRs)

Many a corporate has come out with DVR as a preemptive line of defense against a hostile corporate takeover. Securities that have differential voting rights (DVRs) to shareholders can help a company generate resources through equity without diluting the existing promoters holding. In India, Tata Motors and Jain Irrigation Gujarat NRE Coke and Pantaloon Retail issued DVRs a few years ago.

The fund-raising through DVR shares helps the target companies maintain their promoter's holding making it difficult for the invader to achieve control over the takeover target.

Employee Stock Ownership Plan (ESOP)

A defense which can be built against a hostile takeover bid is to establish an employee stock options plan (ESOPs). Employees of the company holding ownership in the company imply that a greater percentage of the company's ownership is with people who can be expected to vote in favor of the existing promoters. ESOP also reduces the number of shares available for corporate raider.

Poison Pill

This refers to the olden days when agents were instructed to swallow a cyanide pill instead of being captured. When it comes to the corporate world, poison pill is the issuance of shares at a discount to the market price to existing shareholders. Technically, the "rights" to purchase additional shares at a given price attached to each share will be triggered on the announcement of any unwanted takeover bid.

The issue of poison pills, or the right issue at cheaper price, happens with a triggering event, e.g., acquirer gaining more than 20% of the firm's shares without the board's approval or a tender offer for 24% of the target firm's outstanding stock.

Poison pill emerged in the financial literature in the 1980s which involves an arrangement that will make the target company's stock unattractive for the acquiring company. Poison pill provision can be used to deter prospective acquirers.

These rights to purchase additional shares of target in the event of a hostile takeover, at a lower price for each share held by them, make it very expensive for the acquirer to take over a target. The larger number of shares shall require more funds on the part of acquirer making it difficult to acquire. Poison pill is considered to be the most effective defense strategies to thwart a hostile bid.

These Poison Pills Can Be of Various Types Like

Flip-In

One of the most commonly used poison pill is known as "flip-in" which allows existing shareholders to buy more shares at a discount in the event of any takeover attempt. It generally gets triggered when a threshold figure of say 30–40% is hit. The flow of additional cheap shares into the total pool of shares increases the total number of shares which need to be purchased by invading company. In 2004, PeopleSoft was employing the flip-in model against Oracle Corporation's multi-billion hostile takeover bid.

In 2012, Carl Icahn had purchased nearly 10% of the shares of Netflix in an attempt to take over the company. The Netflix board at that time reacted by equity rights issue plan known as flip-into make takeover excessively costly for the invader. The terms of the rights issue were that if anyone bought up 10% or more of the shares of the company, the existing shareholders shall be permitted to buy newly issued rights shares at a heavy discount. This shall automatically dilute that stake of corporate raider.

Flip-Over

A flip-over pill is administered when target shareholders exercise their right to buy acquirers shares. Flip-over is different from flip-in because it occurs when the shareholders of the target company's will be permitted to buy the shares of the acquiring company at a discount after the merger has been completed. This will dilute the company's control in the hands of the acquirer. This kind of clause which the invader comes to know of shall desist him to initiate the takeover bid.

Poison Puts

Poison put is a strategy to ward off any hostile bid by paying off the bondholders of the target in case of a hostile takeover attempt. This is executed through the issuance of specific types of Puttable bonds in which put option is exercisable only upon a hostile takeover which creates a strain on acquirer to re-finance the debt. In the event of an unfriendly takeover bid the bondholders exercise their put option to sell their bonds to the company. By selling off the bonds, large principal payments become due for the target company toward the bondholder.

People Pill

Here, management threatens that in the event of a hostile takeover bid, the existing management team and the core specialists will resign at the same time en-masse. This strategy is highly effective since the highly qualified employees who are crucial in identifying and developing business opportunities will resign from their posts. For example, a company is specialized in high-tech equipment's made by highly professional employees. If any takeover attempt takes place, they all claim that they will leave their job on such occasions. This disables the raiders company as it is not easy to recruit such high-tech employees and it will be difficult to maintain them also.

Jonestown Defense

Borrowing large amounts of money by the target company that the acquiring company would have to later on payoff is known as Jonestown Defense. This excessive borrowing makes it unattractive target, although it can lead to serious financial problems or even bankruptcy. In some cases, a company may decide that it would rather go out of business than be acquired. They intentionally rack up enough debt to face bankruptcy. This is known as the Jonestown Defense.

Staggered Board

Target can stagger their board, allowing only part of it reelected every year. For example, only 2 directors are elected every three years where board has 12 directors. When this kind of staggered board exists in a company, the acquirer is not able to get control of the board at least for few years. For acquiring control, they need to appoint majority of their elected directors who favors the acquisition.

The takeover process gets dragged, owning to this staggered board, because it prevents the entire board from being replaced at the same time. Many companies that are interested in making an acquisition don't want to wait for a long period of time for the board to turn over. Therefore, the staggered board acts as a strong deterrent for any hostile takeover bid.

Supermajority Voting for Mergers

Provision that mergers can be approved only by a huge percentage of shareholders as against normal majority in normal cases might act as a strong deterrent for hostile acquisition. Acquirer hence has to get support of those many shareholders to be able to take over the target.

It is a defense that generally requires 70 or 80% of shareholders to approve of any acquisition. Conducting a takeover by buying enough stock for a controlling interest in this situation becomes almost impossible.

Fair Price Amendment
The provision stating that unless a fair price is offered for the target (determined by some provision), the merger can't be done. This price is specified by the target up front and might be onerous for an acquirer making a hostile bid.

Golden Parachute
One of the most recognizable defenses used in the USA where when the director, manager, or any executive vacates his/her office owing to an unwanted takeover or merger then they take a huge amount of money as compensation. This measure discourages an unwanted takeover. The golden parachute clause gets triggered when there is a change of control over the company and subsequent ouster of the executives by the acquirer. The benefits to be offered to the executives may include stock options, bonuses, or hefty severance pay which is termed as golden parachute.

Golden parachutes can be highly expensive for the acquiring company. This makes the undesirable suitors think twice before acquiring a company.

For example, golden parachute is a provision in a CEO's contract which states that a large bonus in the form of cash or stock shall be given to him if the company is acquired. This clause shall make the acquisition more expensive and therefore less attractive.

Some of the time this strategy is implemented along with other takeover defense strategies. The golden parachute's primary purpose in a hostile takeover is to protect the executives of the target company as well as to make the acquisition unattractive.

3.3.1.3 Lobster Trap
A lobster trap is an anti-takeover strategy used by target firms. In a lobster trap, the target firm prevents individuals with more than 10% ownership of convertible securities from transferring these securities to voting members of the company. This is a preventive measure that makes sure large stakeholders cannot add to their voting stock and thus reduces facilitating the takeover of the target company.

3.3.2   Responsive Takeover Defense Strategies Litigation

A general tactic to delay the takeover process is to file a lawsuit against the acquirer (CCI or MRTP in India) Courts may provide some injunction against the takeover and help the company avoid the hostile acquisition.

3.3.3   Greenmail

Greenmail refers to a company buying a certain amount of its own shares from an individual investor, usually at a substantial premium. This technique was popular during one of the mergers and acquisitions trends in the 1980s. The shares are purchased at a premium over the takeover price. Shareholders of the target company may lose out financially while avoiding a hostile takeover bid because the invader has to be paid out a hefty premium.

3.3.4   Buyback of Shares

Buyback of shares brings about a change in the capital structure of the company dramatically. It makes the company unattractive for the acquirer.

The buyback of the share pushes the price of the stock up and hence makes the target more expensive to be acquired. The proportion of promoters' holding goes up when the company goes for buyback of its own shares.

3.3.5   Crown Jewel

In this takeover defense, the target company sells one of its most valuable assets which make the target company less attractive in the eyes of the raider company.

In this case, the target company gets the right to sell off the company's most valuable assets (crown jewels)—all or only a few, when it faces a hostile bid. Selling such assets will make it less attractive to the possible acquirers and may ultimately force it to retraces its steps.

For example, Company A wants to acquire Company B because Company B has a land site which is situated in special economic zone and very beneficial to Company A. On such a hostile takeover attempt, Company B sells away such land site to prevent itself being taken over by Company A. Company B may incur a great loss by selling off the property, but still could avoid the hostile takeover.

This defensive strategy may be executed when the target company sells its crown jewels to another friendly company (white knight) and later on, when and if the acquiring company has withdrawn its offer, buys back the assets sold to the white knight at a fixed price agreed in advance.

3.3.6   Pac-Man Defense

In this strategy of avoiding a hostile acquisition, the target company counter bids and makes a takeover attempt on the acquirer itself. In this Pac-Man defense, as a last resort, the target company makes a tender offer to acquire the stock of the hostile bidder. It is a very extreme type of anti-takeover defense and usually signals desperation of the target company. This strategy, however, requires financial resources and shareholders' support.

If the acquirer company tries to purchase shares of the target company, then on such notice to defend itself the target company starts buying shares of acquirer company, making the acquirer company step back. In some cases, the purchase of even a small fraction of shares may help in avoiding the takeover bid by the invader.

3.3.7   Propaganda

This may be called a social defense under which the target company takes the help of social media. The company makes public know its arguments against the takeover. The company may strengthen its positive image and emphasize its importance for the region/country. An effective campaign can turn the wind around, and by influencing the shareholders, state bodies, and general public, the target company can escape from the take-over. This propaganda was vehemently adopted by Corus when Tata's made an attempt to acquire it.

3.3.8   White Knight Defense

This is a defense mechanism wherein a friendly third party is sought who can buy the target at an attractive price. This normally results in a price war between the acquirer and the third party, resulting in target shareholders getting better price in the end. Typically, the white knight agrees to pay a premium above the acquirer's offer to buy the target company's stock.

Such a strategy deters the raider as well as benefits the shareholders in the short term, if the terms are favorable, as well as in the long term if the merger with a white knight is a good strategic fit. The friendly company is termed as a white knight. The target may seek out a white knight by itself or with the help of investment bankers.

White knight acquires a minority stake in the company which is big enough to deter acquirer's takeover plans. For example, if the target promoters have 40% holding and contact their friendly organization to buy 15% stake in their company, then their collective holding will be 55% (more than 50%) and it will become impossible for hostile bidder to attain the majority control in the target and execute their takeover plan.

3.3.9   *Scorched Earth Policy*

This is another defensive technique employed by the companies to avert a hostile takeover bid. The strategy is quite similar to crown jewel strategy. Scorched earth tactics include selling off the valuable assets or entering them into long-term contractual commitments.

For example, in 2008, Yahoo offered severance packages to all full-time Yahoo employees to avert a possible takeover from Microsoft. Yahoo managed to stave off Microsoft's offer with a series of other strategies including the scorched earth policy.

3.4   Conclusion

Selection of the defense system against a hostile takeover is a strategically important decision. Careful preparation is of great importance to forestall such unfriendly bids. It is also equally important to remain flexible enough by responding to changing dynamic. There is no "One sizes that fits all" strategy to make the company foolproof against such hostile bids. Therefore, a regular review and understanding of the ever-changing environments is highly important.

Each strategy has its own unique implications. Even if their company is not currently being considered for acquisition, it is prudent for management to put in place preemptive defensive mechanism. Such policies should be seriously pursued by highly profitable companies with strong balance sheet and an attractive cash flow statement or a company with growing market share for its products or services. In addition, if the company exhibits significant barriers to entry and limited competitive environment or minimal bargaining power of suppliers making them more susceptible to hostile takeover, these preemptive techniques become highly important. A thorough understanding of responsive takeover defense mechanisms is equally highly advised.

CHAPTER 4

Deal Structuring and Financing

4.1   INTRODUCTION

In the pursuit of acquisition, certain factors which play an important role are continued growth opportunity provided by the target company, purchase price, and financing terms.

Once valuation for a particular deal is complete, it is necessary to identify how much price has to be paid for acquiring the partial or complete stake. In the case study of Myntra discussed in valuation chapter, we have valued the Myntra at 1189 crores, based on DCF method. Assume that the premium that can be paid for acquisition to be 311 crores. The overall value of the company comes out to be 1500 crores. Now both the companies (Flipkart and Myntra) will start negotiating the deal. Flipkart will not pay anything more than 1500 crores for the company as it will destroy the wealth. On the other hand, Myntra will not accept anything below 1500 crores. Thus, negotiations take place, and price is arrived to make maximum gain for either of the parties. Since valuations are subjective, each company arrive at different values (not necessarily 1189 for both) and agree with the price based on negotiations. Once the price is agreed upon, the structure of the deal has to be negotiated, which is how the deal will be taking place, how the consideration will be paid, legal and other accounting aspects.

A merger or acquisition deal can typically be structured in ways where the acquirer company would create a separate entity just to facilitate a particular M&A deal. An M&A deal may have a complex structure due

© The Author(s) 2019
V. Kumar and P. Sharma, *An Insight into Mergers and Acquisitions*,
https://doi.org/10.1007/978-981-13-5829-6_4

to legal, regulatory, accounting, taxation, and other business considerations. With the simplification of the regulatory frameworks taking place, the legal and accounting complications in structuring are gradually getting reduced.

4.2   Deal Structuring Process

Every deal is structured in a different way depending upon the objectives of the buyer and seller entering into a deal. For example, in case of Facebook acquiring WhatsApp, the objective of Facebook was not to control the operations (as WhatsApp is still run independently), but to ensure its vision of making the world connected and keeping its market share. For WhatsApp, the objective might have been to get a good valuation. The objectives of the parties to the deal can be categorized as follows:

- Control
- Life of the entity
- Ownership status
- Tax status
- Risk

The above-mentioned objectives will help in strategizing a structure for the M&A deal, which is affected by the following:

i.   Acquisition vehicle
ii.   Method of payment
iii. Form of acquisition
iv.   Legal considerations
v.   Accounting and tax considerations

These factors broadly decide how the structure of the deal is going to be, keeping in view the above-mentioned objectives.

4.3   Why Deal Structuring Matters?

To understand why deal structure matters in an M&A, let us consider the following example:

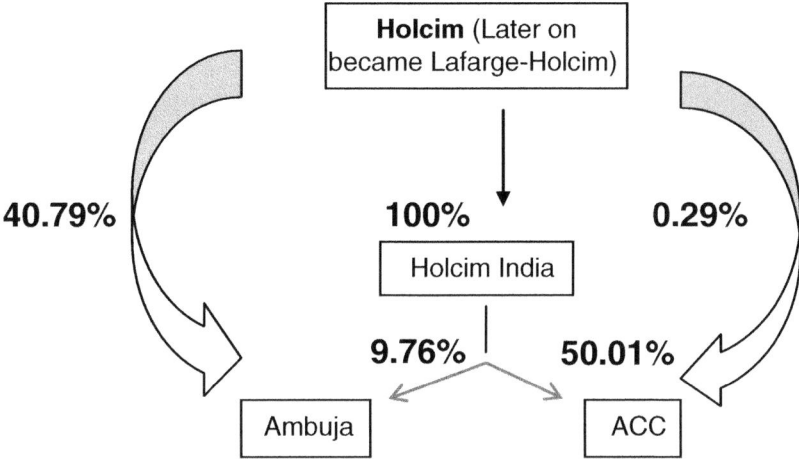

Fig. 4.1 Shareholding pattern

The scheme of Amalgamation between Ambuja Cements and Holcim India Private Ltd.

The intention of Ambuja Cements Ltd. (ACL) was to acquire ACC which could potentially unlock synergies in the form of supply chain and fixed cost optimization. But the existing structure of shareholding in ACL and ACC made it complicated for ACL to acquire ACC directly. Thus, ACL had to go for a reverse merger scheme of its holding company Holcim India Pvt Ltd. (Fig. 4.1).

The above structure implies that both Ambuja and ACC were subsidiaries of Holcim India Private Ltd. (HIPL), which was in turn a wholly-owned subsidiary of LafargeHolcim (Lafarge and Holcim merged). Thus, for Ambuja, buying ACC was a complicated deal.

As a result, Ambuja went on to a reverse merger process where Ambuja would first buy 24% stake in Holcim India Pvt Ltd. by paying cash worth Rs. 3500 Crores. Subsequently, both the entities would get merged (thereby taking indirect control of ACC Ltd.). Post-merger, the shareholding is expected to be (Fig. 4.2).

The merger swap ratio was fixed at one share of Ambuja for every 7.4 shares of Holcim, translating into an implied swap ratio of 6.6 Ambuja shares for every ACC share. Based on the swap ratio, Ambuja Cement

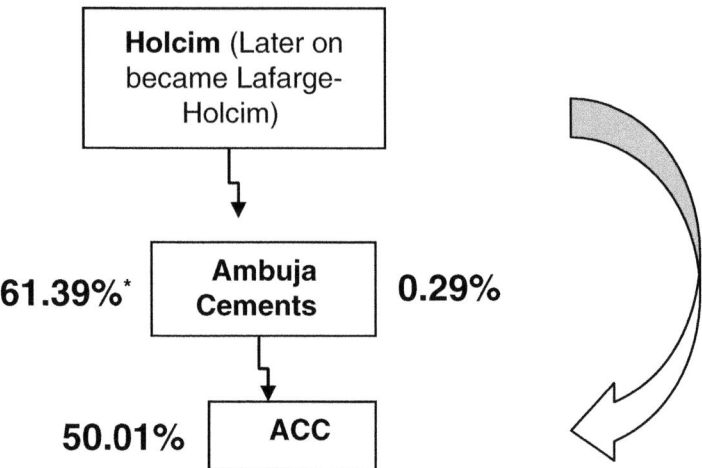

Fig. 4.2 Shareholding pattern post-merger

had to issue Rs. 58.4 crore new equity shares of the company to Holcim as a consideration for the merger. ACL would issue Rs. 8226 Crores (20.6%) worth of its shares to LafargeHolcim to merge HIPL into ACL. Holcim already holds 40.79%, thereby making the total shareholding of Holcim in ACL equal to 61.39%.

Note: *61.39% would be post-merger stake of Holcim in the Ambuja.

This deal was considered to be one of the highly complicated structures by Industry Experts and market analysts, because of the entities involved, post-merger Industry structure, accounting issues, etc.

The deal structures are more often a case of buyer-dominated decision. A buyer who is confident in the acquisition he might not want to share the post-merger profits may prefer to go for all-cash deal. If the buyer feels there is more risk in the business being acquired, he might negotiate and issue its equities to the target shareholder's to make them share the risk of the business after acquisition.

Thus, it can be said that, the appropriate structure, varies from deal to deal given the objectives of the parties involved and consensus between them.

In the above case, since the intention of Ambuja was to gain control over ACC, they entered into a **Reverse Merger** by way of cash and equity issuance, and not acquisition or any other structure.

In 2016 cairn India, India's largest oil producing company merged with the mining and metal giant company Vedanta Ltd. In all share deal of $25 million where the shareholder of cairn India shall get the equity and preference share of Vedanta.

4.4   DEAL FINANCING AND DEAL STRUCTURE

Deal structure deals with "what the buyer is intending to do." The buyer may be interested in

a. Asset purchase,
b. Stock purchase,
c. Merger, etc.

Financing the method of payment of the deal could be:

- Cash deal (Consideration paid in cash)
- Stock deal (Consideration paid in stock)
- Debt (Consideration paid through issuance of bonds of the acquirer)
- Earn-outs (Consideration subject to achievement of specified targets)
- Combination of any of the above

4.5   DEAL STRUCTURING AND FINANCING

Any particular deal is financed as per its structure and as per the risk-reward objective of the entities involved. Thus, it can be said that any particular deal structure is a resultant of the careful thought on financing of the deal (deal type) and other key considerations to derive maximum benefits.

That is, if it makes sense for a deal to be paid out in stock because cash deal would result in immediate tax implications which might not be beneficial for the target shareholders, the deal can be structured as a "Merger" or "Stock purchase through stock swap."

From the above, it can be inferred that all the considerations (factors) should be seen simultaneously before choosing which mode of payments to be opted for. Once it is identified, the structure can be negotiated so as to extract maximum gains for both the parties.

Let us consider the above structures in detail:

4.5.1   Asset Purchase

In case of an asset acquisition, the buyer would acquire all or some of the assets of the target entity. It would typically be any specific asset like technology of one firm, buying the manufacturing plant of a distressed company, etc. In this case, the buying entity is not buying the overall business, but only the assets of the target for a consideration. But it is not necessary that the liabilities should also have to be absorbed by the acquiring entity.

Also, in case of asset purchase the transaction is between the companies. There is no involvement of the shareholders. That is, the consideration will be paid to the target company and not the shareholders of the target, for the asset being purchased.

For example, Jaypee associates have agreed to sell its several cement plants to Birla Group-owned Ultratech Cement at a mutually agreed price of 15,900 Crore. This sale of majority of cement business except the Karnataka cement plant will help the debt-ridden Jaypee Group to reduce its debt. This deal of purchase of assets only shall not result in any payment to the shareholders of the company.

Another type of asset acquisition is the **Slump Sale.** In this type, the acquirer buys a pool of assets for a lump sum consideration. There is no specific value attached to individual assets. Slump sale includes both the assets and liabilities.

For example, Tata Chemicals, during August 2016, announced to sell its urea business to Yara Fertilizers India Private Limited by way of slump sale for an amount of Rs. 2670 Crores. For Tata Chemicals, the deal is a divestiture as it is hiving off its business division. But for Yara Fertilizers India Pvt Ltd., the deal is structured as an asset purchase.

Though Yara is acquiring the business unit, it is structured as asset purchase because the payment of Rs. 2670 Crores is being transferred to Tata Chemicals and not the shareholders of Tata Chemicals. It effectively means that Tata Chemicals has sold its asset for a consideration on a lump sum basis giving away the assets and liabilities related to its urea business.

An asset purchase can happen not only by giving the cash, but also by issuing stocks or debt of the acquirer entity to the acquire company but not to the shareholders of the acquire company.

Asset purchase in respect of the considerations:

Stockholder's approval: For an asset purchase, stockholder's approval is not required as it can be stated as business division not impacting the minority shareholders.

Tax consequences: Taxability is generally seen for the target entity. In case of an asset purchase, the target company receives the consideration (either in the form of cash or stock or both). Thus, it will be treated as a capital gain/loss for the company and the effective tax rate for target will be applicable on the same.

Legal consequences: The legal status of the entities will not be complicated in the case of asset purchase/sale. Asset purchase is literally like a person selling his car or house to the other person. Thus, only the ownership of the asset is transferred and there is no question on the legality of the party involved.

Risk sharing: In an asset purchase, generally, the ownership of the asset is transferred to the acquirer in full. Thus all the risk related to assets has to be borne by the acquirer. In the above case, Yara has to assume all the risk. But, if Yara makes payment through stock for purchase of the asset, the risk will be shared by Tata Chemicals indirectly as Tata Chemicals would become the shareholder of Yara.

Third-party approval: For an asset purchase, there is no need for third-party approvals. Third parties are generally competition commission of India, RBI, Industry regulators, other regulators, etc.

4.5.2   Stock Purchase

Stock purchase is where the acquirer entity purchases the common stock of the target entity. The acquirer entity can even purchase 100% shares of the target entity by making open offers. It effectively means the assets and liabilities of the target are being purchased by the acquirer proportionate to the acquisition.

4.5.2.1 Example IGATE Acquires Majority Stake in Patni Computers

IGATE's 1.2 billion-dollar acquisition of Patni Computers during May 2011, creating a new entity IGATE Patni with over 82.5% stake by IGATE is an example of stock purchase. The rationale behind the acquisition was to increase the revenue by increasing the customer base.

Stock purchase in respect of the considerations:

Stockholder's approval: Shareholders consent of both target and acquirer entities is generally not required as shares are more often but not, purchased from the open market from the shareholders. Any entity can purchase the stocks of target entity without even triggering the open offer to shareholders unless the amount of stakes purchase exceeds 24% (SEBI Takeover Code).

Tax consequences: If the stock purchase is effected by way of cash (which is most likely the case), the target shareholders will be taxed as per their holdings. If it is a long-term capital gain for a shareholder, he/she might not be charged to tax for any gain arising out of the sale of his shares since long-term capital gain from equities is exempted in India. In case of short-term capital gains (shares held for less than a year), capital gain tax will be applied at the prevalent tax rate.

Legal consequences: The legal status of the target entity will remain the same as in case of stock purchase the target would mostly be run as a subsidiary. The acquirer entity will become the holding company. However, if agreed, the legal status can be revoked and the brand name of the target might cease to exist post-acquisition in case of wholly-owned subsidiaries.

Risk sharing: In case of acquisition transactions, the consideration would most likely be cash, implying the transfer of stakes from target shareholders to the acquirer entity. Thus all the risks are borne by the acquirer. However, even acquisition (or) stock purchase can happen through stock swap, where the target shareholders will be given the stocks of the acquirer entity implying that the risk will be proportionately shared by the target shareholders.

Third-party approval: Acquisition generally requires fewer third-party approvals. However, if it is done on a larger scale (acquisition of control) then the approval from RBI, SEBI, Stock Exchanges (if listed), and local regulatory authorities will be required.

Deal-specific considerations: In case of inbound acquisitions or outbound acquisitions, certain deal-specific factors would come into picture. For example, anti-trust laws might get triggered if the deal is set to have a potential conflict of interest.

4.5.3   Merger

Merger is the typical structure wherein the two entities (acquirer and the target) combine into one business. The assets and liabilities of both the entities are collated and become the assets and liabilities of the resultant entity. Post-merger there would be only one surviving entity and the other entity cease to exist (typically the one which is merging into the other).

For Example

Kotak Mahindra Bank and ING Vysya Bank went on to merge in the year 2015. Post-merger, all the assets and liabilities of ING Vysya Bank got transferred to the books of Kotak Mahindra Bank. The deal was structured as a **Merger**, thus, ING Vysya bank ceases to exist. However, Kotak has requested ING group to use the trademark for a certain period of time. The deal was all stock deal wherein the shareholders of ING Vysya got 725 shares of Kotak for every 1000 shares held.

Merger in respect of the considerations:

Stockholder's approval: Shareholders consent of both target and acquirer entities is required in case of a merger. The board of directors of both the company also need to approve the merger, who will then, take the merger process to shareholders for approval.

Tax consequences: Typically, merger happens by way of a stock swap. The merging entity shareholders will get the shares of the entity to which it is being merged into. Ranbaxy shareholders become the shareholders of Sun Pharma post-Ranbaxy's merger. In such cases, there is no immediate tax liability as the shareholders are getting shares of another company. Those minority shareholders who do not agree to the merger will have to sell the share (if merger occurs, assuming majority shareholders agree to the merger). This sale would result in capital gain or loss which would be taxable based on the tenure of holding the shares.

Merger also happens by way of cash financing at times. In that case, there will be immediate taxability at the hands of the target shareholders as they will be exposed to capital gains (short term or long term).

Legal consequences: The legal status of the target entity will cease to exist. The brand name of the entity might prevail in cases where the board of directors of the acquirer entity feels to use the name and logo.

Risk sharing: In case of a merger structure, as mentioned above, the consideration would most likely be shares implying that risk remains with the target shareholders in an indirect form. Till the time they sell the shares of the surviving entity. However, the board of directors of the merging company might become the board of directors of the surviving entity (as their stakes would be higher), thereby, making it a little difficult to part away with the risk easily.

Third-party approval: In case of a merger, the regulatory pressures are higher. Many regulators like RBI, Competition Commission of India, High Court, SEBI (if it is a listed entity), Industry Regulators (e.g., TRAI in case of TELECOM Industry), etc. come into picture. High court approval is considered utmost important as the scheme of merger might potentially lead to conflict of interest of minority shareholders and also leads to concentration in the industry (as congeneric mergers will lead to increased market share by the merging entities hurting other players in the industry).

Deal-specific considerations: Every merger in itself is a new dimension. In the above example of Kotak Mahindra and ING Vysya, the banking employee union of ING Vysya Bank went on a strike expressing their concerns over job security post-merger. Thus, it was necessary to get their approval to facilitate the merger. Such kind of situation arises deal by deal.

4.6   Other Structures

Apart from asset/stock acquisition and merger, an M&A deal might typically be structured as follows:

A. Two-stage stock acquisition
B. Triangular merger
C. Leveraged buyout
D. Single-firm recapitalization

4.6.1   Two-Stage Stock Acquisition

A two-stage stock acquisition is a typical structure in which the intention of the acquirer is to merge the target entity with the acquirer entity.

In this structure, during the first stage the acquirer will buy target's share from the open market via tender offer so as to gain a controlling interest in the target firm (as higher shareholding gives higher say in the management of the company).

Once the controlling interest is obtained, it would be easy for the acquirer to do a backend merger as merger requires the approval of board and shareholders. Practically, these are common cases as some of the target board members might not be interested in a merger deal and the most prominent way for the acquirer is to opt this route and get into board to work out the merger.

For example, Vedanta-Cairn Merger

4.6.2   Triangular Merger

In this structure, the acquirer entity creates a wholly-owned subsidiary/acquisition subsidiary. The subsidiary entity later on merges or gets merged with the target entity. In this structure, there is a third independent entity being involved (subsidiary of the acquirer).

Triangular merger is of two types:

a. *Forward Triangular Merger*: In case of forward triangular merger, the selling entity or the target entity merges with the wholly-owned subsidiary of the acquirer. Thus, the target entity ceases to exist and the wholly-owned subsidiary (acquisition subsidiary) survives.

b. *Reverse Triangular Merger*: In case of reverse triangular merger, the wholly-owned subsidiary of the acquirer mergers with the target entity, resulting in survival of the target entity. The acquisition subsidiary ceases to exist.

4.6.3   Leveraged Buyout

In this structure, the acquirer acquires the target by taking debt serviceable based on the cash flows or assets of the target. It is a structure to deal with more of how the financing is done for a particular deal.

For example,

Nirma Ltd., on July 2016, announced to purchase Lafarge India Pvt Ltd. for about Rs. 9400 Crores out of which Rs. 4000 crores would be raised through bonds from the domestic markets. The balance amount is expected to be raised as equity. The financing of 4000 crores classifies the structure as a Leveraged buyout (LBO).

Structure:

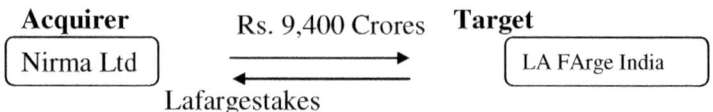

4.6.4   *Single-Firm Recapitalization:*

This is a special structure wherein the acquirer itself is the target entity. Sometimes when the management wants to take complete control of the company or alter its capital structure they enter into merger with such structure.

Under this structure, the acquirer entity creates a wholly-owned subsidiary. Once created, it then merges itself with the subsidiary through scheme of merger wherein the acquirer ceases to exist, post-merger. This will result in minority shareholders of the acquirer going out of the entity as they will be paid cash on sale of their shares.

For example,

Consider that the management of A Ltd. is planning to take control of its firm whose share capital is diversified with lot of minority shareholders. A Ltd. creates a wholly-owned subsidiary called B Ltd. Later on, A Ltd. merges with B Ltd. and A Ltd. ceases to exist post-merger and B Ltd. survives. The majority shareholders of A Ltd. will become the shareholders of B Ltd. and the minority shareholders opposing the merger will move out of the company by selling its shares at the offered price.

4.7   SWAP RATIO

Swap ratio is a "term" associated in Mergers & Acquisition, where the deal consideration is paid through exchange of shares. That is, the number of shares Ranbaxy shareholders gets (post-Sun Pharma–Ranbaxy merger) for every 1 share held by them is known as swap ratio.

Swap ratio entails issue of more shares by the acquiring company to the target company's shareholders, thereby, diluting the share capital of the acquirer. This dilution will have a spiraling effect on financial metrics like the EPS, PE ratio, etc. (post-merger), of the acquiring company.

It is not necessary that only Merger is financed through share swap. Even acquisitions can happen through exchange of shares by the acquirer issuing shares to acquire.

Let us understand the calculation of swap ratio and the impact of it on the financial metrics, with the help of the following example.

4.7.1 Illustration 1

A company says B is a highly successful company and wants to expand by taking over other firms. Its expected growth in earnings and dividends can be seen in its PE ratio of 17. The board of B has been advised that if it was to take over firms with a lower PE ratio than its own, using a share-for-share exchange, then it could increase its reported earnings per share. C Ltd. has been zeroed upon as a possible target for a takeover, which has a PE ratio of 10 and 1,00,000 shares in issue with a share price of Rs. 15. B has 5,00,000 shares in issue with a share price of Rs. 12.

Find the share exchange ratio, change in earnings per share of if it acquires the whole of C Ltd. by issuing shares at its market price of Rs. 12. Assume the price of B's shares remains constant.

4.7.2 Solution

Share exchange ratio $= \frac{\text{Rs. } 15}{\text{Rs. } 12} = 1.25{:}1$

Number of equity shares to be issued to shareholders of C Ltd. $=(1.25 \times 1,00,000 \text{ shares})$
$= 1,25,000$ shares in B Ltd.
PE ratio $=$ MPS/EPS

	B Ltd.	C Ltd.
EPS = MPS	=Rs. 12	=Rs. 15
PE ratio	17	10
	Rs. 0.70588	=Rs. 1.50
Number of equity shares	5,00,000	1,00,000
Earnings available for equity share holders	Rs. 3,52,941	Rs. 1,50,000

Post-merger combined earnings $=$ Rs. 5,02,941
Post-merger number of equity shares $=6,25,000$ (5,00,000 + 1,25,000)
Post-merger EPS $=$ Rs. 0.80471

Change in EPS = Rs. 0.80471 – Rs. 0.70588
= Rs. 0.09883

Calculation of impact on Earnings, Market value of the entity, given the share swap ratio.

4.7.3   Illustration 2

Air India wants to acquire SpiceJet and has offered a swap ratio of 1:2 (0.5 shares for every one share of SpiceJet). Calculate the below with the following information:

	Air India	SpiceJet
Profit after tax	Rs. 18,00,000	Rs. 3,60,000
Equity shares outstanding (Nos.)	6,00,000	1,80,000
EPS	Rs. 3	Rs. 2
PE ratio	10 times	7 times
Market price per share	Rs. 30	Rs. 14

i.   The number of equity shares to be issued by Air India for acquisition of SpiceJet.
ii. What is the EPS of Air India after the acquisition?
iii. Determine the equivalent earnings per share of SpiceJet.
iv. What is the expected market price per share of Air India after the acquisition, assuming its PE multiple remains unchanged?
v.   Determine the market value of the merged firm.

4.7.4   Solution

The number of shares to be issued by Air India:

The exchange ratio is 0.5
So, new shares = 1,80,000 × 0.5 = 90,000 shares.

EPS of Air India after acquisition:

Total earnings (18,00,000 + 3,60,000) = Rs. 21,60,000
No. of shares (6,00,000 + 90,000) 6,90,000
EPS equivalent (21,60,000)/6,90,000) Rs. 3.13

Equivalent EPS of SpiceJet:

No. of new shares 0.5
EPS Rs. 3.13
Equivalent EPS (3.13×0.5) Rs. 1.57

New market price of Air India (PE remaining unchanged):

Present PE ratio of Air India 10 times
Expected EPS after merger Rs. 3.13
Expected market price (3.13×10) Rs. 31.30

Market value of merged firm:

Total number of shares 6,90,000
Expected market price Rs. 31.30
Total value $(6,90,000 \times 31.30)$ Rs. 2,15,97,000

CHAPTER 5

Deal Valuation

5.1 Introduction to Valuation

"Price is what you pay and value is what you get." This famous quote of Warren Buffet signifies the importance of "value" of any particular investment. Whether it is an investment in the shares of the company by an individual investor or investment for the purpose of acquisitions or merger, the importance of value cannot be overemphasized. Price is the cost of investment while and value is the benefit you reaped. Value of any investment, however, shall vary from one appraiser (valuer) to another. One may see a great value in an investment while the other may not. **Valuations are subjective in nature**.

The assessment of value of the assets to be acquired or merged must comprise the value of the synergistic benefits.

For example, assume Company A, which is worth Rs. 1000 crores has paid Rs. 180 crores to acquire Company B, which is worth Rs. 150 at a premium of 20%. Assume the synergy derived is worth Rs. 20 crores. By paying a premium of Rs. 30 crores and fetching synergy worth Rs. 20 crores, Company A has actually destroyed its wealth. This might seem illogical, but is highly common in case of mergers and acquisitions.

Thus, it is very important to critically examine the value of a particular company before entering into merger or acquisition deal.

In terms of investments, it is necessary to estimate the value of a deal. Why so?

© The Author(s) 2019
V. Kumar and P. Sharma, *An Insight into Mergers and Acquisitions*,
https://doi.org/10.1007/978-981-13-5829-6_5

When Fortis acquired Escorts Heart Institute in the year 2005, it was believed that there is a possible synergy since Fortis was able to get expertise in heart care which was not otherwise available to them. This may seem to have created a synergy for sure. But does that lead to creation of value? May be yes or maybe not.

To answer the above question, we need to analyze synergy in quantitative terms and compare it with the price paid by Fortis to decide whether the deal has led to increase in value. Empirical evidence shows that the success ratio of mergers or acquisition deals is minimal. This might be because the acquirer paid a price that was much higher than the benefits derived.

Valuation of target company has to be done by the acquirer to see the real worth or potential benefits after merger or acquisition. The target company also estimates its own value so as to create the premise for price negotiations.

5.2   VALUATION METHODOLOGIES

There are 5 common approaches through which valuations are done, in case of a merger/acquisition.

1. Market value-based valuation.
2. Status quo valuation.
3. Transaction analysis.
   a. Relative valuation/comparable company analysis method.
   b. Transaction-based valuations.
4. Discounted cash flow model.
5. Sum of parts approach.

5.3   MARKET VALUE-BASED VALUATION APPROACH

Asset-based valuation is most often used when a particular firm is expected to get liquidated. It is otherwise the liquidation value of a company. It takes into account the net assets value which is computed as:

NAV = Market value of Assets − Outstanding Liability

The market value of any asset of a business may not be equal to the book value of the business since the book values of tangible and intangible assets are accounted based on historical cost (as per AS 10 and 26 of Indian Accounting Standards). Thus, it is essential to consider the market value of an asset while calculating the "Net Asset Value."

NAV does not take into account the intangible assets since they cannot be seen or valued precisely. Thus, net asset value is the market value of the total tangible assets minus the outstanding liability.

This tells us what a shareholder of a particular company is left with, after selling all its assets and settling claims to outsiders. This approach may prove to be useful when analyzing industries/companies which are capital intensive.

Asset-based valuation proves to be an easy valuation method as it does not take into account the earnings prospects of a business. A company which is being acquired can use asset-based valuation for ascertaining the minimum amount to be received in the deal.

5.4   STATUS QUO VALUATION

This method is a built up on the discounted cash flow (DCF) method. In this method, the valuation of the company is based on free cash flows. The estimated "Free cash Flow to Firm" for the year is ascertained and growth rate is applied in the free cash flows. The resultant figure is discounted with the "Weighted Average Cost of Capital" (WACC) to arrive at the value of the firm.

However, as per status quo method, the value of any enterprise is not only the value of its operations but also the control premium and the value of the synergy. Thus, offer price should include all the three factors viz., discounted FCFF, control premium, and the value of expected synergy.

Ascertaining the control premium:

Control premium is, in simple words, the amount the acquirer is willing to pay for taking over the control of the target company. This would most likely arise if the acquirer feels the target is not properly managed. The acquirer would assume that, apart from synergies from the deal, if the target firm is managed properly it might lead to increase in top-line as well as bottom-line growth after acquisition.

Say, Company A, which is the acquirer company feels that Company B is poorly managed because of which it is operating at lower than optimum capacity, Company A can take over the management and take steps to improve the acquired company's operations to ensure full/optimum capacity utilization. The way Company A would do that is by altering the financial structure, changing existing management policies, hiving off unproductive assets or any other radical change in its operations, etc.

By doing this, Company A can increase the profitability of Company B which would ultimately benefit Company A. Thus, Company A might be willing to pay a premium for Company B for deriving such benefits.

The value of control premium would be:

Control Premium = Value of company if managed by acquirer − Actual value of target

Value of Synergy:

Synergy is the major strategical benefit; an acquirer company is trying to achieve through acquisition or takeover. As a matter of fact, this benefit has to be compensated. Thus, a target firm would require premium for providing synergistic benefits. The amount of premium would be based on negotiations which are in turn based on the value of synergy which the acquirer and target thinks can be obtained.

Value of synergy can be calculated using the same method.

Thus,

Value of the target firm = Value of discounted FCFF + Control Premium + Value of Synergy

Illustration:

Company X is planning to acquire the entire stake in Company Y at the end of FY 15 and is trying to assess the value of Company Y with the following information:

Particulars (for the year FY 15)	Amount (in lakhs)
NOPAT	50
Depreciation and amortization	4
Capital expenditure made during the year	12
Change in working capital	7

Particulars (for the year FY 15)	Amount (in lakhs)
Tax rate	30%
Growth rate in FCFF for first 3 years	15%
Terminal growth rate	7%
Value of firm	500
Value of firm if managed by Company X	580
Synergy expected	400
WACC	12%

Solution:

FCFF = NOPAT + Dep & Amort − Net capex − Change in Working capital
FCFF = 50 + 4 − 12 − 7 = 35
$FCFF1 \rightarrow 35 \times (1.15)^1 = 40.25$
$FCFF2 \rightarrow 35 \times (1.15)^2 = 46.28$
$FCFF3 \rightarrow 35 \times (1.15)^3 = 53.23$
$FCFF4 \rightarrow 53.23 \times (1.07) = 56.95$
Terminal Cash flow $= 56.95/(0.12 − 0.07) \rightarrow 1139$

Discounting all the cash flows by WACC, we get
(Discounting factor $= CF1/(1+r)^1 + CF2/(1+r)^2 + CF3/(1+r)^3 + \ldots + CFn/(1+r)^n$)

Value of discounted $FCFF = 40.25/(1+12\%)^1 + 46.28/(1+12\%)^2 + (53.23 + 1139)/(1+12\%)^3$

$$= 921.44$$

Control Premium = Value of firm if managed by acquirer − Actual value of target

$$= 580 − 500 = 80$$

Value of synergy = 400

Value of target firm = Value of Discounted FCFF + Control Premium + Value of Synergy $= 921.44 + 80 + 400 \rightarrow$ Rs. 1401.44 lakh

5.5 TRANSACTION ANALYSIS

Transaction Analysis of mergers and Acquisitions tries to estimate the value of the target by comparing it with its peers. The underlying principle for transaction analysis is the "Law of One Price."

Law of one price in the context of valuations states that companies that are operating in identical businesses should be priced equally by the market.

Transaction Analysis is of two types:

A. Comparable Company Analysis (or) Relative Analysis.
B. Transaction-Based Valuations.

5.5.1   Comparable Company Analysis

This method is alternatively known as market-based valuation method. As the name implies, the valuation parameters are derived by calculating certain ratios relative to that of market. Those identified parameters are then multiplied with the respectable target's (valuing company's) fundamental parameters to arrive at the intrinsic value of the company.

For ascertaining the intrinsic value under this approach, two measures are used:

   i. Price multiples.
   ii. Enterprise value multiples.

5.5.1.1 Price Multiples

In price multiple valuation, based on the actual price of the stock, the actual multiples such as Price/Sales, Price/Book Value, Price/Cash Flows, Price/Earnings, and Price Earnings/Growth (PEG Ratio) are identified.

These identified multiples are then compared with the benchmark multiples.

Benchmark multiples usually applied are:

   a. Peer group average (or) Median ratio.
   b. Industry average/Median ratio.
   c. Index ratio.
   d. Average historical multiple ratios of the same company.

If the valuing company's equity stock is not listed in the stock exchange, the reverse calculation takes place. That is, the benchmark multiples are found first based on the closest peer group companies and then the average of all the multiples are taken out. Based on the average, the fundamental parameters of the company being valued are multiplied to arrive at the intrinsic value of the takeover candidate.

Once the intrinsic value of the target is ascertained, the takeover premium is estimated and added.

Illustration:
You have been given the following information:

Target firm fundamentals		Average of the comparables	
Sales	100 crores	Price/Sales	5
Earnings	20 crores	Price/Earnings	26
Cash flows	18 crores	Price/Cash flows	20
Book value	165 crores	Price/Book value	3

The takeover premium calculated as an average of the past 15 deals comes out to be 60%. Calculate the value of the deal using price multiple approach.

Answer:

Fundamental metrics		Average multiples	Estimated intrinsic value
Sales	100	5	500 crores
Earnings	20	26	520 crores
Cash flows	18	20	360 crores
Book value	165	3	495 crores

According to the relative parameters, the Estimated Intrinsic Value differs for every multiple. Thus, the average of the Estimated Intrinsic Value has to be calculated and that will become the Final Intrinsic Value of the company.

Average of Estimated Intrinsic Value $= (500+520+360+495)/4 \rightarrow 468.75$ crores
Add: Takeover Premium $= 468.75 \times 60\% \rightarrow 281.25$ crores
Total value of the target company $= 750$ crores

5.5.1.2 Enterprise Value Multiples
Enterprise value multiples are calculated for the total level as these multiples take into account the debt, preferred stock and not just the equity (unlike price multiples). It is a better measure to use along with price multiples in case of a merger and acquisition valuation for companies with differential leverage patterns. Generally, enterprise value as a multiple of EBITDA is used for assessing the worth of the takeover target.

The commonly used **EV multiple is EV/EBITDA** wherein, Enterprise Value = Market Value of Common stock + MV of Debt + MV of Preferred − Cash & Cash Equivalents
EBITDA = Earnings before Interest, Tax, Depreciation and Amortization

5.5.2   Transaction-Based Valuation

This method of valuing a target company is almost similar to that of comparable company except that, under this method, the fundamental metrics of the target are not multiplied by the benchmark (or) industry average/median, rather it is multiplied by the average relative valuation ratios of the similar comparable M&A deals. Therefore, this method typically requires the usage of judgment by the appraiser to assign weightage to the valuation metrics.

Under this method, there is no need to add a takeover premium at the end, since the valuation is arrived after considering comparable M&A transaction deals and thus already includes the takeover premium.

Let us consider the following example:

Illustration:

Nestle India Ltd. is planning to acquire 100% stakes in Coffee Products Ltd. and has asked you to estimate the price that can be paid for the proposed deal. You have gathered the following information of the past transactions that have taken place in the FMCG sector.

Fundamental metrics	Unilever PLC and Hindustan Unilever	Hatsun Agro and Jyothi Diary	Dabur India and Northern Aromatics	Target firm
Acquisition share price	120	200	70	??
Earnings per share	6.48	9.52	4.66	18.5
Book value per share	95	70.8	22.2	150
Cash flow per share	12.8	15.5	6.12	22
Sales per share	35	40	15	55

Note All the values are mentioned above are hypothetical

FMCG sector is the fastest-growing sector where sales and cash flows of a company are the most important valuation measures. Thus, give sales and cash flows a weightage of 40% each and 10% each for the rest of the two measures.

The fundamental metrics of the target are:
EPS $\rightarrow$ 18.5, BVPS $\rightarrow$ 150, CFPS $\rightarrow$ 22, Sales per Share $\rightarrow$ 55

Answer:

The first step is to calculate the average relative valuation ratios for the comparable transactions using the above table.

Relative valuation ratios	Transaction 1	Transaction 2	Transaction 3	Average
Price/Earnings	18.5	21	15	**18.17**
Price/Book value	1.26	2.82	3.15	**2.41**
Price/Cash flows	9.38	12.9	11.44	**11.24**
Price/Sales	3.43	5	4.67	**4.37**

Once the mean relative valuation ratios (using past M&A transactions are estimated, the fundamental metrics of the target should be multiplied with the respected ratios).

Fundamental metrics of the target		Relative ratios		Estimated intrinsic value (X)	Weights (W)	Price W × X
Earnings per share	18.5	PE	18.17	336.15	0.1	33.615
Book value per share	150	P/BV	2.41	361.5	0.1	36.15
Cash Flow per share	22	P/CF	11.24	247.28	0.4	98.91
Sales per share	55	P/S	4.37	240.35	0.4	96.14
						264.815

Weighted Average $= \Sigma WX / \Sigma W = 264.815/1 \Rightarrow 264.815$

Multiplying the intrinsic value by the weights,
Weighted Average Intrinsic Value $= 10\%$ (Earnings) $+ 10\%$ (Book Value) $+ 40\%$ (Cash Flow) $+ 40\%$ (Sales)

$= 10\% (336.15) + 10\% (361.5) + 40\% (247.28) + 40\% (240.35)$
$= 33.615 + 36.15 + 98.91 + 96.14$
$= 264.815$ per share

As mentioned earlier, since the intrinsic value or the price for the deal is obtained by using the relative valuation metrics of the past M&A transaction, there is no need to add a takeover premium.

5.6   Discounted Cash Flow Model

As the name implies, the DCF model requires the use of discounting the cash flows. The future cash flows that the target company (which is being valued) would generate are estimated through various assumptions with regard to its earnings and cash-generating capabilities. The estimated future cash flows, however, stand at different time zones. In order to know the current value of those future cash flows, they should be discounted with the appropriate discount rate.

Below is the basic timeline of how the DCF would look like:

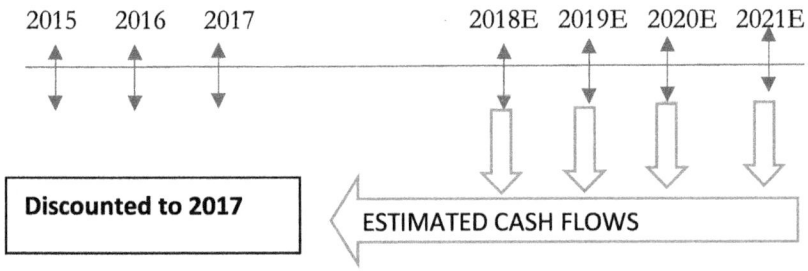

Assume that we are estimating the value of an XYZ company in 2017. The cash flows of the previous years 2014, 2015, 2016, and 2017 are taken. With the trend and other estimates, the cash flows of 2018–2021 are estimated. However, a company will generate cash flows beyond 2021 as well. And standing by the basic "going concern" principle of accounting the company is expected to generate cash flows forever, i.e., perpetually.

But it is highly difficult to predict the cash flows beyond a certain period of time (2021 in the above case). Thus, a simplistic assumption is taken that the cash flows will grow at a certain constant rate (known as the **terminal growth rate**) from 2022. Those cash flows which are produced from 2021 will be **discounted separately** and the present value of those comes at 2021. This discounted cash flow is called the **Terminal Value**. Thus, practically 2021 has two cash flows, one is the cash flow generated for that year and the other is the terminal value.

Then all the cash flows, that is, 2018, 2019, 2020, and 2021 (along with terminal value) are discounted to the year 2017. This becomes the discounted cash flow value or the intrinsic value of a company.

Free cash flow discount model is used in case of M&A valuations because free cash flows are the funds that are being generated internally by a company and are available to the investors of the company.

5.6.1   *Free Cash Flow Discount Model*

Free cash flows are the funds that are available to the investors of a company. There are two types of free cash flows. They are:

a. Free cash flow to equity (FCFE).
b. Free cash flow to firm (FCFF).

5.6.1.1 *Free Cash Flow to Equity (FCFE)*
Free cash flow to equity is the cash available for equity shareholders after meeting all the operating requirements of the company. This is a cash flow net of debt financing.

$$\textbf{FCFE} = \textbf{FCFF} - \textbf{Interest} \times (\textbf{1} - \textbf{Tax Rate}) + \textbf{Net borrowings}$$

5.6.1.2 *Free Cash Flow to Firm (FCFF)*
This is the cash available for the company as a whole. That is, for its bondholders as well as shareholders.

This is the perfect measure for valuing a company in case of M&A, since the acquirer would only be interested in the total funds generated for all the fund providers rather than cash flow left for shareholders.

Calculation of FCFF:

Free cash flow is calculated by making various adjustments to the reported or estimated operating income of the company.

$$\textbf{FCFF} = \textbf{EBIT} \times (\textbf{1} - \textbf{Tax Rate}) + \textbf{Depreciation} - \textbf{FC}_{\textbf{Inv}} - \textbf{WC}_{\textbf{Inv}}$$

where
  $EBIT$ = Earnings before Interest and Tax
  FC_{Inv} = Fixed capital Investments or Capital Expenditures (capex)
  WC_{Inv} = Working capital Investments

EBIT x (1−Tax Rate) is alternatively known as Net Operating Profit after tax (NOPAT)

Estimating the Terminal Value:

As stated earlier in the discounted cash flow timeline, terminal value is the discounted value of cash flows which grow at a constant rate. It has arrived at the end of the forecast horizon.

Terminal value is calculated as follows:

Terminal Value $= \text{FCFF}_{\text{End}}\,(1+g)/(\text{WACC}-g)$

where

$\text{FCFF}_{\text{End}} =$ Free cash flow to firm at the end of the forecast period (2021 in our timeline example)

WACC = Weighted average cost of capital

$g =$ Terminal Growth rate (constant rate)

Estimating the Discounting Rate:

Once the free cash flows are calculated, these need to be discounted with the appropriate discount rate. For free cash flow to firm, the appropriate discounting rate is the weighted average cost of capital.

WACC is calculated using the following formula,

$$\text{WACC} = \text{Wd} \times \text{Kd}\,(1-\text{Tax Rate}) + \text{We} \times \text{Ke} + \text{Wp} \times \text{Kp}$$

where

Wd = Weight of Debt

Kd = Cost of Debt

We = Weight of Equity

Ke = Cost of Equity

Wp = Weight of Preference Shares

Kp = Cost of Preference

However, most of the companies in India do not issue preference shares.

Thus,

$$\text{WACC} = \text{Wd} \times \text{Kd}\,(1-\text{Tax Rate}) + \text{We} \times \text{Ke}$$

Weights are calculated either by the target company's capital structure or by the cost of funding.

Wd = Market Value of Debt/(Market Value of Debt + Market Value of Equity)

We = Market Value of Equity/(Market Value of Debt + Market Value of Equity)

Calculation of Cost of Equity:

Though cost of debt is directly available as it is the rate at which a company borrows money, cost of equity is not readily available. It has to be calculated using the following formula:

$$Ke = Rf + \beta\ (Rm - Rf)$$

where

Ke = Cost of Equity

Rf = Risk-free rate in the country

β = The sensitivity of the company with respect to Market

Rm = Return of the Market (country's Index)

Let us consider the following example to calculate WACC

Illustration:

ABC Ltd. is planning to acquire the controlling stake in XYZ Ltd. and is trying to estimate the value of XYZ Ltd. For the purpose of funding the acquisition, ABC is planning to raise 40% of the funds through equity and the remaining 60% through debt. Since ABC Ltd. is a stable company, it is able to obtain loan from big banks at a lower rate of interest of 9%. What is the WACC to be used for discounting the cash flows of XYZ Ltd. given the following information:

Risk-free rate in India is 6.5%.

Nifty index of India has given 15% rate of return.

The beta between XYZ Ltd. and Nifty is 1.2.

Corporate tax rate is 30%.

Answer:

$$\begin{aligned}
\text{Cost of Equity} &= Rf + \beta\ (Rm - Rf)\\
&= 6.5\% + 1.2\ (15\% - 6.5\%)\\
&= 16.7\%\\
\text{WACC} &= Wd \times Kd\ (1 - \text{Tax Rate}) + We \times Ke\\
&= (0.6) \times (0.09)\ (1 - 0.3) + (0.4)\ (0.167)\\
&= (0.054) \times (0.7) + (0.0668)\\
&= 0.0378 + 0.0668\\
\text{WACC} &= 0.1046\ \text{or}\ 10.46\%
\end{aligned}$$

5.7   Sum of Parts Approach

In this method, the value of a particular business division is ascertained individually. In case of conglomerate companies, sum of parts valuation tends to be a better valuation approach. It is done mostly when a company hives off its non-profitable or non-core business segment or demerges. This creates a necessity for the appraiser to look at that particular segment of the business which is demerging or spun off.

For example, Reliance Industries is present in various business segments like refining, petrochemicals, oil & gas, organized retail, textiles, telecom, etc. Assume the value assigned by the market to Reliance Industry is roughly 3.5L crores. Does this mean the value of every segment put together is 3.5L crores?

The answer is no. If you calculate the value of telecom business, organized retail business and other business divisions separately it might be, say, 4L crores. Market had discounted 0.5L crores which are known as conglomerate or diversification discount. This is done because of various reasons like the lack of management focus in one domain, complicated business specifications, etc.

Thus, it is necessary to value the various individual business segments independently of others and add all the valuations to arrive at the exact valuation of the company.

As stated, this method is used for valuing a demerger which is generally done for unlocking the value in the conglomerate entity. Some companies which have done this are L&T, Reliance Industries Ltd., Siemens Ltd., JK Lakshmi Cement Ltd., SRF, etc.

5.8   Case Study on Valuation

5.8.1   *Acquisition of Myntra by Flipkart*

In one of the biggest consolidations in the e-commerce industry, Flipkart, a largest retailer, acquired its fashion rival firm Myntra for an approximate deal value of Rs. 2000 crores (though the deal value hasn't been disclosed).

Binny Bansal, co-founder of Flipkart, has said the "acquisition would help Flipkart grab bigger market share and compete better" as this would lead Flipkart to venture into Online Fashion Retailing through

Myntra which has already set up its strong presence. This would also help Flipkart compete with major giants like Amazon by consolidating the industry.

As it is an acquisition, Myntra will continue to run as an independent entity while Flipkart will be operating its fashion/apparel segment headed by Mukesh Bansal, the co-founder and CEO of Myntra. With this acquisition, investors such as Tiger Global, Sofina Capital, and Accel Partners having investments in both the entities separately would be able to consolidate its shareholding in Flipkart.

5.8.2   Valuation of Myntra

Given various methods to value a target company for takeover or acquisition, one of the most reliable and prominent methods is by discounting the future cash flows (DCF).

This case study of Flipkart and Myntra would help us understand the DCF method of valuing a company in a detailed manner.

Note: Though E-commerce companies are priced through GMV multiples and DCF is generally not used to value E-commerce companies like Flipkart, Myntra, Ola, etc., due to their negative cash flows. However, DCF technique is widely used in the valuation of companies specifically for M&As. Here the valuation of Myntra using DCF has been an effort to appraise the reader with the methodology.

5.8.3   Deal Overview

E-commerce one of the fastest-growing sectors in India is currently valued at around $38 billion and is expected to touch $120 billion in the year 2020, as predicted by ASSOCHAM India in their 2016 year report. The valuation in the year 2014 was pegged at $13.6 billion. This was majorly contributed by the sale of branded apparels, jewels, accessories, and gifts. Myntra having the acumen in branded apparels was expected to touch highs with quality product, easy return backed by good customer support. On the other hand, Flipkart, one of the highly valued e-commerce players, was losing its presence in the apparel segment.

This has perfectly paved way for Flipkart acquiring Myntra, so as to reap the benefits of entering the apparel segment.

According to Grant Thornton Deal Tracker report 2015, it was estimated that Flipkart would have paid $340 million for acquiring 100% stake in Myntra.

Whenever a company acquires another company, it can acquire it at a premium or at a discount to market value based on the target company's expected performance and the existing status. Given Myntra, being placed at a driving position, Flipkart must have paid premium to acquire Myntra.

Thus, the total deal value of $340 million includes the intrinsic value of Myntra and the premium paid for acquisition.

5.8.4   Process of Calculating the Intrinsic Value Through DCF (from Flipkart Point of View)

Every DCF model requires us to take certain assumptions for forecasting the financial statements. The efficiency of the model depends on how sound (or) logical the assumption is. Thus, this model is also filled with such assumptions where the logics for such assumptions are also stated alongside for your reference.

It is also assumed that Flipkart would have valued the company before the merger talks was initiated during Jan 2014, thus valuing Myntra based on 2013 and prior year financials.

When valuing for merger or acquisition, it is necessary to look at the enterprise value of the company since it is the actual economic value at a given point of time.

Enterprise value = Market Cap + Total Debt + Minority Interest + Capital Lease − Cash & Cash Equivalents. (When you want to purchase a company, you will have to pay to the equity shareholders for their stakes, repay the debt, and pay its minority holders as well as to settle the capital lease. Of course, you will get the cash the target company is having at that point of time, which can be used for settling the debt.)

For calculating the market cap, the requirement to calculate the intrinsic value of the company arises. The intrinsic value is calculated using discounted free cash flows. That is, the free cash flows at various future time zones discounted to current time period. Then the intrinsic value is assumed to be the market cap of the target company. Thus, it is alternatively known as implied market value.

For estimating the future cash flows, there are lots of ways. This model uses one such way as stated below:

$\text{FCFF} = \text{EBIT} \times (1 - T) + \text{Depreciation} + \text{Amortization} - \text{Capex} - \text{Change in Working Capital}$

Once free cash flows are calculated using this formula, it is then discounted with the appropriate discounting rate, which is, the weighted average cost of capital. The present value of all the cash flows discounted will give the intrinsic value of the company.

The basic assumption used when calculating the free cash flows is that the company will continue to run forever. But it is practically not possible to forecast the cash flows generated by the company for more than 5 or 10 years. Thus, we project the cash flows individually till the time we feel we can project (5 years in this case) and assume the final "FCFF" (at the end of 5th year) will grow at a certain constant rate, based on the industry growth, economic prospects, etc.

It is not necessary to forecast every item in the financial statement to arrive at the free cash flows. It is sufficient to forecast the items which are required, as given by the formula. That is, earnings before interest and tax (EBIT), tax rate, depreciation, amortization, capex, and change in working capital. Projections of the above are interlinked, and it requires careful heeding toward the steps involved.

5.8.4.1 Projecting the EBIT

Usually, projecting the earning takes in two forms. Projection as per historical trend and projection as per the market structure, management expectation about the business, etc. The latter method is more relevant as past trend may not be same as the future performance. However, the expectation in the market for certain financial statement items will not be available, thus, requiring the usage of historical trend. Thus, to say, projection should be a mix of historical trend and future expectations which is more subjective in nature, which differs from person to person.

So, for projecting the future we need to analyze the trend of the historical data as well. Usually, previous 3 years data can be used for analyzing the historical trend. Sometimes it can be 5 years if there is too much volatility in the industry, requirement of the appraiser, availability of data, etc. Forecasted income statement is given below along with the explanations:

Exhibit 1: Forecasted Income Statement

	Company Name	Year End		Ticker	Scenrio				
	Myntra Pvt Ltd	31/12/2013		Gen	Base				
	Income Statement INR (In Lakhs)								
	Particulars	Historical			Forecast				
		2011	2012	2013	2014E	2015E	2016E	2017E	2018E
	Revenue from operations	1649.21	6254.66	20325.87	40651.74	73173.13	113418.34	175798.43	272487.57
(Includes cost of packing)	Cost of goods sold	1369.93	5242.63	19891.99	39783.97	68185.23	103392.04	140638.75	190741.30
	Gross Profit	279.28	1012.03	433.88	867.76	4987.89	10026.30	35159.69	81746.27
	Employee benefit expens	751.78	1963.91	4912.16	8130.35	10975.97	11341.83	17579.84	27248.76
(Included in other expenses due to change of format)	Advertising and sales promotion	356.67	3124.49	0.00					
	Other expenses	740.88	1282.40	9131.83	16260.69	25610.59	34025.50	35159.69	40873.14
	EBITDA	-1570.04	-5358.78	-13610.10	-23523.28	-31598.67	-35341.03	-17579.84	13624.38
	Less: Depreciation	90.10	138.82	371.05	645.48	1069.45	1771.88	2935.69	4863.92
	Less: Amortization	8.10	56.89	205.14	261.91	403.00	620.09	954.12	1468.10
	EBIT	-1668.25	-5554.49	-14186.29	-24430.67	-33071.12	-37733.01	-21469.66	7292.37
Note: Exceptional or extraordinary items have to be excluded since it is one time in nature.	Less: Finance cost	10.99	33.31	213.28					
	Add: Other income	162.41	461.49	979.97					
	Earnings before Tax	-1516.83	-5126.31	-13419.60	-24430.67	-33071.12	-37733.01	-21469.66	7292.37
	Less: Tax expense								2187.71
	Earnings after tax	-1516.83	-5126.31	-13419.60	-24430.67	-33071.12	-37733.01	-21469.66	5104.66
			2.38	1.62	0.82	0.35	0.14	-0.43	-1.34
	Basic EPS	-44.53	-143.05	-364.18					
	Diluted EPS	-44.53	-143.05	-364.18					

The primary step in forecasting financial statements is to arrange them as per the convenient order based on the operational aspect. In the above, the data of 2011, 2012, and 2013 are actual figures obtained from the annual report of the company. EBIT is the operating profit, and EBITDA is the cash operating profit. Forecast is done majorly till these levels. Thus, any item which is not operational but classified in the company's financial statement before EBITDA should be removed and included after EBIT. Various heads can also be clubbed so as to make the model easy for forecast. It is also necessary to **not consider** extraordinary or exceptional item since it is one time in nature and the probability of occurrence of such items cannot be predicted.

Exhibit 2: Historical Analysis

Assumptions	Historical			Forecast				
	2011	2012	2013	2014E	2015E	2016E	2017E	2018E
Sales Growth Rate		379%	325%	100%	80%	55%	55%	55%
Cost of Goods Sold as a % of Sales	83%	84%	98%	98%	93%	91%	80%	70%
Employee Benefit Expense as a % of Sales	46%	31%	24%	20%	15%	10%	10%	10%
Other Expenses as a % of Sales	67%	70%	45%	40%	35%	30%	20%	15%
Depreciation as a % of Gross Tangible Assets	30%	12%	19%	20%	20%	20%	20%	20%
Amortization as a % of Intangible Assets	25%	19%	29%	24%	24%	24%	24%	24%

As mentioned earlier, for forecasting certain sound assumptions has to be made. The historical analysis helps us in making those assumptions. Various factors such as sales growth rate, cost of goods sold as a % of sales are calculated. If you see that the COGS has a consistent increasing trend. However, COGS cannot keep on increasing forever as higher variable cost will lead to lower or negative gross margins which will not be entertained by the company. Apparel is a business where gross margins are near about 30%. Though the margins should be 30%, however COGS cannot be reduced suddenly, thus it is reduced over a period of 5 years (from 2014 to 2018).

Employee benefit expense as a % of sales (of those respective years) shows a constant fall as the company is becoming more efficient and cutting down on the cost. Thus, we can say that the trend may continue in the future as well, where we can assume a gradual fall and keep it constant from the terminal year onwards (since logically employee expense can never become zero as company requires staff). Same is the case with other expenses.

Though many use to calculate depreciation and amortization as a % of sales, it should not be so because both the expenses are arising out of assets. Thus, it is necessary to link those to total gross assets. Both the expenses are volatile in nature, as we could see from the figures. Thus, it is better to take average of the prior trend and keep it constant throughout (20 and 24%, respectively). The figures are obtained by dividing the depreciation by gross tangible assets during the year.

Once all the futuristic rates for forecast are ascertained, it needs to be linked with the respective years to calculate the amount. That is, sales for 2014 would be equal to sales of 2013 multiplied by 1 plus 2014 sales growth rate assumed, and so on. Mathematically,

Sales of 2014 = 20,325.87 × (1+100%) → 40,651.74, Sales of 2015 = 40,651.74 × (1+80%) → 73,173.13, and so on.

Once sales are calculated for the forecast period (2014–2018), COGS, employee benefit expenses and other expenses can be calculated. For example, COGS for 2014 is 98% of sales of 2014, which comes out to be 39,783.97. Similar is the case with other years and other items.

However, since depreciation and amortization are not linked with sales, we need to first find out the gross assets by preparing an **Asset schedule** so as to calculate the exact amount of depreciation and amortization expense to be shown in income statement.

Exhibit 3: Asset Schedule

Fixed Asset Schedule	Historical			Forecast					
	2011	2012	2013	2014E	2015E	2016E	2017E	2018E	
Gross Tangible Assets (PP&E)	139.46	304.42	1,157.74	1,918.16	3,178.05	5,265.46	8,723.92	14,453.98	
Additions	166.68	912.74	766.93	1,259.89	2,087.41	3,458.46	5,730.06	9,493.68	
Disposals	(1.72)	(59.42)	(6.50)	-	-	-	-	-	
Total Gross Tangible Assets	304.42	1,157.74	1,918.16	3,178.05	5,265.46	8,723.92	14,453.98	23,947.66	
Less: Accumulated Depreciation	72.84	125.26	264.08	909.56	1,555.04	2,624.49	4,396.37	7,332.06	(Adjusted for disposal)
Net Tangible Assets (PP&E)	141.48	893.66	1,283.04	1,623.01	2,640.97	4,327.55	7,121.92	11,751.68	
Depreciation for the year	90.10	138.82	371.05	645.48	1,069.45	1,771.88	2,935.69	4,863.92	
Intangibles	21.42	32.96	304.36	706.01	1,086.33	1,671.52	2,571.95	3,957.41	
Additions	11.54	271.39	401.66	380.32	585.19	900.42	1,385.47	2,131.80	
Total Gross Intangibles	32.96	304.36	706.01	1,086.33	1,671.52	2,571.95	3,957.41	6,089.21	
Less: Accumulated Amortization	6.44	14.54	71.43	333.35	736.35	1,356.44	2,310.56	3,778.66	
Net Intangibles	18.42	232.92	429.44	491.07	755.61	1,162.64	1,788.94	2,752.61	
Amortization for the year	8.10	56.89	205.14	261.91	403.00	620.09	954.12	1,468.10	
Capex	178.22	1,184.13	1,168.59	1,640.21	2,672.60	4,358.89	7,115.52	11,625.47	
Tangible assets		151%							
Growth in Tangible Assets		280%	66%						
Intangible assets		277%							
Growth in Intangible Assets		54%	823%						

Similar to that of income statement, the historical asset data of 2011, 12, and 13 have been gathered from annual reports. The gross tangible assets have increased by 280% (1157.74/304.42 − 1) during 2012 and

66% during 2013. (End value/Beginning value − 1 formula is used to calculate growth.) The compounded growth rate for the years comes out to be 151% using CAGR formula.

That is, CAGR = (End Value/Start Value) ^ (1/(Periods − 1)) − 1
CAGR = (1918.16/304.42) ^ (1/((2013 − 2011) − 1)) − 1 → 151%

The business model of Myntra is asset light in nature, implying that the assets cannot grow in future at such higher rates. Thus, the lower of the rates has been taken for forecasting tangible as well as intangible asset, which is 66 and 54% respectively.

Applying the rates, the gross tangible assets for the year 2014 would be, 1918.16 × (1+66%) → 3178.05. The same can be continued for the years 2015–2018. The additions made during the year would be the total gross tangible assets of current year minus the gross tangible assets of the previous year.

Additions for the year 2014 = 3178.05 − 1918.16 → 1259.89
Additions for the year 2015 = 5265.46 − 3178.05 → 2087.41 and so on.

Depreciation for the year would be the total gross tangible assets for the year multiplied by the rate of depreciation forecasted during the year (obtained from income statement).

Depreciation for the year 2014 = 3178.05 × 20% → 645.48
Depreciation for the year 2015 = 5265.46 × 20% → 1069.45 and so on.

SAME methodology is applied for calculating intangible assets and amortization.

Once the tangible and intangible assets are forecasted, the **addition** for the two would be clubbed and taken as capital expenditure or capex. That is, capex for the year 2014 = Additions in Tangible assets + Additions in Intangible assets

= 1259.89 + 380.32 → 1640.21 and so on.

Then the calculated values are fed in the income statement to calculate the EBIT (as shown in Exhibit 1).

5.8.4.2 *Ascertaining the Change in Working Capital*

For calculating the free cash flow to firm, the things required are EBIT, tax rate, depreciation, amortization, capex, and changes in working capital. In the earlier step, we would have calculated all of the required items except changes in working capital.

Exhibit 4: Changes in Working Capital

		2011	2012	2013	2014E	2015E	2016E	2017E	100,000.00 2018E
Number of Days	365								
Net Sales		1,649.21	6,254.66	20,325.87	40,651.74	73,173.13	113,418.34	175,798.43	272,487.57
Cost of Goods Sold		1,369.93	5,242.63	19,891.99	39,783.97	68,185.23	103,392.04	140,638.75	190,741.30
Working Capital Balances									
Inventories		211.14	3,658.67	5,471.77	10,354.73	16,812.80	24,077.60	30,824.93	39,193.42
Trade Receivables		424.49	2,359.93	3,989.24	5,568.73	8,018.97	9,322.06	9,632.79	7,465.41
Other Current Assets		4,298.81	2,807.93	6,064.29	8,130.35	10,975.97	11,341.83	8,789.92	13,624.38
Total Non Cash Current Assets		4,934.44	8,826.53	15,525.31	24,053.81	35,807.74	44,741.49	49,247.64	60,283.21
Trade Payables		401.59	2,259.76	5,252.11	9,809.75	15,878.75	22,661.27	28,898.37	36,580.52
Other Current Liabilities		384.10	1,171.20	2,821.21	5,642.43	9,670.49	14,663.75	19,946.33	27,052.21
Short Term Borrowings		384.92	50.20	672.24	4,376.24	7,500.38	11,373.12	15,470.26	20,981.54
Short Term Provisions		20.80	23.45	75.91	164.88	282.58	428.48	582.84	790.48
Total Current Liabilities		1,191.41	3,504.61	8,821.48	19,993.29	33,332.19	49,126.63	64,897.81	85,404.76
Net Working Capital/ (Deficit)		3,743.03	5,321.92	6,703.83	4,060.52	2,475.55	(4,385.14)	(15,650.16)	(25,121.55)
(Increase)/ Decrease in Working Capital			1,578.89	1,381.91	(2,643.31)	(1,584.98)	(6,860.69)	(11,265.02)	(9,471.38)
Assumptions:									
Accounts Receivable, net (Collection period in days)		93.95	137.72	71.64	50.00	40.00	30.00	20.00	10.00
Inventory (Days outstanding)		56.26	254.72	100.40	95.00	90.00	85.00	80.00	75.00
Other Current Assets (% of Net Sales)		261%	45%	30%	20%	15%	10%	5%	5%
Accounts Payable (Days Payable)		107.00	157.33	96.37	90.00	85.00	80.00	75.00	70.00
Short term Provisions		1.52%	0.45%	0.38%	0.41%	0.41%	0.41%	0.41%	0.41%
Other Current Liabilities (% of COGS)		28%	22%	14%	14%	14%	14%	14%	14%
Short term Borrowings		28%	1%	3%	11%	11%	11%	11%	11%

Determining the changes in working capital requires us to prepare a separate working capital schedule, as seen in the above exhibit.

Working capital is the difference between the current assets and the current liabilities, while change in working capital is the difference between current year working capital and the previous year working capital.

The primary step in working capital schedule is linking the sales and cost of goods sold from the years 2011–2018 (historical and forecast, calculated in income statements). It is because the current assets and current liabilities are mostly dependent on sales and COGS. For example, accounts receivable is the amount the company has to receive from its customers on account of sales made, while accounts payables are the amount a company has to pay to its suppliers on account of raw material purchase (which is the COGS).

Once the historical data are fed in, ratios such as Inventory days, accounts receivable days, accounts payable days, etc. have to be calculated as shown in exhibit (as assumptions).

Inventory days = (Inventory × 365)/Cost of Goods Sold
Receivable days = (Receivables × 365)/Sales
Payable days = (Payables × 365)/Cost of Goods Sold
Other Current Assets as a % of Sales = Other current Assets/Sales
Short-term provisions as a % of COGS = Short-term provisions/Cost of Goods sold
Other current liabilities as a % of COGS = Other current Liabilities/Cost of Goods sold
Short-term borrowings as a % of COGS = Short-term borrowings/Cost of Goods sold

Note: Provisions and borrowings are linked to COGS since short-term borrowings are majorly taken for meeting the working capital requirements or in other words to pay money to their suppliers of raw materials.

Once the ratio is calculated for the year 2011, 2012, and 2013, the trend of such ratios is ascertained for the future years (either by logical assumptions or continuing the historical trend).

It is generally believed that a company would improve its efficiency over a period of time. As company starts growing, it will have control over its deal negotiations with the suppliers and customers. As such, the receivable and payable days will gradually come down. Inventory days also starts declining as the sales volume picks up. Thus, the trend for Inventory days, accounts payable days, and accounts receivable days is gradually reduced from the 2013 levels.

For other items such as short-term borrowings and provisions, the same logic may not work as the capacity is not the only determinant. A company might have cash in hand to meet the working capital requirements, but would still try to avail credit maybe due to cheaper cost of credit or its credit policies. Thus, it is better to go ahead with the trend of those line items for projections.

In Myntra's case, the company is not a cash surplus company; it has to fund its working capital through taking loans. Thus, the other current liabilities are kept at constant levels though it is declining and short-term borrowings are kept at average levels since it is volatile. (It is entirely subjective and can be kept at any levels backed by logic.)

The other current assets seem to be constantly decreasing from 261% to 45% and 30%. So the trend can be continued by reducing it gradually and then keep it constant over a period of time. When it comes to short-term provisions, it is already at lower levels. Thus, it is not legitimate to reduce it further. The historical ratios can be averaged out and kept constant throughout.

Once the future trends are established, the reverse calculation is done to estimate the individual set items.

That is, in case of Inventory days, since the future "Inventory period" is projected, the Inventory for that particular year can be calculated as $(COGS \times Inventory\ days)/365$.

For example, the projected Inventory days for 2014 is 95.

Inventory for $2015 = (COGS\ of\ 2014 \times Inventory\ days\ of\ 2014)/365$
Inventory for $2015 = (39{,}783.97 \times 95)/365 \rightarrow 10{,}354.73$

Similarly, the calculated value of Inventory, accounts receivable, accounts payable, short-term borrowings, etc. is given in the above exhibit.

Once the individual items are forecasted for the future years, the working capital which is the difference between the current assets and current liabilities is calculated.

Working capital for the year $2014 =$ Current assets of $2014 -$ Current liabilities of 2014

$$= 24{,}053.81 - 19{,}993.29 \rightarrow 4060.52$$

Working capital for 2015–2018 is calculated using the same formula.

The last step in working capital schedule is calculating the change in working capital. **As dictated by the FCFF formula, change in working capital is only taken into consideration for calculating the free cash flows and not the working capital.**

Change in working capital is calculated as follows:

Δ Working Capital = Working capital for the current Year − Working capital of the previous Year
Δ Working capital of 2014 = Working capital of 2014 − Working capital of 2013

$$= 4060.52 - 6703.83 \rightarrow (2643.31)\ and\ so\ on.$$

5.8.4.3 Discounted Cash Flow Calculation
Free Cash Flows:

The above-calculated inputs such as EBIT, depreciation, amortization, change in working capital, and capex is used for calculating the free cash flows.

Exhibit 5: Free Cash Flows

INR (In Lakhs)						
	2013	2014E	2015E	2016E	2017E	2018E
EBIT		(24,430.67)	(33,071.12)	(37,733.01)	(21,469.66)	7,292.37
Tax Rate						0.00
EBIT(1-T)		(24,430.67)	(33,071.12)	(37,733.01)	(21,469.66)	5,104.66
Dep		645.48	1,069.45	1,771.88	2,935.69	4,863.92
Amort		261.91	403.00	620.09	954.12	1,468.10
Change in WC		2,643.31	1,584.98	6,860.69	11,265.02	9,471.38
Capex		(1,640.21)	(2,672.60)	(4,358.89)	(7,115.52)	(11,625.47)
FCFF	0	(22,520.18)	(32,686.30)	(32,839.24)	(13,430.34)	9,282.58
	0	(22,520.18)	(32,686.30)	(32,839.24)	(13,430.34)	9,282.58

$$FCFF = EBIT \times (1 - T) + \text{Depreciation} + \text{Amortization} - \text{Change in Working Capital} - \text{Capex}$$

$$FCCF \text{ for } 2014 = (24,430.67) \times (1 - 0\%) + 645.48 + 261.91 - (2643.31) - 1640.21$$
$$= (22,520.18)$$

Note: Though change in working capital is negative as per our calculations, it is added in the spreadsheet as formula requires to deduct a negative number.

Tax rate is zero for the years 2014–2017 because the company was incurring losses. In the year 2018, the company went on to show profitability thereby requiring to pay taxes. For the purpose, statutory tax rate of 30% is applied.

5.8.4.4 Calculating Appropriate Rate for Discounting

For discounting the free cash flows, an appropriate rate has to be calculated. It might be the cost of capital of the acquirer. (Since, that is, the cost at which he has funded the deal). But generally, WACC can be used if it is a cash or a stock deal or a combination of the two.

In Myntra's case, the founder of Myntra is expected to join Flipkart board, implying that the deal would have been funded by way of Equity. Thus, WACC has to be used for discounting the cash flows.

Calculation of WACC:

$$WACC = Wd \times Kd \times (1 - T) + We \times Ke$$

Exhibit 6: Weighted Average Cost of Capital (WACC)

WACC Calculation		
Wd	0	Since debt is 2-3% on Equity Debt is negligible for calculation purposes.
We	100.0%	Therefore, Ke can be taken as WACC for discounting
Ke	30.24%	(Removing the negative sign of beta because of risk involved)
Rf	7.53%	
Rm	25.92%	
Risk Prem		
Beta	-1.234540801	Negative Beta Represents only the inverse relationship
Adjusted Beta	-0.497142336	On a long term basis, the beta of the company tends to move in line with the market beta of 1
Thus Adjusted beta needs to be taken for discounting the Terminal cash flow.		
WACC	30.24%	
WACC with Adjusted Beta	17%	
Growth rate for next 5 years	35%	
Terminal Growth rate	15%	

Myntra's debt to equity ratio was pegged at around 0–2.5% during 2011–2013. Since the debt portion is smaller, it is assumed to be 0 for the purpose of calculation of WACC. Alternatively, assuming equity to be 100%.

Tax rate is not essential since debt is assumed to be zero.

Once the weights are calculated, the cost of equity and cost of debt need to be calculated.

Cost of equity can be calculated using CAPM Model.

where $Ke = Rf + \beta \times (Rm - Rf)$

Calculation of Cost of Equity:

Step 1: Find the rate of 10-year government bond yield on the day in which the valuations are done, which will be the "Rf" for CAPM. (7.53%)

Step 2: Calculate the Beta by regressing the earnings of the company with Nifty index earnings. The resultant slope is the Beta. Beta comes out to be −1.23. This means that the earnings of Myntra and earnings of Nifty are inversely proportionate and the sensitivity is 1.23 times.

Step 3: Calculation of Adjusted Beta. Over a period of time, the Beta of the stock tends to merge with the market Beta implying the requirement for adjusting the regression beta.

Adjusted Beta = Regression Beta × (2/3) + Market Beta × (1/3)

Adjusted Beta = −1.23 × (2/3) + 1 × (1/3) → −0.49

Used only for discounting the terminal cash flow.

Step 4: Calculate the Market Return (Rm). It is done by taking the average returns of the previous 10 years (to cover the impact of all market cycles). The average index return of Nifty comes out to be 25.92%.

Step 5: Estimate the cost of equity by using the formula "$Ke = Rf + \beta \times (Rm - Rf)$"

$Ke = 7.53\% + 1.23 \times (25.92\% - 7.53\%) \rightarrow 30.24\%$

Note: Negative Beta cannot be used since it would make the "Ke" lesser than the "Rf" which is practically not true.

5.8.4.5 Extended Forecast & Terminal Value

The requirement for extended cash flow forecast arises in the case of Myntra since the growth rate assumed during the years 2014–2018 is higher, and it is practically not good to drop it suddenly to the terminal growth rate. Thus, the growth rate has to be reduced.

Exhibit 7: Terminal Value

INR (In Lakhs)		Note: Extended Forecast on Free Cash Flows to Firm					
	2018E	2019E	2020E	2021E	2022E	2023E	
EBIT	7,292.37						
Tax Rate	0.00						
EBIT(1-T)	5,104.66						
Dep	4,863.92						
Amort	1,468.10						
Change in WC	9,471.38						
Capex	(11,625.47)						
FCFF	9,282.58	12,531.48	16,917.50	22,838.62	30,832.14	41,623.39	
	9,282.58	12,531.48	16,917.50	22,838.62	30,832.14	2,896,192.88	
						Inclusive of Terminal Value	

The free cash flow for the year 2018 comes out to be 9282.58. The growth rate for the next 5 years is assumed to be 35% (given in Exhibit 6).

That is, FCFF for $2019 = 9282.58 \times (1+35\%) \rightarrow 12,531.48$ and FCFF for 2023 will be $30,832.14 \times (1+35\%) \rightarrow 41,623.38$

Calculation of Terminal Value:

Terminal value is the value at the end of the forecast horizon (2023 in our case). Beyond forecast horizon, we will take a simplifying rate of growth in the free cash flows (which is expected to go perpetually).

For perpetual growth, we use the formula, $FCFF_1/(Ke - g)$

where $FCFF_1$ is the cash flow at the end of the forecast horizon multiplied by the long-term growth rate.
$$(FCFF_1 = 41,623.38 \times (1+15\%) \rightarrow 47,866.89)$$

g is the long-term growth rate (15% assumed, given in Exhibit 6).

Ke is the cost of equity calculated through CAPM model using the **adjusted beta** and **not** the regression beta (17%).

Applying the figures,

$$\text{Terminal Value} = 47,866.89/(17\% - 15\%)$$
$$= 2,854,569.49$$

The calculated terminal value is added to the last cash flow of 2023.

Discounting the Cash Flows:

Once all the cash flows are calculated, the NPV of the cash flows is calculated which will become the present value of the future cash flows. The discounting rate applied will be the cost of equity as calculated as per Step 2. **The NPV comes out to be, 125,558.06**

Finding the Enterprise Value:

The final step in the valuation process is finding the enterprise value.

EV = Implied Market Value + Total Debt + Minority Interest + Capital Lease − Cash & cash Equivalents

Implied Market Value—125,558.06
Debt—Nil
Cash & Equivalents—6619.33 (2013 cash balance of Myntra)
Minority Interest—Nil
Capital Lease—Nil

EV = 125,558.06 − 6619.33 → 118,938.73 (or) 1189 crores (since the figure were in lakhs).

Thus, valuation of Myntra comes out to be INR 1189 crores as per the applied DCF model.

As per the VC Circle news dated March 28, 2014, Myntra was valued at $200 million in the funding rounds just prior to its acquisition. By applying the prevailing rate of dollar @ 1$ = INR 60, at that time, this valuation is equal to INR 1200 crores. By applying the Grand Thorton Deal Price of $340 million (INR 2040 crores), the acquisition premium paid by Flipkart comes out to be equal to INR 840 crores.

The valuation of Myntra as per VC Circle is quite closer to the valuation of Myntra calculated as per our DCF model. Thus based on our DCF valuation, Flipkart acquisition price of Myntra at $340 million (INR 2040 crores) includes the intrinsic value of INR 1189 crores and deal premium of INR 851 crores.

CHAPTER 6

Accounting for Mergers and Acquisition

6.1 Introduction to M&A Accounting

Accounting for M&A in India cannot be described in terms of a single standard of Accounting; rather, it covers various standards that are applied on a case to case basis. Some accounting standards which covered the M&A Accounting in India hitherto have been accounting standards (AS) of the Institute of Chartered Accountants of India such as AS 14, AS 10 (for assets), and AS 21 (for process). Although AS 14 governs major aspects of accounting for the M&A, it remains a tedious task in terms of comparison, compliance, and lot more.

Adhering to the global standards for the purpose of uniformity, the Indian Accounting Standards have been converged with the IFRS standards of IASB. This convergence has led to creation of IndAS (FULL FORM). Post-convergence, accounting for mergers and acquisitions would be entirely covered under IndAS 103.

6.2 M&A Accounting as per Accounting Standard AS-14

AS 14 recognizes amalgamation in two forms, "Amalgamation in the nature of merger" and "Amalgamation in the nature of purchase."

© The Author(s) 2019
V. Kumar and P. Sharma, *An Insight into Mergers and Acquisitions*,
https://doi.org/10.1007/978-981-13-5829-6_6

6.2.1   Amalgamation in the Nature of Merger

A transaction will be recognized as merger if the following conditions are satisfied:

All the assets and liabilities of transferor (target) company will be transferred to transferee (acquirer) company.

More than or equal to 90% of the shareholders of target become the shareholders of acquirer.

The mode of payment is largely in the form of equity shares of acquirer issued to target shareholders or to target company. Only partial payment may be in the form of cash to account for fractional shares. Suppose if the swap ratio is 1:3, and a particular target shareholder owned 100 shares, he is entitled to receive 33.33 shares of acquirer. He would be receiving 33 shares of acquirer and for the 0.33 shares he might be paid in cash.

The business of the target will be carried by the acquirer after the merger.

No adjustments will be made in the book value of assets and liabilities of target, except to bring uniformity in the accounting policies followed.

In cases where the two companies are following different accounting policies for charging depreciation or inventory valuation methods, etc., steps are taken to bring uniformity. Supposing target company follows straight-line method of depreciation and the acquirer follows WDV method, adjustments can be made to convert the target company's books to match the WDV method of depreciation of the acquirer.

Example 1

In a particular merger and acquisition transaction, the target company's books have a particular asset which was bought 3 years ago, and the cost price of asset was 10 lacs and useful life was 5 years. If the target follows the straight-line method and acquirer follows the written down value method of depreciation, then to collate the books of two entities, following adjustments have to be made in the book value of this asset.

Solution:

Step 1: Calculation of book value and accumulated depreciation of this asset as per SLM method:

Cost Price of this asset $= 10$ Lacs

Useful life $= 5$ years

Yearly depreciation as per SLM method $= 10$ lacs$/5 = 2$ lacs

Accumulated depreciation for three years = 2 lacs × 3 = 6 lacs
Book Value of the asset at the time of merger = 10 lacs−6 lacs = 4 lacs

Step 2: Calculation of book value and accumulated depreciation of this asset as per WDV method (rate of depreciation applied is 20%):
Cost Price of this asset = 10 Lacs
Depreciation in 1st Year (20% of 10 lacs) = 2 lacs
WDV at the end of 1st Year = 8 lacs
Depreciation in 2nd Year (20% of 8 lacs) = 1.6 lacs
WDV at the end of 2nd Year = 6.4 lacs
Depreciation in 3rd Year (20% of 6.4 lacs) = 1.28 lacs
WDV at the end of 3rd Year = 5.12 lacs

Thus at the end of third year, book value of target asset and accumulated depreciation would have been 5.12 lacs and 4.88 lacs, respectively, as per WDV method in contrast to 4 lacs and 6 lacs, respectively, as per SLM method.

In order to collate the books of the acquirer and the target companies, the differential amount caused by two methods of charging depreciation (which is 1.12 lacs in this case) has to be adjusted in the book value of assets of target.

If all of the above conditions are satisfied, the transaction would be categorized as merger and pooling of interest method will be applied for accounting purpose.

6.2.2   *Amalgamation in the Nature of Purchase/Acquisition*

If any of the conditions mentioned above, in merger methods, is not satisfied then the transaction would be categorized as amalgamation in the nature of purchase. In this case, for accounting purpose, the purchase method will be followed.

6.3   POOLING OF INTEREST METHOD

Under this method, the assets, liabilities, and reserves of target company will be recorded by the acquirer at their book value/carrying value.

No adjustments have to be made in the assets, liabilities, and reserves of target, except to account for any difference arising out of differential accounting policies. The identity of all the reserves will be preserved. For example, general reserve of target will be transferred as general reserve, in the consolidated books and so on.

The difference in the reported values of assets/liabilities and reserves caused by differential accounting policies has to be reported as a prior period item, and the change in net profit/loss due to such adjustments has to be reported alongside. The financial statements have to give clarity on the accounting policies being followed post-merger. The financials of the post-merger unit have to be reported with uniform set of accounting policies.

Thus in the Example 1, discussed in the beginning of this chapter, asset will be recorded at 5.12 lacs (as per WDV method) instead of 4 lacs (as per SLM method) to bring uniformity in accounting policies. The difference in the accumulated depreciation of 1.12 lacs caused by difference in methods will result in increased profits of target and will be reported as prior period item.

Example 2

Pooling of interest method—balance sheet of A Ltd. and B Ltd. is given as follows:

A Ltd.—Balance Sheet as on March 31, 2015

Liabilities		Assets	
Share capital (2 lacs shares at Rs. 10 each face value)	2,000,000	Building	1,800,000
Reserves & surplus	500,000	Plant & machinery	500,000
Term loan	200,000	Stock	200,000
Trade creditors	100,000	Bills receivable	100,000
		Cash & bank	200,000
	2,800,000		2,800,000

B Ltd.—Balance Sheet as on March 31, 2015

Liabilities		Assets	
Share capital (1 lac shares at Rs. 10 each face value)	1,000,000	Plant & machinery	700,000
Reserves & surplus	200,000	Patent	200,000
Debentures	100,000	Stock	150,000
Trade creditors	100,000	Bills receivable	225,000
		Cash & bank	125,000
	1,400,000		1,400,000

The balance sheet of combined entity after the merger of A Ltd. and B Ltd., as per pooling of interest method, will be prepared as follows:

Merged Entity—Balance Sheet as on March 31, 2015

Liabilities		Assets	
Share capital (3 lac shares at Rs. 10 each face value)	3,000,000	Tangible fixed assets	3,000,000
Reserves & surplus	700,000	Intangible fixed Assets	200,000
Long term liabilities	300,000	Stock	350,000
Trade creditors	200,000	Bills receivable	325,000
		Cash & bank	325,000
	4,200,000		1,400,000

Thus in pooling of interest method, no change will be made in the book value of assets and liabilities of target entity. All assets and liabilities will be added at their carrying book value in the balance sheet of combined entity.

6.4   Purchase/Acquisition Method

Under this method, the fair value at the time of acquisition of all the assets and liabilities of the target will be calculated and the same will be incorporated in the consolidated books of accounts. Where fair value is the value negotiated by a knowledgeable buyer and seller of that particular asset/liability. For this purpose, the acquirer will apply his judgment for the assessment of fair value based on the market value of the asset, specific usage of the asset for consolidated business, etc.

Post-revaluation, the reserves would get eliminated since all the assets and liabilities are valued at fair value. If the purchase price is higher than the revalued assets and liabilities of the target company, then goodwill would be created in the consolidated books of accounts. The goodwill, if any created, would be amortized over a period of 5 years or justified useful life as per AS 14.

If the consideration paid to target is less than the net asset value of the target, then capital reserve would be created as liability/shareholders equity. The minority shareholding, if any, post-acquisition, would be appearing in the consolidated books under "Minority Interest."

Example 3

Target is acquired 100% by issuing shares worth 12,000.

Particulars	Acquirer	Target	Target (fair value)
Capital	4000	300	
Reserves	21,000	1600	
Shareholder's equity	25,000	1900	
Long-term liabilities	12,000	1500	1300
Non-current liabilities	4000	500	500
Current liabilities			
Accounts payable	6000	200	200
Other current liabilities	2000	400	400
Assets			
Machinery	10,000	1300	2000
Plant and equipment	15,000	1000	2200
Goodwill	2000	200	300
Current assets			
Cash	8000	300	300
Inventory	4000	500	800
Trade receivables	10,000	1200	2200

Solution:

Fair value of the target = Fair value of Identifiable net assets−Liabilities
$$= \text{(Machinery + Plant and Equipment + cash + Inventories}$$
$$+ \text{Trade receivables)} - \text{(Long-term liabilities + Non-current liabilities}$$
$$+ \text{Accounts Payable} + \text{Other current Liabilities)}$$
$$= (2000 + 2200 + 300 + 800 + 2200) - (1300 + 500 + 200 + 400)$$
$$= 7500 - 2400$$
$$= 5100$$
Purchase consideration $= 12,000$
Goodwill $= 12,000 - 5100 \rightarrow 6900$

Balance Sheet of the Combined Entity

Particulars	Acquirer	Target	Combined entity
Capital	4000	300	16,000
Reserves	21,000	1600	21,000
Shareholder's equity	25,000	1900	37,000
Long-term liabilities	12,000	1500	13,300
Non-current liabilities	4000	500	4500
Current liabilities			

Particulars	Acquirer	Target	Combined entity
Accounts payable	6000	200	6200
Other current liabilities	2000	400	2400
Assets			
Machinery	10,000	1300	12,000
Plant and equipment	15,000	1000	17,200
Goodwill	2000	200	8900
Current assets			
Cash	8000	300	8300
Inventory	4000	500	4800
Trade receivables	10,000	1200	12,200

Assets and liabilities of acquirer and target (fair value) are added to get the combined B/s.

6.5   IFRS AND INDAS

Globalization has highlighted the need to have a uniform set of accounting practices. The growing complexity of transactions has led to emergence of non-comparable financial statements among the results from different parts of the globe. It is avoid such complexities that the need to develop a uniform standard. Accordingly, a uniform set of accounting standards, The International Financial Reporting System (IFRS), has been developed by International Accounting Standards Board (IASB).

The ICAI has not adopted the IFRS because of the lack of compatibility of IFRS with Companies Act, Income-Tax Act, and several other acts prevailing in India. Instead of directly adopting the IFRS, ICAI has converged the Indian Accounting Standards with IFRS, and a new set of accounting standards "IndAS" has been developed by modifying few of the key policies In India. IndAS will be implemented in two phases:

In phase 1, the companies which are listed and have a net worth of 500 crores or more and its holding, subsidiaries, joint venture and associate companies (AND) unlisted companies with net worth of 500 crores or more and their holding, subsidiaries, joint venture and associate companies, have to adopt the IndAS from the financial year 2016–2017.

The companies having net worth of 500 crore or more as on March 31, 2014 would be falling under this category and thus have to abide by the provisions of IndAS from phase 1. If classified, the financials for the year FY 14–15, 15–16 have to be refurbished as per IndAS for the purpose of comparing the financials FY 16–17 reported under IndAS.

In phase 2, all the listed companies (irrespective of their net worth), and unlisted companies with net worth between 250 and 500 crores along with their holding, subsidiaries, joint venture and associate companies will have to adopt IndAS from the financial year 2017–2018.

Those companies which are unlisted and have a net worth of less than 250 crores are expected to be covered under the provisions in the near future. For them, the roadmap is yet to be outlined.

In this context, the accounting for mergers and acquisitions will be governed by the provisions of "IndAS 103 – Business Combinations."

6.6   Provisions of IndAS 103—Business Combinations

A company which is abiding by the provisions of IndAS 103 need not refer various accounting standards for M&A Accounting, which was the case prior to IndAS 103 as it covers the accounting aspects for most of the business combinations.

6.6.1   Business Combination

IndAS 103 specifically defines a business combination, which was not the case in the existing accounting standards. According to IndAS 103, any transaction which gives the acquirer the power to control one or more business of another entity, by way of transferring cash, incurring liabilities, contracts, etc., it will be classified as a business combination.

The below mentioned are the common forms through which business combination takes place:

- If two or more businesses become the subsidiaries of the acquiring entity.
- If two entities combine their net assets to form a new entity.
- If one entity merges its net assets with the assets of the acquiring entity.

IndAS covers only the business combinations, where business is defined as entity which has an input, process, and output. Where input means any economic resource which leads to creation of output, and process being the systems, procedures, rules, etc., being applied to input which aids in creation of output. Output means combined effect of input and process which provides the returns in the form of dividends, cost savings or any other economic benefits.

However, IndAS does not cover strategic alliances. If any transaction deals only with acquisition of assets like plant, machinery, etc., which does not qualify the criteria of input, process, and output, it will not be governed by IndAS 103 and instead will be governed by the provisions of SEBI Takeover Code and other IndAS.

As per IndAS 103, for all the business combinations, purchase/acquisition method will be applied except the businesses under common control for which pooling of interest method will be applicable.

6.6.2 Purchase/Acquisition Method

The purchase/acquisition method given under AS 14 previously is more or less similar to that of purchase/acquisition method under IndAS 103. However, the below mentioned is the overall method/framework under IndAS 103, Acquisition method.

- Identification of Acquirer:

Acquirer is the entity who has issued the shares for most of the transactions as payment consideration, except in case of reverse mergers. If the payment mode is in cash, the entity paying the cash is considered as acquirer. Acquirer is the entity who controls the operations and runs the business of the combined entity.

Where control is defined as the ability to appoint the board of directors and influence the decisions, policies, and operations of the business.

- Determination of Acquisition Date:

It is generally the date on which control is obtained by the acquirer, which will normally be the day on which the consideration is transferred to the transferor entity and assets and liabilities of the transferor are acquired by the acquirer. From that day, books of accounts will collate. However, if the control is obtained prior to payment of consideration through agreements, etc., that particular day would be considered as the acquisition date.

- Recognizing and measuring the identifiable assets acquired, the liabilities assumed and any non-controlling interest in the acquired firm:

After recognition, all the assets and liabilities will be measured at the fair value as at acquisition date. The non-controlling shareholders stake will also be measured at fair value of net assets on acquisition date, and those non-controlling shareholders will be either issued proportionate share of ownership instruments in the combined entity or the fair value would be paid in cash.

- Recognizing and measuring goodwill or a gain from a bargain purchase:

If the payment consideration (final amount paid by the acquirer company to transferor) is in excess of the net asset value acquired, it will give rise to goodwill. The difference will be shown as goodwill in the asset side of the combined entity and will be tested for impairment periodically. For example, X Ltd. pays 1 crore for acquiring 100% stakes in Y Ltd. The fair value of the net assets of Y Ltd. as on acquisition date is 80 Lakhs. Then the goodwill will be equal to 20 Lakhs.

Bargain Purchase: If the payment consideration is less than the net asset value, then the transaction is treated as bargain purchase. The gain of the acquirer is recognized as comprehensive other income to acquirer company and will be reported as capital reserve in the consolidated financial statements (balance sheet).

In the above example, if the fair value of the net assets of Y Ltd. as on acquisition date is 1.30 Crores, then the capital reserve would be equal to 30 Lakhs.

Calculation of Net Asset Value:

Net asset value has to be calculated as the difference of fair value of identifiable assets and liabilities of the transferor company as on the acquisition date. No asset which is non-identifiable should be considered for calculation of NAV.

Calculation of Payment Consideration:

The aggregate of the following will be the payment consideration:

Amount of consideration paid in cash, assets, financial instruments like shares, preference shares, etc., or liabilities incurred by acquirer toward transferor shareholders excluding the existing holding of acquirer in transferor (like contingent liabilities/deferred payments).

Non-controlling Interest Assumed:

Acquisition date fair value of previous shareholding of acquirer in transferor if acquisition takes place in stages. For example, Vedanta and Cairn (proposed merger).

Illustration: Calculation of Goodwill:

Suppose, Vedanta proposes to merge with Cairn India in which they already hold 40% stake. The non-controlling interest in Cairn India is, say, 10%. What would be the amount of goodwill that would be recognized in the consolidated books given the following information? (Table 6.1).
    Reserve includes 40% of shareholding by Vedanta, amounting to 400. Assume the payment made in cash is 1200. The fair values of the assets are as follows:

Answer: Purchase consideration $= 1200$
    Net Asset Value $=$ Total assets $-$ Existing Goodwill $-$ Liabilities
                $= 1600 - 100 - 500$
                $= 1000$
    Goodwill $= 1200 - 1000 \rightarrow 200$

- Measurement Period:

All these accounting steps have to be completed in a reasonable time frame after the acquisition date. If it is not completed before the

Table 6.1 Goodwill calculation

Shareholders equity and liability		Assets	
Particulars	*Amt*	*Particulars*	*Amt*
Shareholders equity and liability	100	Machinery	550
Reserves	900	Plan, property and equipment	550
Non-controlling Interest	100	Goodwill	100
Liabilities	500	Patents	100
		Current assets	300
	1600		1600

reporting date of financial year in which combination took place, then provisional values calculated by the accountant based on available data of the related items will be reported. In the subsequent period, proper measurements will be done and the provisional figures will be revised.

Measurement period ends when the accountant reasonably feels that they have obtained all the information and reporting for business combination can be done appropriately with the obtained information.

In no case, this measurement period should exceed more than 1 year (from the acquisition date).

6.6.3   Pooling of Interest Method

Accounting for business combinations under common control would be done through the usage of pooling of interest method.

Business combinations under common control means that combining entities are controlled by the same party both before and after the combination, where controlling entity may be a business entity or a person or a group of persons who have the powers to control the financial and operating policies of the business. Examples of combinations under common control may be merger of subsidiaries with parent entity or combination of business entities within the same group.

6.6.3.1 Method of Accounting for Common Control Business Combinations

Assets, liabilities, and reserves of combining entities will be transferred at their carrying/book value. No adjustments will be made to the book values of assets and liabilities except to account for the uniformity of accounting policies between the combining entities. Identity of reserves will be preserved.

The consideration for combination may be paid in the form of securities, cash or net assets. Securities will be valued at their nominal value; assets except cash will be valued at their fair value.

If the consideration paid is more than the share capital of transferor, then the excess will be adjusted from the capital reserve. If capital reserves are not present in the balance sheet, then it will be adjusted from the general reserve. If there is deficiency in the consideration paid in comparison with share capital of transferor entity, then the difference will be recorded as capital reserve in the books of transferee entity.

Example 4

Below mentioned is the balance sheet of acquirer and transferor company.

in '000

Equity and Liability	Acquirer	Target	Assets	Acquirer	Target
Shareholders Funds			Non current Assets		
Share Capital	15,000	4,000	Fixed Assets		
Reserves	6,000	2,000	Machinery	11,000	3,500
Minority Interest	300	100	Plant, Property and Equipment	8,000	2000
			Goodwill	1,000	800
Non current Liabilities			Non current Investments	2000	400
Long term borrowings	3000	800			
Current Liabilities			Current Assets		
Short term borrowings	900	300	Inventories	600	120
Trade payables	450	120	Trade Receivables	1600	300
Other current liabilities	600	200	Cash and Cash Equivalents	950	250
			Other current Assets	1100	150
Total	26250	7520	Total	26250	7520

The transferor was taken over by the acquirer at the end of the financial year. The payment consideration made is as follows:

Acquirer entity has issued its debt to replace the debt of transferor debt holders. Acquirer has also issued 500,000 equity shares of Rs. 10 each to pay the shareholders and non-controlling interest of the acquire company. Prepare the consolidated balance sheet of acquirer company as per pooling of interest method.

Solution:

Equity Issuance—500,000 × 10 → 5,000,000
Share capital of the transferor—4,000,000
Minority Interest of the Transferor—100,000
Amount paid in Excess—5,000,000−(4,000,000+1,00,000) → 900,000

Since the amount paid by the acquirer is in excess of the transferor's share capital and payment for minorities, it has to be adjusted in the general reserve of the merged entity.

Reserve account	Amount
Acquirer general reserve	6000
Transferor reserve	2000
Less: Excess amount paid	(900)
Total balance	7100

Balance Sheet of the Combined Entity

Equity and liability	Amount (in '000)	Assets	Amount (in '000)
Share capital (15,000 + 5,000)	20,000	Machinery (11,000 + 3500)	14,500
*Reserves	7100	Plant, property and equipment (8000 + 2000)	10,000
Minority interest (300)	300	Goodwill (1000 + 800)	1800
Long term borrowings (3000 + 800)	3800	Non-current investments (2000 + 400)	2400
Short term borrowings (900 + 300)	1200	Inventories (600 + 120)	720
Trade payables (450 + 120)	570	Trade receivables (1600 + 300)	1900
Other current liabilities (600 + 200)	800	Cash and cash equivalents (950 + 250)	1200
		Other current assets (1100 + 150)	1250
Total	33,770	Total	33,770

6.7   DIFFERENCE BETWEEN AS 14 AND IndAS 103

AS 14	IndAS 103
Two methods for accounting amalgamation. That is, pooling of interest method and purchase method	Majorly purchase method is prevalent, except for such business combinations having common control (for which pooling of interest method applies)
Goodwill arising out of purchase method is amortized over a period of 5 years	Goodwill is tested for impairment annually but not amortized
No precise guidance in respect of the acquisition date	Clear picture on the acquisition date. That is, the date in which the acquirer obtains control over the acquired entity
No guidance on the measurement period	The accounting process cannot exceed more than one year from the date of acquisition

6.8   Difference Between Purchase Method and Pooling of Interest Method

Pooling of interest method	Purchase method
All the assets and liabilities will be recorded at the book value or the carrying value	All the assets and liabilities will be recorded at the fair value
Reserves of the acquired entity will also get recorded at the carrying value	Reserves of the acquired entity would get eliminated since all the assets and liabilities are revalued
Any difference arising out of the consideration paid, and the share capital of the acquired entity will be adjusted in the reserves of the merged entity	Any difference arising out of the consideration paid, and the fair value of the net assets will be treated as goodwill or capital reserve
[a]Would be used only for business combinations under common control and joint venture	[a]Would be used for all types of business combinations except common control

[a]Effective from 2017 for the firms who are following IndAS 103

CHAPTER 7

Performance Evaluation of M&A

7.1 Introduction

Mergers and acquisitions are considered as one of the fastest routes to growth. Companies indulge in M&A with the objective of expanding and growing at a faster rate in comparison with their competitors. But the same needs to be carried out with utmost care by having proper due diligence so as to ensure that shareholder's wealth does not get eroded. If organizations pursue M&A deals which are strategically fit, priced right, and carefully implemented, they are set for achieving good growth. The long-term profitability of such enterprises is bound to expand with shareholders wealth multiplying significantly.

However, in most cases, the management team involved in the process of finalizing the deals of a merger or an acquisition really forget that their decision should be governed by the sole objective of maximizing shareholders wealth. When the empire building perspective dominates the profitability angle, the merger and acquisition deal may prove to be winners curse. M&A activity attempts to satisfy the hunger of companies to expand their size, aid in intense market penetration, and facilitating fast-growing top line. However, such an aggressive growth strategy often leads to unsuccessful mergers followed by a deterioration in shareholder wealth over the long run.

There are contradictory opinions emerging from varied empirical researches as to whether M&A activity creates value or destroys value.

© The Author(s) 2019
V. Kumar and P. Sharma, *An Insight into Mergers and Acquisitions,*
https://doi.org/10.1007/978-981-13-5829-6_7

7.2   WHO SAYS M&A DOESN'T CREATE VALUE—"ACCENTURE REPORT 2012"

Although majority of empirical research including Hogarty (1978), Philippatos et al. (1985), Pawaskar (2001), Sharma and HO (2002), and Ken C. Yook (2004) says that M&A does not create value, the Accenture report published in 2012, however, argues that M&A creates value. The extent of value creation may vary among different industries depending upon the individual industry dynamics.

While mergers in some industries result in more value than that of those in other industries, top-quartile performers in every industry create value from M&A activities.

Acquirer Total Return to Shareholders (TRS) versus Industry Index, by industry Top 500 deals from June 2002 to September 2009 (Fig. 7.1).

(TRS measured 24 months after deal announced)

This research shows a wide range of value-creation potential across industries, from a median Total Return to Shareholders (TRS) of 25

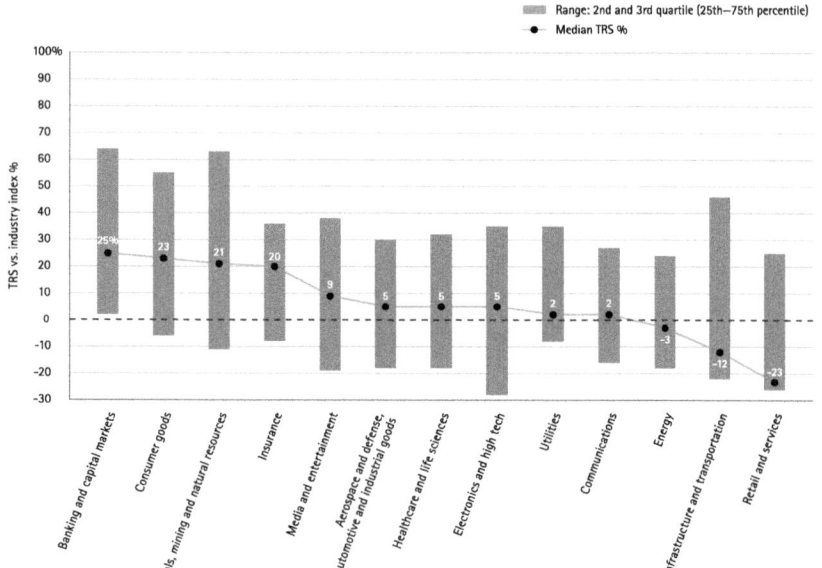

Fig. 7.1   Returns vis-à-vis industry (*Source* Accenture analysis)

percent for deals in banking and capital markets to a discouraging negative 23 percent in retail and services (as given in chart).

On analyzing the dynamics of the two industries—banking and capital markets and retail and services—we find that both have bricks-and-mortar branches and are moving to web-based interactions with their customers, differing their outlook toward growth. This variation in growth outlook easily explains the banking segments ability to create and enhances shareholder value while demonstrating the struggle of retailers.

Bankers relentlessly acquired and consolidated from 2002 to 2009, generating more M&A volume than any other industry as consumers across the globe valued established banking brands.

Retailers, on the other hand, continued to think small and focused on inward operations. Leading retail players have had to face well-documented challenges in trying to move into newer markets to capture growth. Consequently, the retail segment did not find any place in the 500 largest deals registered between 2002 and 2009.

The nature of an industry and the number of players in it are also very important as less concentrated industries tend to create more value from M&A than heavily concentrated industries, as measured by the Herfindahl–Hirschman Index. The findings of the Accenture report, however, show that this relationship is fairly loose—after all, banking and retail are both relatively fragmented. The report states that "But it's possible that we would have found more evidence of this trend if we hadn't confined our research to the 500 largest deals."

As a number of previous researchers have reported, less concentrated industries offer prospective acquirers a target-rich environment where they can find and take over smaller best-fit companies that meet their desired screening criteria—an advantage that's somewhat blunted if the acquirer is determined to do a deal on large scale. Previous researchers have also found and reported that less concentrated industries tend to be less mature and less regulated than more concentrated industries, making changes easier to work during a deal's all critical merger integration phase.

7.3   Evaluation of M&A Performance

In order to evaluate, whether Merger & Acquisition has been a successful strategy or not, several empirical studies have been conducted in the different parts of the world. They include event studies conducted around the merger announcement to gauge whether such announcement leads to abnormal return to the shareholders of acquirer and target entities.

The results of most of the event studies show that shareholders of target companies benefit while the acquirer shareholders get negative returns or at the most their wealth remain unaffected.

Further, several studies were conducted to evaluate the long-term financial performance of merging entities through comparison of pre- and post-merger financials over a long period of time.

In order to assess the financial performance of a specific merger and acquisition, pre-merger financial parameters of merging entities have to be compared with the post-merger financials of the combined entity. If the improvement is found to be accretive, then the merger is said to be successful.

The performance can be evaluated based on the following parameters:

a. Earnings per Share (EPS)
b. Return on Assets (ROA)
c. Return on Equity (ROE)
d. Market Price/Market Value (MPS/MV)
e. Net Present Value (NPV), etc.

This can be understood with the help of the following examples:

Example 1

Q Ltd. is merging with P Ltd. P Ltd. will issue its shares to the shareholders of Q Ltd. at the current market value of Q Ltd. What will be post-merger EPS and Value of combined entity, if the following information is given:

Company	Number of shares	Market prices	Earnings
P Ltd.	4000	25	
Q Ltd.	2500	15	
Combined			8000

Solution

Market Value of Q Ltd. $=$ Number of Shares $\times$ Market price
$$= 2500 \times 15 = 37,500$$
Number of Shares to be issued by P Ltd. $=$ Market Value of Q Ltd./ Market Price of P Ltd.

$$= 37,500/25 = 1500$$

Total number of shares of combined entity = existing shares of P Ltd. + Shares issued to Q Ltd.
$$= 4000 + 1500 = 5500$$
EPS of combined Entity = Combined Earnings/no. of shares
$$= 8000/5500 = 1.45 \text{ Rs. per Share}$$
Value of combined entity = Total no. of shares × market price
$$= 5500 \times 25 = 137{,}500$$

Example 2

If A Ltd. acquires B Ltd. for Rs. 350 Crore while the Fair Net Asset Value of B Ltd. is Rs. 300 Crore as A Ltd. perceived the post-merger value combined entity to be Rs. 900 Crore. Where the value of A Ltd. was Rs. 400 Crore, calculate the value of synergy created from this merger transaction and the gains to A Ltd.

Solution

Value of Synergy = Value of combined entity – total value of merging entities before merger
$$= \text{Rs. 900 Crore} - (\text{Rs. 400 Crore} + \text{Rs. 350 Crore}) = \text{Rs. 150 Crore}$$
Gain to A Ltd. = Value of Synergy created – merger premium paid
$$= \text{Rs. 150 Crore} - (\text{Rs. 350 Crore} - \text{Rs. 300 Crore}) = \text{Rs. 100 Crore}$$

Example 3

XYZ Ltd. acquires PQR Ltd. by issuing 0.8 shares of XYZ Ltd. for each share of PQR Ltd. Calculate the EPS of combined entity and gains to the shareholders of each company. Details are given as follows:

Company	Number of shares	Market prices	Earnings	EPS
XYZ Ltd.	10,000	25	20,000	2
PQR Ltd.	5000	15	10,000	2
Combined			30,000	

Solution

Number of Shares issued by XYZ Ltd. to the Shareholder of PQR Ltd.
$$= \text{Number of PQR Ltd. shares} \times \text{exchange ratio}$$
$$= 5000 \times 0.8 = 4000 \text{ shares}$$
EPS of combined entity = Combined Earnings/Total number of Shares
$$= 30{,}000/(10{,}000 + 4000) = \text{Rs. 2.14 per Share}$$

Increase in the EPS of XYZ Ltd. shareholders = EPS of combined firm-pre-merger EPS of XYZ Ltd.

= Rs. 2.14 − Rs. 2 = Rs. 0.14 per Share

Increase in the EPS of PQR Ltd. shareholders = EPS of combined firm − pre-merger EPS of PQR Ltd.

= Rs. 2.14 − Rs. 2 = Rs. 0.14 per Share

Calculation of Gains to Shareholders

Post-merger share price of combined entity if XYZ Ltd. maintains its PE ratio = existing PE ratio × new EPS = (25/2) × 2.14 = Rs. 26.78

Value of Combined Entity = Total No. of Shares of combined entity × New Share Price

$$= 14{,}000 \times 26.78 = \text{Rs. } 374{,}920$$

Total value of XYZ Ltd. and PQR Ltd. before merger = Sum of (Number of Shares × Market Price) of both companies

$$= (10{,}000 \times 25) + (5000 \times 15) = \text{Rs. } 325{,}000$$

Gains from Merger = Post-merger value − Pre-merger value 374,920 − 325,000 = Rs. 49,920

Calculation of division of total gains of Rs. 49,920 between the acquirer and the target entity:

Gains to XYZ Ltd. = Proportionate Post-merger value of XYZ Ltd. − Pre-merger value

$$= (10{,}000 \times 26.78) - (10{,}000 \times 25) = \text{Rs. } 17{,}800$$

Gains to PQR Ltd. = Proportionate Post-merger value of PQR Ltd. − Pre-merger value

$$= (4000 \times 26.78) - (5000 \times 15) = \text{Rs. } 32{,}120$$

7.3.1   Performance Evaluation: BootStrapping Effect

In the above, we would have seen that any increase in the EPS of the combined entity over and above Acquirer's EPS is said to be accretive and the merger is said to have created value. However, there is an exception to it.

At times, the EPS of the combined entity would have been increased at the initial levels itself, merely due to acquisition of firms with lower PE multiples and not necessarily due to synergistic benefits. This is popularly referred to as bootstrapping effect.

Consider the below example.

Company A buys Company T with an exchange ratio of 1:2.

Assuming market applies pre-merger PE of Company A to post-merger earnings the position of the combined entity stands to be:

Parameters	Company A	Company T	Post-acquisition Company A
Net profit	10,000	8000	18,000
No. of shares	1000	800	1400
EPS	10	10	12.86
PE	18	12	18
Price per share	180	120	231.4
Market value	180,000	96,000	324,000

In the above case, Company A, having higher PE multiple, purchased Company T with lower PE multiple (at a cheaper valuation). The EPS of the combined entity comes out to be 12.86 with an increase of 2.86 or 28.6% from the Acquirer's EPS. This increase is not due to realization of synergy or increase in the operating performance of the combined entity.

This is just an increase attributable to favorable swap ratio used by Company A for purchasing Company T's earnings. This resulted in lower number of outstanding shares for combined entity while the net profit remained same for the combined entity which in-turn led to increase in EPS.

Note: EPS = Net profit/Number of Shares (since the number of shares reduced, EPS increased).

Thus, we cannot conclude that M&A has created value just by seeing an increase in combined EPS.

7.4 Empirical Evidence on Long-Term Financial Performance Evaluation of M&A

Several empirical studies have been conducted to evaluate the financial performance of mergers and acquisitions. Empirical evidence does not support the M&A as a successful strategy for growth. The studies found that in most of the cases M&A doesn't create value. Rather benefit is transferred from the acquirer shareholders to target shareholders in most of the cases. The wealth of the target shareholders goes up because of the hefty premiums paid by the acquirers. In contrast, the wealth of acquirer shareholders increases marginally or remains the same and in some cases it may even decline. Only in few cases, M&A has been found to be a value-creating exercise leading to increase in wealth of both target and acquirer entities shareholders. The results of few empirical studies are given here.

7.4.1   Study on Performance Evaluation of M&A in the USA

In 1922, Healy, Palepu, and Ruback looked at the issue of whether mergers improved performance, and if they did so, what were the recorded economic gains.

They observed an increase in the post-merger operating cash flow returns vis-à-vis the firms' pre-merger performance. The improvements in operating cash flows post-merger were mainly due to the enhancement of asset productivity.

In some of their further studies, Healy, Palepu, and Ruback found that most of the mergers were not value creating once the merger premium paid by acquirers was taken into account.

Another study by Sharma and Ho (2002) investigated, whether corporate acquisitions create synergies reflected in corporate operating performance measures.

They found that corporate acquisitions did not lead to significant post-acquisition improvements in corporate operating performance. Their study also inferred that the type of acquisition (conglomerate versus non-conglomerate) and the form of acquisition financing (cash, share, or a combination) do not mightily influence post-acquisition performance. Also, the size of the acquisition and the payment of a premium (goodwill) do not impact post-acquisition performance.

7.4.2   Indian Study

Ramakrishnan (2008) tested the hypothesis that mergers in India have helped firms perform better in the long term.

Sample Details

The final sample size used for analyzes was 87 pairs of mergers consisting of 174 firms (87 each of targets and bidders). The average relative size of the target to the bidder firm was 0.59, where size was measured as the total assets of the firm.

Result

Ramakrishnan concluded that, broadly, merged firms in India seem to have performed better financially post the merger, as compared to their performance in the pre-merger period. This improvement in performance can be credited to the merger.

7.5   PERFORMANCE EVALUATION OF A SAMPLE OF INDIAN COMPANIES: AN EMPIRICAL RESEARCH WORK

A detailed study has been conducted by Authors where the objective was to find out whether the Mergers and Acquisition deals entered in past have led to any significant difference in the financial performance of the combined firms. This has helped us deduce whether M&A is a successful strategy for corporate growth or not. The same methodology has been used for the performance evaluation of individual mergers.

7.5.1   *Period of Study and Performance Measurement*

For the purpose of this study, the domestic mergers and acquisitions that took place during the period from 2001 to 2007 were considered for evaluation. Cross-border Mergers were dropped, and the final sample size of 67 domestic M&A deals (Annexure-I) was selected from Economic Times Intelligence Group M&A database. The sample contains the deals from diverse industries. The performance of these deals is analyzed for the period 5 years prior to acquisition and 5 years after the acquisition with the help of ratios and cash flow-based parameters.

The study also included the analysis whether post-merger performance is influenced by the following factors:

1. Pre-merger performance
2. Mode of payment
3. Relatedness (industry in which both the entity operates)
4. Relative size of target
5. Promoters stake in acquirer entity
6. Debt in the capital structure of acquirer.

The results indicate that M&A does not lead to any significant improvement in the performance of merged entities. Further, it was found that except pre-merger performance of merged entities no other factors mentioned above have a bearing on post-merger performance of combined entity. Thus, it was concluded that mergers as a strategy for growth may not be a successful strategy in all the cases.

The sample which was used for the study is given as annexure.

ANNEXURE-I: LIST OF SAMPLE MERGERS AND ACQUISITIONS FOR EMPIRICAL STUDY

S.No.	Acquirer company	Target company
1	AI Champdany Inds. Ltd.	Champdany Industries Ltd.
2	Aarti Industries Ltd.	Alchemie Organics Ltd.
3	Aban Offshore Ltd.	Hitech Drilling Services India Ltd.
4	Ambuja Cements Ltd.	Ambuja Cement Rajasthan Ltd.
5	Ambuja Cements Ltd.	Ambuja Cement Eastern Ltd.
6	Asahi India Glass Ltd.	Floatglass India Ltd.
7	Bharat Petroleum Corpn. Ltd.	Kochi Refineries Ltd.
8	Bilt Paper Holdings Ltd.	Janpath Investments and Holdings Ltd.
9	Cadila Healthcare Ltd.	German Remedies Ltd.
10	Chambal Fertilisers & Chemicals Ltd.	India Steamship Co. Ltd.
11	Clariant Chemicals (India) Ltd.	Clariant (India) Ltd. and Vanavil Dyes and Chemicals Ltd.
12	Coromandel International Ltd.	Godavari Fertilisers and Chemicals Ltd.
13	Cosmo Films Ltd.	Gujarat Propack Ltd.
14	Dr. Reddy's Laboratories Ltd.	Cheminor Drugs Ltd.
15	Eveready Industries (India) Ltd.	Powercell Battery India Ltd.
16	Forbes & Co. Ltd.	FAL Industries Ltd.
17	Gateway Distriparks Ltd.	Snowman Frozen Foods Ltd.
18	Gillanders Arbuthnot & Co. Ltd.	GIS Ltd.
19	Gitanjali Gems Ltd.	Gemplus Jewellery India Ltd.
20	GlaxoSmithKline Pharmaceuticals Ltd.	Smithkline Beecham Pharmaceuticals (India) Ltd.
21	GlaxoSmithKline Pharmaceuticals Ltd.	Burroughs Wellcome (India) Ltd.
22	Gujarat Narmada Valley Fertilizers Co. Ltd.	Narmada Chematur Petrochemicals Ltd.
23	Henkel India Ltd.	Henkel Spic India Ltd.
24	Himachal Futuristic Communications Ltd.	HTL Ltd.
25	Hindalco Industries Ltd.	Indian Aluminium Co. Ltd.
26	Hyderabad Industries Ltd.	Malabar Building Products Ltd.
27	ITC Ltd.	ITC Bhadrachalam Paperboards Ltd.
28	ITC Ltd.	ITC Hotels Ltd.
29	ITC Ltd.	Wimco Ltd.
30	IVRCL Ltd.	Hindustan Dorr-Oliver Ltd.

S.No.	Acquirer company	Target company
31	Indian Oil Corpn. Ltd.	Bongaigaon Refinery & Petrochemicals Ltd.
32	Indian Oil Corpn. Ltd.	Chennai Petroleum Corpn. Ltd.
33	Indian Oil Corpn. Ltd.	IBP Co. Ltd.
34	Ispat Industries Ltd.	Ispat Metallics India Ltd.
35	JSW Steel Ltd.	Jindal Iron & Steel Co. Ltd.
36	Mahindra & Mahindra Ltd.	Mahindra Hinoday Inds. Ltd.
37	Mahindra & Mahindra Ltd.	Punjab Tractors Ltd. and Swaraj Engines Ltd.
38	Matrix Laboratories Ltd.	Medicorp Technologies India Ltd. and Vorin Laboratories Ltd.
39	Megasoft Ltd.	Visualsoft Technologies Ltd.
40	Mirc Electronics Ltd.	Onida Savak Ltd.
41	NRB Bearings Ltd.	SNL Bearings Ltd.
42	Nirma Ltd.	Saurashtra Chemicals Ltd.
43	Novartis India Ltd.	Ciba Ckd Biochem Ltd.
44	Pfizer Ltd.	Parke-Davis (India) Ltd.
45	Philips Electronics India Ltd.	Philips Glass India Ltd. and Punjab Anand Lamp Inds. Ltd.
46	Punjab Chemicals & Crop Protection Ltd.	Alpha Drug India Ltd.
47	Punjab Chemicals & Crop Protection Ltd.	I A & I C Chem Pvt. Ltd.
48	RSWM Ltd.	Cheslind Textiles Ltd.
49	Raymond Ltd.	Ring Plus Aqua Ltd.
50	Reliance Industries Ltd.	Indian Petrochemicals Corpn. Ltd.
51	Reliance Industries Ltd.	Reliance Infrastructure Ltd.
52	Salzer Electronics Ltd.	Salzer Controls Ltd.
53	Siemens Ltd.	Siemens VDO Automotive Ltd.
54	Spentex Industries Ltd.	Amit Spinning Inds. Ltd.
55	Sterlite Industries (India) Ltd.	Bharat Aluminium Co. Ltd.
56	Sterlite Industries (India) Ltd.	Hindustan Zinc Ltd.
57	Sundaram-Clayton Ltd.	TVS Motor Co. Ltd.
58	Sundram Fasteners Ltd.	TVS Autolec Ltd.
59	Supreme Industries Ltd.	Siltap Chemicals Ltd.
60	TVS Motor Co. Ltd.	Lakshmi Auto Components Ltd.
61	Tata Chemicals Ltd.	Hind Lever Chemicals Ltd.
62	Tata Sons Ltd.	CMC Ltd.
63	Tata Steel Ltd.	Tata SSL Ltd.
64	Torrent Power Ltd.	Torrent Power AEC Ltd. and Torrent Power SEC Ltd.
65	Uflex Ltd.	FCL Technologies & Products Ltd. and Flex Engineering Ltd.
66	United Spirits Ltd.	Shaw Wallace & Co. Ltd.
67	VIP Industries Ltd.	Blow Plast Ltd.

CHAPTER 8

Regulatory Insights for M&A in India

8.1 Overview of M&A Regulations

Corporate restructuring not only impacts the individual company involved in the process, but also the economic or business environment around it. If a company with 30% market share merges with another company with 25% market share in the industry, it may lead to dominance in the market by the combined entity, which in turn might result in concentration in the industry affecting the local businesses. Thus, the merger decision of a company impacts the whole industry and the related counterparts. Legal frameworks are put in place to make sure that the process goes on according to the best interest of the business/society and adhere to the law satisfying the concerning authority norms.

Mergers and acquisitions have not only evolved over a period of time, but also undergone structural changes in their legal frameworks. Initially, the mergers were governed by Companies Act 1956, which was replaced by the new Companies Act 2013 on December 15, 2016. The regulatory aspect pertaining to mergers and acquisition is now being taken care of by The Companies Act 2013 (for merger), under sections 230 to 240 and SEBI Takeover Code-2011 (for acquisition). Mergers and acquisitions are also governed by the provisions of **Competition Act, FEMA (for Cross-Border deals)** and several other regulations.

© The Author(s) 2019
V. Kumar and P. Sharma, *An Insight into Mergers and Acquisitions,*
https://doi.org/10.1007/978-981-13-5829-6_8

8.2   COMPANIES ACT 2013:
IMPORTANT PROVISIONS PERTAINING TO M&A

Section 230 to 240 of Companies Act 2013 covers the procedural frameworks for mergers and acquisitions in India.

Companies Act 2013 has brought some remarkable improvements to the M&A regulations, which includes: (1) recognition of cross-border mergers, (2) fixation of time limit for expressing objection/opinion by various regulatory authorities like SEBI, RBI, etc., (3) separate procedure for merger according to types of companies (small companies, wholly-owned companies, etc.), and (4) provision related to mandatory filings to ensure compliance with different regulatory requirements.

8.2.1   Companies Act 2013

Amalgamation, under the Act, is defined as any combination where a company or an undertaking transfers its property, assets, and liabilities either to an existing company or to a new company and the transferor company loses its entity and gets dissolved without winding up.

As per the Companies Act 1956, merging entities have to prepare the scheme of merger and the entire proceedings of mergers have to be conducted through high courts of the states where the registered offices of merging entities are located. However, the Act of 2013 calls for the formation of new regulator "National Company Law Tribunal (NCLT)" which would replace the high courts for sanctioning approval for mergers. Thus it is no longer required for companies intending to merge to go to the court for approval. They can get this done with this new authority NCLT.

NCLT has been formed in the year 2016 and in December 2016 notification of MCA all cases pending with high courts pertaining to M&A, and other cases will be transferred to NCLT and now all company-related legal matters including the approval of mergers will be dealt by NCLT rather than high courts. Formation of NCLT will reduce the load on high courts, and this will result into speedy proceedings of corporate legal matters by this specified tribunal.

8.2.1.1 Procedural Changes
The Companies Act 1956 does not specifically ask for the merging entities for getting consent/approval from various regulators such as SEBI, Stock Exchanges (in case of listed companies), RBI, Ministry

of Corporate Affairs, FEMA, and Competition Commission of India. It only talks about getting approval from shareholders and creditors. However, the Companies Act 2013 specifically asks for obtaining sanctions from the above-mentioned regulators. The timeline with which the regulators should revert back their concern or approve is 30 days. If any regulator does not respond within 30 days from the date of receiving the scheme of merger documents, it is deemed as the regulator has approved of the Merger.

Once the scheme of merger is filled with the high courts then court gives the date for holding the shareholders and debt holders meeting for approval of the scheme of merger. As per the Companies Act 1956, for casting their votes for such approval, members had to be present in the meeting. However, as per the new act, when the merger scheme gets proposed to the shareholders or the creditors of the company, the respective shareholders/creditors can cast their votes through postal ballot or in electronic form, which in case of Companies Act 1956 was available to only those presenting in person for the meeting. This permission for ballot/e-voting will result into wider representations from shareholders/creditors toward approval of the scheme of merger.

According to the Act of 2013, only those shareholders who have the ownership of 10% or more and the debt holders having 5% or more of total debt of the company are entitled to express their objection. However, this was not the case earlier. Any shareholder having even a single stock was allowed to file the objection. This used to result into frivolous objections on the part of stakeholders causing the unnecessary delay in the process. Now the condition of a minimum holding in the company will help to reduce such frivolous objections and process will be smoothened and only those stakeholders who have vested interest and genuine concern will be allowed to raise the objections.

Many experts believe that, the limit of 10 and 5% holding for shareholders and debt holders, respectively, seems to be quite high and even sometimes the large institutional investors like LIC, GIC may have less than 10% stake in a company and such a high limit may prove as deterrent in raising genuine concerns by such large institutional/retail investors who have quite large holding in the company but less than the specified limits.

The Companies Act of 2013 mandates for attaching the valuation report along with scheme of merger documents, which was not specifically mentioned in the Companies Act 1956. The valuation report has to be prepared by a registered investment banker and attached with the scheme of merger. This will help the approving entities to understand the basis of fixing the deal price and evaluate the impact of merger on the stakeholders of both the companies.

The Companies Act of 2013 also mandates all the listed and unlisted companies to provide the auditor's certificate for compliance with the accounting standards for the purpose of accounting treatment. This clause results into proper adherence to prevailing accounting standards.

8.2.1.2 Special Cases

Companies Act of 2013 has separately laid down provisions for cross border, merger of small companies and merger of holding with wholly-owned subsidiary companies. This was not covered individually in the Companies Act 1956.

8.2.1.3 Cross-Border Mergers

The new Companies Act of 2013 provides for cross-border mergers of all types (inbound and outbound mergers). Earlier the act was recognizing cross-border merger only in case of outbound merger, where a foreign company is merged into an Indian company. The act was silent about an Indian company merging into foreign company. The new act recognizes both inbound and outbound deals.

According to the 2013 Act, the payment for cross-border merger can be either in form of cash or depository receipts (DRs) or in both (since shares cannot be issued). Since the payments are made in cash, tax comes into picture. However, in case of outbound merger, the Income-tax Act grants tax exemptions but it is silent in the case of inbound merger. Under such cases, one has to refer to corresponding foreign exchange or tax laws prevailing at the time of deal.

8.2.1.4 Small Companies

The Companies Act 2013 allows that small-sized companies with a paid up capital of maximum 5 Million or companies with turnover of maximum 20 Million, need not file for approval from NCLT Tribunal. Any company falling in the above category, if approved for merger by 90% shareholders and 9/10th of debt holder's approval along with the approval of Ministry of Corporate Affairs is not required to get the NCLT proceedings done. However, if the MCA feels the necessity for taking the case to tribunal, it can do so. This was not the case in 1956

Act, companies irrespective of their size had to get approval from the court and now NCLT.

This provision will be very helpful for the small companies seeking growth via M&A route and whose mergers did not have a bearing on industry concentration and competition because of their small size but still had to go through the lengthy procedure of merger approval through courts. This exemption of merger approval from courts and only requirement of shareholder and debt holder approval for merger will go a long way, in today's dynamic corporate world, in boosting the growth of small size companies which want to opt for M&A route of growth.

This is same for holding companies intending to merge with their wholly-owned subsidiary companies

8.2.1.5 Merger of Listed Company with Unlisted Company

As per the provisions of new act, if a listed (transferor) company merges with an unlisted entity (transferee), then it does not result into automatic listing of Transferee Company. For the purpose of listing the transferee company has to separately apply to stock exchanges and has to comply with the regulations of exchange in order to get listed.

Further, if any shareholders of transferor company want to opt out of this and want to exit, then they have to be duly paid. The price to be paid to them has to be decided as per SEBI guidelines.

8.2.1.6 Offer to Minority Shareholders

If the shareholding of the transferee company reaches to the level of 90% or more in transferor company then in such a case, transferee company has to bring offer for buying the shares of minority shareholders. The offer price has to be based on basis of the valuation done by a registered valuer.

8.3   Regulatory Process
for Mergers and Scheme of Merger

When two companies decide to merge with each other, they have to prepare the scheme of merger which has to be approved by NCLT. For the completion of merger, they have to follow the step-wise procedure mentioned hereunder:

Step 1: Getting the valuation done by an independent valuer.

Step 2: Getting the fairness opinion from a merchant banker.

Step 3: The transferor company and transferee company will pass the resolution in the meeting of the board of directors for the purpose of merger and acquisition.

Step 4: Preparation of the scheme of merger.

Step 5: Submission of the scheme of merger documents to the respective high courts in the jurisdiction of corporate office of target and acquirer. (Going forward this approval will be done by NCLT.)

Step 6: Sending the scheme of merger for approval to all the regulatory authorities which include stock exchanges, RBI, Competition Commission of India, SEBI, industry-specific regulators such as TRAI and FSSAI.

Step 7: Calling the meeting of shareholders and creditors/lenders on the date given by the high court and getting their approvals.

Step 8: Once the scheme is approved by all the parties concerned, the process of transfer of assets and liabilities of transferor company to transferee company will be initiated, in exchange of consideration, which in case of mergers would mostly be in the form of shares of a transferee company and will be cash in case of acquisitions.

Step 9: Once the process is complete, the transferor company will automatically get dissolved, without the process of winding up. Its business and undertaking will be transferred as going concern to the transferee company. (Everything including all the assets and liabilities will be transferred.)

8.3.1   Example: Scheme of Merger Sun Pharma–Ranbaxy Merger

Let us understand the complete process with the help of Sun Pharma and Ranbaxy Merger proceedings.

On April 6, 2014, the board of directors of Ranbaxy Laboratories Ltd. passed the resolution for the merger of Ranbaxy into Sun Pharma Industries Ltd. The merger was subject to various approvals.

April 1, 2014, was decided as appointed date (the date from which the merger process starts). The valuation report dated April 6, 2014, of Ranbaxy was prepared by M/s. Walker Chandiok & Co. LLP (Independent Chartered Accountants). As per the report, 5 Equity shares of Ranbaxy of Rs. 5 each shall be exchanged into 4 Shares of Sun Pharma of 1 Re each (Annexure I).

For this valuation report, fairness opinion report dated April 6, 2014, was taken from the merchant banker-ICICI Securities Ltd. (Annexure II).

Scheme of Merger for the amalgamation of two companies was prepared and submitted to the court. The major contents of the scheme of merger are as follows:

1. *Preamble* It includes the description of transferor (Ranbaxy) and transferee company (Sun Pharma Industries Ltd.), rationale for the merger and acquisition, details about board of director's resolution and the definitions of all the terms used in the scheme of merger.
2. Details of Share capital of transferor company and transferee company as on March 31, 2014.
3. Complete process of transfer and vesting of undertaking of Ranbaxy into Sun Pharma.
4. *Transfer of Net Assets* All the assets and properties of Ranbaxy Ltd., movable as well as immovable, as on appointed date shall become the assets and properties of Sun Pharma. All the liabilities, including secured and unsecured will be absorbed by the Sun Pharma Industries Ltd.
5. *Execution of Contracts and deeds* Any contract entered in, by Ranbaxy, concluded prior to the appointment date or negotiated prior to appointment which got concluded post-appointment date but before execution date would be executed by Sun Pharma.
6. The same is the case for legal obligations.
7. This scheme shall be operative from effective date. The conduct of business of Ranbaxy Ltd. and Sun Pharma Industries Ltd. between the appointed date and effective date will be conducted as agreed between the two parties.
8. The consideration to be made by transferee company (Sun Pharma Ltd.) to the Shareholders of Ranbaxy whose name was there as on the record date.
9. The detail on the number of shares that can be withheld by Sun Pharma to issue, in case of Sun Pharma holding shares in Ranbaxy Ltd.
10. The clause on cancelation of shares of Ranbaxy post issue of consideration to the shareholders.
11. *Reduction of capital and Reserve and Surplus of the transferor company (Ranbaxy Ltd.)* That is, Ranbaxy's capital/reserves will

be reduced by the amount of debit balance in Profit & Loss A/c as on date used for accounting purpose (March 31, 2014).

12. Accounting treatment of Assets/Liabilities and Reserve and Surplus of Ranbaxy in the books of Sun Pharma. Details on usage of pooling of interest method as per AS 14. That is, the assets and liabilities will be recorded at their existing carrying amount in the same form as at the appointed date in the books of Sun Pharma Ltd.

13. *Dissolution of Ranbaxy Ltd.* On the effectiveness of the scheme the Ranbaxy Ltd. will be dissolved without winding up and the board of directors, any committee, etc., will also be dissolved.

14. Details on change in memorandum and articles of association and the share capital of Sun Pharma, if any, required for the purpose of facilitating the merger.

15. Both the entities will apply to their respective high courts for approval. If required, the modifications/amendments as directed by the court might be pursued.

16. This scheme is subject to approval by various authorities. If this scheme is not sanctioned by the court, then it will stand canceled. If any part of the scheme is approved but not found to be possible for implementation, the validity of the scheme is not impacted, subject to mutual agreement between the parties.

17. This was the example of Sun Pharma scheme of merger which was later approved by the high courts, and merger was completed in 2015 when this scheme of merger came into effect and trading in the scrips of Ranbaxy was suspended in April 2015.

8.4   SEBI (Substantial Acquisition of Shares and Takeovers) Regulations, 2011

Another Important Regulation which governs the takeovers is SEBI Takeover Code-2011. Important provisions of the code are discussed hereunder:

8.4.1   *Meaning of Acquisition*

Acquisition is the purchase of controlling stake in an entity by a person or group of persons or by another entity. Acquisition also includes the purchase of all the assets or liabilities of an entity. Here controlling stake means either absolute majority stake or proportionate majority stake which enables the acquiring entity to exercise control on the affairs of target entity. The control can also be exercised by disproportionate voting rights acquired by the acquirer.

This acquisition of shares can be done either through an agreement between the acquirer and majority shareholders or by making an offer of purchase directly to all the shareholders or through open purchase of shares from the market.

SEBI Takeover Code 2011 applies to the transactions pertaining to acquisition of substantial shareholding or voting rights in a target company or acquisition of controlling interest either directly or indirectly.

- Target Company

For the purpose of SEBI Takeover Code, a target company is a company which is listed on stock exchange and the share or voting rights of such entity are acquired/being acquired by some other company or individual or group of persons, etc. If the control of such listed entity is acquired/ being acquired in some other manner, then also it will be categorized as target company.

- Acquirer

An acquirer is a company/individual/group of persons/person acting in concert or any other legal entity which is acquiring/planning to acquire the majority shares or voting rights or control in some target company.

- Person Acting in Concert (PAC)

PAC is the persons/group of persons/companies or other legal entities acting together for the common purpose. The common purpose is to acquire substantial quantity of shares or voting rights or control over some target company. They can act together for this common purpose out of mutual understanding or through some formal agreement.

Some entities are automatically considered to be acting in concert, and there is no need to prove that they are jointly attempting to acquire the target company, for example holding and subsidiary companies, group companies, Trustee and Sponsor Company in case of mutual fund, etc.

- Meaning of Control

A company/person/group of person, etc. are said to have control over target company if they have right to appoint majority of directors. Control is also established if the acquirer can control the management or influence the strategic decisions in the target company.

- This Control Is Exercisable By

The acquirer can exercise the control if they hold controlling number of share, majority voting rights or management rights, shareholder's agreement or in some other manner.

There are two different reasons for which meaning of substantial quantity of shares has been defined by SEBI Takeover Code:

a. **An acquirer of shares has to make disclosures if it touches the defined threshold quantity of shares**: For this purpose, substantial acquisition of shares means acquirer is touching the threshold limit of acquisition of shares beyond which he is required to make proper disclosure to stock exchange, to the company whose shares are being acquired and to other regulatory authorities.

    If an acquirer acquires some shares in an entity and after that his total shareholding or voting rights in that company crosses 5/10/14/54/74% limits, then at each of these stages, the acquirer is required to make disclosures. Such disclosure has to be made to target entity and the stock exchange where the target entity is listed.

b. **Acquirer has to make an open offer if its shareholding in target reaches Trigger point**: If the acquirer touches this threshold limit of acquiring the shares of target company, then he is obligated to make an open offer to all the shareholders to buy an additional specified percentage of shares at the prescribed price as per the regulation.

8.4.2   Mandatory Open Offer in Case of Acquiring More Than 25% Shareholding of a Company

An acquirer is permitted to hold 24.99% shares or voting rights in target company if it doesn't acquire the control over the affairs of target entity.

If acquirer acquires more than 25% of the target, then it has to make an open offer of at least 26% additional stake to be bought from the existing shareholders. (The number was 15% in the previous regulation.)

In 2012, SEBI granted an exemption for the above-mentioned regulation in case of an Indirect Acquisition by APS Trust which acquired 25.61% of the shares of Dr. Reddy's Laboratories Ltd. This was granted on the underlying that there isn't a change in control since the parties to the trust are the same promoters of the target company thereby resulting in no change in promoter group shareholding.

8.4.3   *Mandatory Open Offer in Case of Consolidation of Holding*

If an acquirer already has 25% or more stake of a target company and wishes to consolidate his holdings, then it is permissible to acquire additional 5% stake in a financial year. The acquirer in this manner can consolidate his holdings maximum to the level permitted for non-public shareholding. As per SEBI regulations maximum, permissible non-public shareholding is 75% for Public Ltd. Companies.

If an acquirer crosses this limit of 5% for consolidation of holding in a financial year, it will trigger a mandatory open offer for such acquisition.

The above mentioned 5% creeping acquisition is calculated on gross basis. It means any reduction in voting rights resulting from dilution of stakes on account of new issues or disposal of shares doesn't count in 5%. **This creeping acquisition limit for the main promoter is only 3% and not 5%**.

8.4.4   *Mandatory Open Offer in Case of Acquiring Control*

Irrespective of the quantum of voting rights held, or holding of shares, if an acquirer is acquired/planning to acquire the control over a target company then it has to make an open offer to all the shareholders. This condition of open offer will be applicable whether the control is acquired directly or indirectly.

Control means by virtue of having controlling stake/majority voting rights or in some other manner the right to appoint majority of directors or control the management of influence the policy decisions of target entity. A director might not be considered as the controller of a particular company just by holding such position.

Thus in case of acquisition, mandatory open offer to all shareholders will be triggered, and acquirer has to buy additional 26% stake in target company if any of the following condition arises:

1. If the acquirer acquires 25% or more shareholding or voting rights or control in any other manner in the target company.
2. If an acquirer already has 25% or more shareholding and it acquires additional 5% or more shareholding in a financial year.
3. Irrespective of existing shareholding/voting rights if an acquirer acquires control over a target company either directly or indirectly.

8.4.5   *Direct and Indirect Acquisition*

Direct acquisition means when acquirer directly acquires the control in the target company through purchase of shareholding/voting rights or in some other manner. However, indirect control means where acquirer doesn't purchase the stake in target entity or directly doesn't acquires control in it but through some other transactions indirectly control comes in the hands of acquirer then such acquisition is called indirect acquisition. For example, if acquirer acquires the control over a holding company, then automatically it will acquire the control over the subsidiary where this holding company has controlling stake.

Indirect acquisition deemed to be direct: An indirect acquisition is deemed to be a direct acquisition, if, on the basis of recent audited financial statements, proportionate sales turnover, or the net asset value, or the enterprise value (EV) of the target is in excess of 80% of the consolidated net assets or sales turnover or enterprise value of the entity or the business being acquired. Or in other words, the assets/sales turnover/EV of the company which is being acquired mainly comprises of the assets/sales turnover/EV of the target only, and therefore, this acquisition will be deemed to be the direct acquisition of target entity for the purpose of SEBI Takeover Code-2011.

- Voluntary Open Offer

Any shareholder of a target company who is willing to consolidate his holdings can announce the open offer to all shareholders voluntarily. Minimum offer in such case can be 10% of total shares of target company. The offer can be as less as 10% of the total shares of the target company while the maximum is the maximum limit of non-public share-holding of 75% for Public Ltd. firms as prescribed by Security Contract Regulations.

• Offer Size

In case of mandatory open offer, offer size is minimum 26% of total shareholding calculated at the end of 10th working day after the closure of open offer. In case of voluntary offer, minimum of 10% and the maximum of the limit permitted by Security Contract Regulations for non-public shareholding would stand as the offer size.

• Offer Price

In case of direct acquisition, minimum open offer price has to be calculated based on the following methods. It has to be highest out of all the prices calculated by these methods.

– Highest Price which is negotiated between the acquirer and majority shareholders of target entity under a share purchase agreement.
– Volume-weighted average price paid/payable by the acquirer during 52 weeks prior to announcement of open offer.
– Highest price of the shares during the 26 weeks immediately preceding the date of PA, paid or payable by the acquirer.
– If the shares are regularly traded then volume-weighted average market price during 60 trading days prior to announcement of open offer. In case shares are not traded regularly then price would be calculated based on the valuation parameters like book value, comparable PE and negotiation by both the parties, namely acquirer and the manager to open offer.
– If the acquisition is deemed to be direct acquisition, i.e., the value of the target company as percentage of sales, enterprise value or net assets exceeds 80% of the business acquired, then the consideration is per share value computed for this indirect acquisition purpose.
– In case of indirect acquisition, it is the highest of above parameters along with the highest price paid from the announcement of primary acquisition and the date of public announcement of open offer.

8.4.6   Example for Calculation of Offer Price

Offer price is calculated based on above-explained four methods:

1. In case of an acquisition, the date of Public Announcement is January 20, 2013. Price paid, under share purchase agreement between acquirer and target, is Rs. 140.
2. 52 Weeks Volume-Weighted Price is calculated as follows:

Date	Price (A)	Number of shares (B)	Value of traded shares $C = (A \times B)$	Volume-weighted price $D = \Sigma C / \Sigma B$
01.02.2012	130	1000	130,000	**140.50**
28.06.2012	140	1200	168,000	
12.10.2012	150	1200	180,000	
20.12.2012	145	900	130,500	
04.01.2013	135	800	108,000	
Total		5100	716,500	

3. Calculation of highest price of the shares during the 26 weeks immediately preceding the date of PA:

Date	Price paid	Highest price paid
15.01.2013	140	**142**
01.10.2012	142	
07.07.2012	141	

4. Calculation of volume weighted average market price during 60 trading days immediately prior to date of Public Announcement

Date	Price (A)	Number of shares (B)	Value of traded shares $C = (A \times B)$	Volume-weighted price $D = \Sigma C / \Sigma B$
05.11.2012	140	1200	168,000	**138**
10.12.2012	138	1000	138,000	
04.01.2013	135	800	108,000	
Total		3000	414,000	

8.4.7   Open Offer Price

As per SEBI Takeover Code, minimum Offer Price for the open offer has to be the <u>highest</u> of the above four prices, which is Rs. 142.

- Mode of Payment

The offer price can be made either through cash, issue of shares, issue of convertible debt securities, and issue of secured investment grade debt instruments or any combination of them. The prerequisite condition for the above is that those shares have to be listed for at least 2 years and has to be frequently traded. It has to comply with the applicable law prevailing in the country.

- Open Offer Process

Prior to the public announcement, the acquirer has to appoint an investment banker and open depositary account for shares tendered. Public announcement (PA) to be made as per the mode of acquisition stated under the regulation. The chronology of events has to as follows:

Number of day after public announcement	Activity
PA + 2 days	Opening of Escrow account
PA + 5 days	Detailed Public Statement (DPS) to be published
PA + 10 days	Draft of letter of offer to be submitted to SEBI, due diligence certificate and draft loo has to be sent to target and stock exchange
PA + 20 days	Competing offer (if any)
PA + 25 days	Comments from SEBI
PA + 32 days	Dispatch of the final Letter of Offer to the shareholders. From this day till 3 days preceding to beginning of tendering period any upward revision in prices or number of shares can be done by intimating the same to SEBI, stock exchange, target company, and the general public
PA + 35 days	Independent directors of the target company make/may make the comment on the offer
PA + 36 days	Advertisement for the opening of tendering period. Disclosure of acquisition during the offer period has to be done
PA + 37 days	Commencement of offer
PA + 47 days	Closure of offer
PA + 57 days	Payment of consideration to the shareholders on account of acquisition
PA + 87 days	Release of remaining Escrow funds by the merchant banker

Annexure I

Walker Chandiok &Co LLP

SPIL, a specialty pharmaceutical company, manufactures and markets pharmaceutical formulations and APIs in India and internationally. SPIL offers formulations in various therapeutic areas, such as psychiatry, neurology, cardiology, diabetology, nephrology, gastroenterology, anti-asthmatic and anti-allergic, musculo-skeletal and pain, gynecology and urology, orthopedics, and ophthalmology. It also provides APIs, such as anti-cancers, peptides, sex hormones, and controlled substances. SPIL was founded in 1983 and is based in Mumbai, India. The equity shares of SPIL are listed on Bombay Stock Exchange and National Stock Exchange of India. For the period ended 31 December 2013, SPIL reported consolidated revenue from operations of INR 150,932.9 million, earnings before interest tax depreciation and amortization of INR 66,949.6 million and reported consolidated net profit (after adjustment for minority interest) of INR 26,038.5 million.

The managements of the Companies propose to consolidate the business operations of RLL with SPIL through a Composite Scheme of Arrangement and Amalgamation under the provisions of Sections 391-394 of the Companies Act, 1956 (including any statutory re-enactment thereof) ("Scheme") as under:

- merge RLL into SPIL on a going concern basis with effect from xx April 2014 (the "Appointed Date") (hereinafter referred as "Proposed Merger").
- The shareholders of RLL will be issued equity shares of SPIL as a consideration for the Proposed Merger.

In this connection, WCC has been requested by RLL to submit a report recommending a fair share exchange ratio in the event of the Proposed Merger for the consideration of the Board of RLL. This report will be placed before the Audit Committee of RLL, as per the SEBI Circular CIR/CFD/DIL/5/2013 dated 4 February 2013, as amended by CIR/CFD/DIL/8/2013 dated 21 May 2013 and the Board of RLL and to the extent mandatorily required under applicable laws of India, maybe produced before judicial, regulatory or government authorities, in connection with the Proposed Merger.

The scope of our services is to conduct relative valuation for recommending a fair share exchange ratio for the Proposed Merger in accordance with generally accepted professional standards.

We have considered financial statements and other information relating to the Companies upto 30 December 2013 in our analysis and made adjustments for facts made known (past or future) to us till the date of our report.

This report is our deliverable in respect of our recommendation of fair share exchange ratio for the purpose of the Proposed Merger.

This report is subject to the scope, assumptions, exclusions, limitations and disclaimers detailed hereinafter. As such, the report is to be read in totality, and not in parts, in conjunction with the relevant documents referred to therein.

Walker Chandiok &Co LLP

SOURCES OF INFORMATION

In connection with this exercise, we have used information available in the public domain as well as the following information from the official website of the Companies:

- Audited consolidated financial statements of RLL for the years ended 31 December 2011 and 2012 and unaudited consolidated financial statements for the four quarters ended 31 December 2013.
- Audited consolidated financial statements of SPIL for the years ended 31 March 2012 and 2013, unaudited consolidated financial statements for 6 months ended 30 September 2013 and consolidated income statement for the 9 months ended 31 December 2013.
- Other relevant information and documents for the purpose of this engagement.

RLL has been provided with the opportunity to review the draft report (excluding the recommended ratios) for this engagement to make sure that factual inaccuracies are avoided in our final report.

SCOPE LIMITATIONS, ASSUMPTIONS, QUALIFICATIONS, EXCLUSIONS AND DISCLAIMERS

Provision of valuation opinions and consideration of the issues described herein are areas of our regular practice. The services do not represent accounting, assurance, accounting / tax due diligence, consulting or tax related services that may otherwise be provided by us or our affiliates.

This report, its contents and the results herein (i) are specific to the purpose of valuation agreed as per the terms of our engagement; (ii) are specific to the date of this report and (iii) are based on the balance sheet as at 30 September 2013 of SPIL and 31 December 2013 of RLL. A valuation of this nature is necessarily based on the prevailing stock market, financial, economic and other conditions in general and industry trends in particular as in effect on, and the information made available to us as of 5 April 2014. Events occurring after this date may affect this report and the assumptions used in preparing it, and we do not assume any obligation to update, revise or reaffirm this report.

The recommendation(s) rendered in this report only represent our recommendation(s) based upon information available in the public domain as well as information sourced from international data bases and the said recommendation(s) shall be considered to be in the nature of non-binding advice (our recommendation will however not be used for advising anybody to take buy or sell decision, for which specific opinion needs to be taken from expert advisors). We have no obligation to update this report.

In the course of the valuation, we have assumed and relied upon, without independently verifying, (i) the accuracy of the information that was publicly available and formed a substantial basis for this report and (ii) the accuracy of information sourced from data bases. In accordance with our engagement letter and in accordance with the customary approach adopted in valuation exercises, we have not audited, reviewed or otherwise investigated the historical financial information available in the public domain. Accordingly, we do not express an opinion or offer any form of assurance regarding the truth and fairness of the financial position as indicated in the historical financial statements.

Walker Chandiok & Co LLP

The report assumes that the Companies comply fully with relevant laws and regulations applicable in all its areas of operations unless otherwise stated, and that the Companies will be managed in a competent and responsible manner. Further, except as specifically stated to the contrary, this valuation report has given no consideration to matters of a legal nature, including issues of legal title and compliance with local laws, and litigation and other contingent liabilities that are not recorded in the audited/unaudited balance sheet of the Companies.

This report does not look into the business / commercial reasons behind the Proposed Merger nor the likely benefits arising out of the same. Similarly, it does not address the relative merits of the Proposed Merger as compared with any other alternative business transaction, or other alternatives, or whether or not such alternatives could be achieved or are available.

No investigation / enquiry of the Companies' claim to title of assets has been made for the purpose of this report and the Companies' claim to such rights has been assumed to be valid. No consideration has been given to liens or encumbrances against the assets, beyond the loans disclosed in the accounts. Therefore, no responsibility is assumed for matters of a legal nature.

The fee for the engagement is not contingent upon the results reported.

We owe responsibility to only the Boards of Directors of RLL under the terms of our engagement, and nobody else. We do not accept any liability to any third party in relation to the issue of this report. It is understood that this analysis does not represent a fairness opinion.

This valuation report is subject to the laws of India.

Neither the valuation report nor its contents may be referred to or quoted in any registration statement, prospectus, offering memorandum, annual report, loan agreement or other agreement or document given to third parties, other than in connection with the Proposed Merger, without our prior written consent. In addition, this report does not in any manner address the prices at which RLL or SPIL's shares will trade following the announcement of the Proposed Merger and we express no opinion or recommendation as to how the shareholders of the Companies should vote at any shareholders' meeting(s) to be held in connection with the Proposed Merger.

SHARE CAPITAL DETAILS OF THE COMPANIES

Ranbaxy Laboratories Limited

The current equity share capital of RLL is INR 2,118.9 million consisting of 423,779,063 equity shares of face value of INR 5 each. For the purpose of determining the fair share exchange ratio, we have considered the fully diluted equity share capital of RLL.

The shareholding pattern as at 31 March 2014 is as follows:

Category	% shareholding
Promoters and Promoter Group	63.4
Others	35.1
Custodians (GDR)	1.5
Total	100.0

Walker Chandiok & Co LLP

Sun Pharmaceutical Industries Limited

The current equity share capital of SPIL is INR 162,229.8 Mn consisting of 2,071,163,910 equity shares of face value of INR 1 each. For the purpose of determining the fair share exchange ratio, we have considered the fully diluted equity share capital of SPIL..

The shareholding pattern as at 31 December 2013 is as follows:

Category	% shareholding
Promoters and Promoter Group	63.7
Others	36.3
Total	**100.0**

APPROACH - BASIS OF PROPOSED MERGER

The scheme contemplates the Proposed Merger of the Companies pursuant to the Composite Scheme of Arrangement and Amalgamation under sections 391 to 394 of the Companies Act, 1956. Arriving at the fair share exchange ratio for the Proposed Merger would require determining the relative values of the concerned businesses and shares of the Companies. These values are to be determined independently but on a relative basis, and without considering the effect of the Proposed Merger.

The Proposed Merger envisages the merger of RLL into SPIL with equity shares of SPIL being issued to the shareholders of RLL. This requires the relative valuation of equity shares of RLL and SPIL for determination of a fair share exchange ratio for the Proposed Merger.

Hence we have carried out a relative valuation of the shares of RLL and SPIL in order to determine the fair share exchange ratio for the Proposed Merger.

There are several commonly used and accepted methods for determining the fair share exchange ratio for the Proposed Merger, which have been considered in the present case, to the extent relevant and applicable, including:

1. Net Asset Value method
2. Market Price method
3. Discounted Cash Flows method

It should be understood that the valuation of any company or its assets is inherently subjective and is subject to certain uncertainties and contingencies, all of which are difficult to predict and are beyond our control. In performing our analysis, we made assumptions with respect to industry performance and general business and economic conditions, many of which are beyond the control of the companies. In addition, this valuation will fluctuate with changes in prevailing market conditions, the conditions and prospects, financial and otherwise, of the companies, and other factors which generally influence the valuation of companies and their assets.

The application of any particular method of valuation depends on the purpose for which the valuation is done. Although different values may exist for different purposes, it cannot be too strongly emphasized that a valuer can only arrive at one value for one purpose. Our choice of methodology of valuation has been arrived at using usual and conventional methodologies adopted for transactions of a similar nature and our reasonable judgment, in an independent and bona fide manner based on our previous experience of assignments of a similar nature.

Walker Chandiok & Co LLP

Net Asset Value (NAV) Method

The asset based valuation technique is based on the value of the underlying net assets of the business, either on a book value basis or realizable value basis or replacement cost basis. The Net Asset Value ignores the future return the assets can produce and is calculated using historical accounting data that does not reflect how much the business is worth to someone who may buy or invest in the business as a going concern. This valuation approach is therefore mainly used in case where the firm is to be liquidated or in case where the assets base dominates earnings capability. A scheme of demerger / amalgamation would normally be proceeded with, on the assumption that the companies / businesses demerge / amalgamate as going concerns and an actual realization of the operating assets is not contemplated. The operating assets are therefore considered at their book values. In such a going concern scenario, the relative earning power is of importance to the basis of demerger / amalgamation, with the values arrived at on the net asset basis being of limited relevance.

We have considered the latest available balance sheets of RLL and SPIL are as at 31 December 2013 and 30 September 2013 respectively to compute the Net Asset Value of equity shares of RLL and SPIL. However, we have not assigned any weight to this method on account of the fact that companies in the pharmaceutical sector have significant intangible assets which are not reflected in the NAV. Assets are not an appropriate indicator of the fair value of a pharmaceutical company.

Market Price Method

The market price of an equity share as quoted on a stock exchange is normally considered as the value of the equity shares of that company where such quotations are arising from the shares being regularly and freely traded in, subject to the element of speculative support that may be inbuilt in the value of the shares. But there could be situations where the value of the share as quoted on the stock market would not be regarded as a proper index of the fair value of the share especially where the market values are fluctuating in a volatile capital market. Further, in the case of a merger, where there is a question of evaluating the shares of one company against those of another, the volume of transactions and the number of shares available for trading on the stock exchange over a reasonable period would have to be of a comparable standard. This method would also cover any other transactions in the shares of the company including primary / preferential issues / open offer in the shares of the company as envisaged in the overall scheme of arrangement and reported to the stock exchanges / available in the public domain.

In the present case, the equity shares of RLL and SPIL are listed on BSE and NSE and there are regular transactions on the bourses in their equity shares. Accordingly in the present case, the volume weighted average share price over reasonable periods for the shares of the respective Companies, as deemed appropriate for the purpose of our valuation analysis, have been considered for determining the value of the shares of the Companies under the market price methodology.

Discounted Cash Flows (DCF) Method

The DCF method uses the future free cash flows of the firm discounted by the cost of capital to arrive at the present value. In general, the DCF method is a strong and widely accepted valuation tool, as it concentrates on cash generation potential of a business. Considering that this method is based on future potential and is widely accepted, we have used this approach in the valuation in the present exercise. .

Walker Chandiok & Co LLP

Using the DCF analysis involves determining the following:

Estimating future free cash flows:

Free cash flows are the cash flows expected to be generated by the company that are available to all providers of the company's capital – both debt and equity.

Appropriate discount rate to be applied to cash flows i.e. the cost of capital:

This discount rate, which is applied to the free cash flows, should reflect the opportunity cost to all the capital providers (namely shareholders and creditors), weighted by their relative contribution to the total capital of the company. The opportunity cost to the capital provider equals the rate of return the capital provider expects to earn on other investments of equivalent risk.

To arrive at the total value available to the equity shareholders of RLL and SPIL, the values arrived above under DCF method for RLL and SPIL are adjusted for, inter-alia, the value of loans, cash, surplus / non-operating assets/liabilities as deemed appropriate for the purpose of our valuation analysis. The total value for equity shareholders is then divided by the fully diluted equity shares of the respective companies in order to work out the value per equity share of RLL and SPIL.

BASIS OF FAIR SHARE EXCHANGE RATIO

The fair basis for the Proposed Merger would have to be determined after taking into consideration all the factors and methodologies mentioned hereinabove. Though different values have been arrived at under each of the above methodologies, for the purposes of recommending a swap ratio, it is necessary to arrive at a single value for the shares of the concerned companies. It is however important to note that in doing so, we are not attempting to arrive at the absolute equity values of the shares of the companies but at their relative values to facilitate the determination of the swap ratio. For this purpose, it is necessary to give appropriate weights to the values arrived at under each methodology.

The Valuer has carried out a relative valuation of the shares of RLL and SPIL and has given weights to the values arrived at under different methodologies, based on their evaluation and judgement of the businesses of the Companies, in order to arrive at the fair share exchange ratio for the Proposed Merger.

In the ultimate analysis, valuation will have to be arrived at by the exercise of judicious discretion by the Valuer and judgments taking into account all the relevant factors. There will always be several factors, e.g. quality of the management, present and prospective competition, yield on comparable securities and market sentiment, etc. which are not evident from the face of the balance sheets but which will strongly influence the worth of a share. This concept is also recognised in judicial decisions.

The fair share exchange ratio of equity shares of RLL and SPIL has been arrived at on the basis of a relative valuation of RLL and SPIL based on the various methodologies explained herein earlier and various qualitative factors relevant to each company and the business dynamics and growth potentials of the businesses of the Companies, having regard to information base, key underlying assumptions and limitations.

Walker Chandiok &Co LLP

In the light of the above, and on a consideration of all the relevant factors and circumstances as discussed and outlined hereinabove, in our opinion the fair share exchange ratio for the Proposed Merger is as follows:

- fair share exchange ratio for the Proposed Merger - 5 (Five only) equity shares of RLL of INR 5/- each fully paid up for every 4 (Four only) equity shares of SPIL of INR 1/- each fully paid up.

Yours faithfully,

For **Walker Chandiok & Co LLP**
Chartered Accountants

Khushroo B. Panthaky
Partner
Membership No.: F42423
Date: 6 April 2014

ANNEXURE II

6 April 2014

To,

The Board of Directors,
Ranbaxy Laboratories Limited
Plot 90, Sector 32,
Gurgaon-122001,
Haryana,
India

<u>Sub: Fairness opinion on the Fair Share Exchange Ratio for the proposed Composite Scheme of Arrangement and Amalgamation between Ranbaxy Laboratories Limited into Sun Pharmaceutical Industries Limited, and their respective shareholders and creditors</u>

This has reference to our engagement letter wherein Ranbaxy Laboratories Limited (hereinafter referred to as "RLL") has requested ICICI Securities ('I-Sec') to provide a fairness opinion on the Fair Share Exchange Ratio for the proposed Composite Scheme of Arrangement and Amalgamation between Sun Pharmaceutical Industries Limited (SPIL), RLL and their respective shareholders and creditors.

BACKGROUND, PURPOSE AND USE OF THIS REPORT

We understand that the managements of RLL and SPIL (referred to as "Companies') are proposing a Composite Scheme of Arrangement and Amalgamation between SPIL, RLL and their respective shareholders and creditors, with effect from the Appointed Date of 31 March 2014 under the provisions of Sections 391-394 of the Companies Act, 1956 read with Sections 100 - 103 of the Companies Act, 1956 or any corresponding provisions of the Companies Act, 2013. (hereinafter referred to as the "Proposed Scheme"). As part of the Proposed Scheme the entire business of RLL will be merged with SPIL ("Proposed Merger")

We understand from the management of RLL that the shareholders of RLL will be issued shares of SPIL as consideration for the Proposed Scheme.

For the aforesaid purpose, the management of RLL have appointed Walker, Chandiok & Co LLP (referred as "Valuer" or "WC") to prepare a report recommending the Fair Share Exchange Ratio for the Proposed Merger for allotment of SPIL shares to the shareholders of RLL pursuant to the Proposed Scheme, to be placed before the Board of Directors of RLL, as per the requirement of SEBI Circular CIR/CFD/DIL/5/2013 dated 4 February 2013 as amended by CIR/CFD/DIL/8/2013 dated 21 May 2013.

In this connection we have been requested by RLL to render our professional services by way of a fairness opinion referred to under clause 24(h) of the Listing Agreement on the Fair Share Exchange Ratio to the Board of Directors of RLL, as to whether the Fair Share Exchange Ratio, as recommended by the Valuer, in their report dated 6 April 2014, is fair and reasonable.

This report is intended only for the sole use and information of RLL, and only in connection with the Proposed Scheme including for the purpose of obtaining judicial and regulatory

approvals for the Proposed Scheme. We are not responsible in any way to any other person / party for any decision of such person or party based on this report. Any person / party intending to provide finance / invest in the shares / business of any of the Companies or their subsidiaries/joint ventures/associates shall do so after seeking their own professional advice and after carrying out their own due diligence procedures to ensure that they are making an informed decision. It is hereby notified that any reproduction, copying or otherwise quoting of this report or any part thereof, other than in connection with the Proposed Scheme as aforesaid can be done only with our prior permission in writing. We acknowledge that this report will be shared to the extent as may be required, with the relevant High Court, stock exchanges, advisors of the Companies in relation to the Proposed Scheme, as well as with the statutory authorities.

As per Valuer's recommendation the holders of outstanding equity shares of RLL will receive 0.80 (Zero point Eight) fully paid up equity shares of SPIL with the face value of Rs. 1 (One) each for every 1 (One) fully paid up equity shares of RLL with the face value of Rs. 5 (Five) each for the Proposed Merger ("Fair Share Exchange Ratio").

SOURCES OF INFORMATION

In arriving at the opinion set forth below, we have relied on:
- (a) Discussions, workings and Valuation report by WC, recommending the Equity swap ratio for the proposed Transaction
- (b) Annual Reports of RLL for the financial years (CY) ended CY 11 and CY 12
- (c) Annual Reports of SPIL for the financial years (FY) ended FY 11, FY12 and FY 13
- (d) Unaudited financial results of RLL for 12 months ended CY 13
- (e) Unaudited financial results of SPIL for 9 months ended FY 14
- (f) Bloomberg consensus projections of RLL and SPIL for the period FY 15 to FY 16
- (g) Reported market price and volume data of RLL and SPIL on NSE
- (h) Reported shareholding pattern of SPIL and RLL on NSE
- (i) Discussions with management of RLL regarding the current operations, future plans, capital expenditure
- (j) Information, discussions (including orally) and documents as provided by RLL as well as the Valuer for purpose of this engagement

SCOPE LIMITATIONS

Our report is subject to the scope limitations detailed hereinafter. As such the report is to be read in totality, and not in parts, in conjunction with the relevant documents referred to therein.

Our work does not constitute an audit, due diligence or certification of the historical financial statements including the working results of the Companies or their businesses referred to in this report. Accordingly, we are unable to and do not express an opinion on the accuracy of any financial information referred to in this report.

Our analysis and results are specific to the purpose of the exercise of giving our fairness opinion on the Fair Share Exchange Ratio for the Proposed Scheme. It may not be valid for any other purpose or if done on behalf of any other entity.

Our analysis and results are also specific to the date of this report and based on information as at 5 April 2014. We have relied on publicly available data for the purpose of this engagement. We have no responsibility to update this report for events and circumstances occurring after the date of this report.

We express no opinion whatever and make no recommendation at all to RLL and SPIL's underlying decision to effect the Proposed Scheme or as to how the holders of equity shares or preference shares or secured or unsecured creditors of the Companies should vote at their respective meetings held in connection with the Proposed Scheme. We do not express and should not be deemed to have expressed any views on any other term of the Proposed Scheme. We also express no opinion and accordingly accept no responsibility or as to the prices at which the equity shares of RLL or SPIL will trade following the announcement of the Proposed Scheme or as to the financial performance of RLL or SPIL following the consummation of the Proposed Scheme.

No investigation of the Companies' claim to title of assets has been made for the purpose of this exercise and the Companies' claim to such rights has been assumed to be valid. No consideration has been given to liens or encumbrances against the assets, beyond the loans disclosed in the accounts. Therefore, no responsibility whatsoever is assumed for matters of a legal nature. Our report is not and should not be construed as our opinion or certifying the compliance of the Proposed Scheme with the provisions of any law including companies, taxation and capital market related laws or as regards any legal implications or issues arising from such Proposed Scheme.

We have not conducted or provided an analysis of due diligence or appraisal of the assets and liabilities of the Companies.

In the ordinary course of business, ICICI Securities Limited and its affiliates is engaged in securities trading, securities brokerage and investment activities, as well as providing investment banking and investment advisory services. In the ordinary course of its trading, brokerage and financing activities, any member of ICICI Securities Limited may at any time hold long or short positions, and may trade or otherwise effect transactions, for its own account or the accounts of customers, in debt or equity securities or senior loans of any company that may be involved in the Proposed Scheme.

It is understood that our report is for the benefit of and confidential use by the Board of Directors / shareholders of RLL for the purpose of this Proposed Scheme and may not be relied upon by any other person and may not be used or disclosed for any other purpose without obtaining our prior written consent.

RATIONALE & CONCLUSION

We are given to understand by RLL that the Fair Share Exchange Ratio has been recommended by the Valuer, after taking into account various factors such as the serviceability of capital after taking into account the potential earning capacity of the business once the Proposed Scheme comes into effect.

In the circumstances, having regard to all relevant factors and on the basis of information and explanations given to us, we are of the opinion on the date hereof, that the proposed Fair

Share Exchange Ratio as recommended by the Valuer, for the Proposed Scheme, is fair and reasonable.

Yours faithfully,
For ICICI Securities Limited,

Ravi Talwar
Senior Vice President
Investment Banking
ICICI Securities
Mumbai

Date: 6/4/2014

CHAPTER 9

Overview of Select M&A Deals

The use of mergers and acquisitions to expand the operations of the company in a short span of time and to increase the shareholder value has become common in the past few decades. An M&A deal can be evaluated on two important metrics.

A deal might be successful in terms of absolute growth, but may have failed to add value to its shareholders. The correct way to look at the success of the deal is seeing it from the viewpoint of the shareholders. There might be growth, but it may not be profitable to them. This is referred to as a **value gap**.

For example, Facebook's acquisition of WhatsApp helped Facebook grow leap and bounds through user base integration (where Facebooks vision of connecting the world has intensified). However, since WhatsApp doesn't charge from its customers the acquisition hasn't created any value till now resulting into "Value Gap."

Evaluation of the performance of the past few deals has provided an idea that majority of the M&A deal fail to create value to the shareholders (or) the company because of various reasons such as unjustified valuations, integration issues, culture clash, management wars, and issues related to turnaround. However, this doesn't necessarily mean that a company must restrain itself from entering into a deal because there is a history of unsuccessful mergers and acquisitions. Companies also need to know that those deals which really created value had been able to increase the operational capabilities of both the acquirer and the targets.

© The Author(s) 2019
V. Kumar and P. Sharma, *An Insight into Mergers and Acquisitions,*
https://doi.org/10.1007/978-981-13-5829-6_9

This makes it that, ALL DEALS ARE NOT BAD.

There are certain operational aspects which the companies ought to focus upon, in order to make up for a sustainable growth. M&A therefore has emerged as a good way to grow in the corporate world.

The following activity in terms of number as well as value of the deals indicates the argument that the way to growth is through mergers and acquisitions.

This went as a key area of study among the experts, and the findings are concluded below.

9.1   ACCENTURE AND THE CONFEDERATION OF INDIAN INDUSTRY (CII) REPORT

Accenture and the CII partnered to investigate the trends in the Indian M&A Strategies to uncover the new M&A dynamics and their impact on the operations. The survey constituted of 66-C level executives from Indian companies which had undergone M&A as a strategy over the past 5 years.

Expenses on supply chain integration, which plays a pivotal role in any M&A deal, can account for as high as 70% of costs, but are not really accounted by the respondents. Only 11% were able to identify the importance of supply chain integration during an M&A planning and execution.

89% of the respondents believed that their merger has lived up to the expectation. However, only 45% of the respondents believed it to be arising out of successful supply chain integration.

The findings also concluded the following in order to achieve a sustainable growth:

- The strategic importance of operational synergies (supply chain integration) has to be given more focus by having relevant leadership by experts throughout the process.
- The execution risk has to be mitigated by way of proper planning and frequent tracking of appropriate metrics pertaining to operational synergies.
- Keeping in place the IT infrastructure and networks and not underestimating the technological efforts.

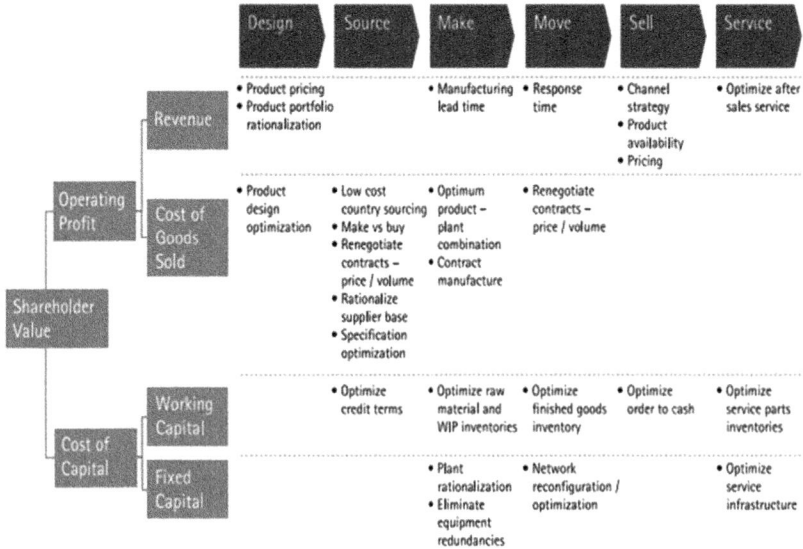

Fig. 9.1 Impact of supply chain on the levels shareholders value (*Source* Accenture, CII Report https://www.criticaleye.com/inspiring/insights-servfile. cfm?id=531, p. 20)

Figure 9.1 summarizes the way in which the supply chain integration (operational synergies) play an important role in adding value to the shareholders.

An M&A deal can add value to its shareholders in two ways, one through increasing operating profit and the other through the betterment of cost of capital of the firm.

9.1.1   Operating Profits

Operating profits arise by way of higher revenue and lower cost as combination of companies would help add value at each and every stage from production till after sale service. The efficiency increases at every stage as the integrating companies might have specialized in varied segment(s) which can be utilized in totality.

For example, during the service stage (i.e.,) post sales, the efficiency comes by way of optimization of after sale service. This would make the end customer stay committed toward the company's product and may suggest even to others which would pen ultimately add to the revenue stream.

During the selling stage, channel strategy, product availability, and pricing would help in increasing revenue. A company which may not have presence in North India might get through acquiring a North Indian company, thereby making its products available to the customers. Some mergers might increase the pricing power of the company like L&T and Grasim cement due to the concentration of market power. These would help in increased revenue.

9.1.2   Cost of Capital

A merger or an acquisition might strengthen the balance sheet of the resultant entity thereby helping it acquire working capital loans or long-term debt with better credit terms. Even here, the terms can improve with respect to the every single stage in which the company operates.

For example, during manufacturing stage, the fixed assets like machineries, plant and building, etc., will be put to utmost use. Any redundancies of equipment would get eliminated.

Thus, the operational synergy (supply chain integration) must be given key importance by any company which is striving for increasing the shareholder value.

9.2   Overview of Select Deals

9.2.1   Fortis and Escorts Heart Institute and Research Centre

9.2.1.1 Overview

On September 28, 2005, Fortis Healthcare Ltd. acquired 90% stakes of Escorts Heart Institute and Research Centre (EHIRCL) for Rs. 585 Crores in an all-cash deal. EHIRCL operates with four network hospitals, namely Escorts Hospitals and Research Centre Ltd., Escorts Heart Centre Ltd., Escorts Heart and Super Specialty Institute Ltd., Escorts Heart and Super Specialty Hospital Ltd., in Delhi, Amritsar, and

Faridabad. Apart from this, Escort was also operating the fifth hospital in collaboration with the Government of Chhattisgarh.

The acquisition also included the Heart command and satellite centers across the country. The deal was financed by taking debt, which was later refinanced by Fortis Healthcare from the IPO proceeds (2007).

9.2.1.2 Escorts Ltd.

Escorts Ltd. was a diversified group operating in auto ancillary products, railway equipment, construction equipment, healthcare services, telecom, etc. EHIRCL, being a part of Escorts Ltd., was operating in its healthcare service segment.

Escorts Ltd. was facing severe cash crunch where it was found struggling to maintain its working capital requirements and debt repayments. This created a need for the group to divest its stakes from its non-core businesses. The acquisition value of Rs. 585 Crores came as a savior for Escorts Ltd. which used Rs. 100 Crore for funding its working capital and the balance for debt repayments. This was the only rationale behind the divestiture by Escorts Ltd.

According to the group chairman, the disinvestment would help Escorts in its overall restructuring initiative, which would replace high-cost and short-term debt into low-cost and long-term debt. The cash inflow would be adequate to fuel the business in order to build the shareholder wealth.

9.2.1.3 Fortis Healthcare

Fortis Healthcare Ltd. (FHL), incorporated in the year 1996, is one of the largest private healthcare chains in terms of bed capacity with 1200 beds. It operates in areas like cardiac care, renal care, neurosciences, orthopedics, etc. However, the presence in cardiac care and diabetics was comparatively lower.

The primary vision of FHL is to become a globally respected healthcare organization known for its Clinical Excellence and Distinctive Patient Care. Fortis started its first hospital in Mohali in the year 2001.

9.2.1.4 Rationale for the Deal

The acquisition of EHIRCL was of utmost strategic importance to Fortis Healthcare Ltd. as it was in line with the core values of FHL.

The acquisition was expected to help Fortis expand its capacity from 1200 to 2200 as EHIRCL was operating at a capacity of 1000 beds. The acquisition also helped Fortis to expand its presence in the field of heart care and diabetics.

Fortis's acquisition of EHIRCL was also expected to give FHL a strong presence in the Northern India thereby increasing its market power.

9.2.1.5 Post-deal Outcome

The deal turned out to be successful. However, it took 3 odd years for FHL to restructure EHIRCL as it was a loss-making unit. EHIRCL was able to help FHL foray into cardiac care with dominating presence as it performed near about 5000 open heart surgeries, 5000 angioplasties and 15,000 angiographies in the fiscal year 2006.

The deal helped Fortis expand its capacity at a rapid phase as EHIRCL offered a steady stream of cash flows for the business. Now, FHL operates with nearly 55 facilities and a potential capacity of 10,000 beds.

Escorts also helped FHL increase in brand value by getting various awards such as Best Single Specialty Hospital—Cardiology, Premier Institute for Cardiology (Fig. 9.2).

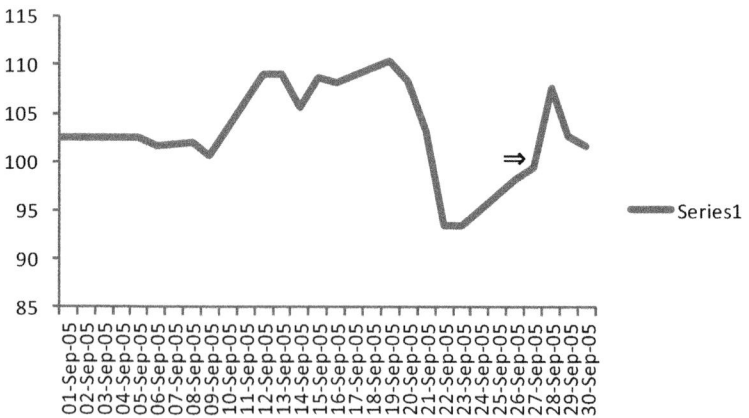

Fig. 9.2   Market returns

The shareholders of Escorts Ltd. reacted positively to the deal as was evident in a 8.35% spike in the company's share price on September 28 when the deal was executed.

9.2.2   P&G and Gillette

"This merger is going to create the greatest consumer products company in the world. It's a dream deal"—said, Warren Buffett, a Legendary Investor.

9.2.2.1 Overview

During the month of June 2005, P&G announced its intention to acquire 100% stakes in Gillette for $57 billion. The deal would make the company the world's largest consumer goods company. The deal was structured as a mix of cash and stock swap where 0.975 shares of P&G would be given to every 1 share held in Gillette. This valued the acquisition at a premium of nearly 20%.

The potential dilution of stakes caused by the acquisition was overcome by buyback of stakes by P&G over a period of 3 years making it a 40% cash deal and 60% stock deal.

The $57 billion deal which was one of the largest in the consumer products segments was considered a perfect marriage as P&G was having its expertise in Women products while Gillette in Men's products.

9.2.2.2 Proctor and Gamble

P&G, in the year 1983, started its operations by selling soaps and candles and is now a worldwide leader and manufacturer of consumer goods. P&G was operating in varied business verticals such as **beauty and healthcare, baby care and family care, home care products, coffee and snacks**. The total revenue for the year ended December 31, 2004, stood at $50 billion roughly.

Some of its popular brands are Crest, Head & Shoulders, Pampers, Vicks, Pringles, etc.

9.2.2.3 Gillette

Gillette was a market leader in men care segment with several product lines including oral care, blades and razors, and batteries. Gillette total sales for the year ended December 31, 2004, stood at $10.5 billion. Some of its popular brands are Gillette, Oral-B, Duracell, etc.

9.2.2.4 Rationale for the Deal

- The deal would make P&G the world's largest consumer goods company. Post-deal P&G would have 21 billion dollar brands (Gillette and P&G brands put together).
- The deal was entered not to enhance the scale but to become more innovative as P&G and Gillette both are innovation-based companies.
- The deal would result in a cost saving of about $14–16 Billion by way of combination of growth opportunities and backroom operations. The per year cost saving was expected to be $1 billion, 3 years from the integration.
- The deal would give Gillette exposure to the Chinese market, while the exposure of products in India and Brazil would be materialized by P&G through Gillette.
- Both the companies would be able to add more and more new products to its portfolio by accessing the highly efficient technology and marketing of each other.

9.2.2.5 Post-deal Outcome

The expectation of the deal had an immediate effect of increase in forecast of revenues of P&G to 5–7% from 4–6%.

On an immediate basis, it was able to triple its revenue in the second-quarter of 2006, which is the fastest growth ever achieved in a decade. P&G reported a jump of revenue by about 27% which would have been only 10% without the impact of Gillette. Bottom-line (Profit) grew by 29% largely due to increase in revenue and reduction in cost attributable to Gillette.

The deal was also helpful in increasing the bargaining power of the combined entity with retailers like Walmart. This also helped P&G focus on integration without having to worry much about the competition as the combined entity got a significant market share. This also compelled other companies to go for M&A to consolidate their positions.

9.2.2.6 Market Reaction

The acquisition announcement came as a positive shock to the market for Gillette as the shares soared nearly 12% while the shares of P&G fell 2% on account of valuations.

Though the deal was considered a win-win for both the companies, the acquisition cost was considered a bit high though not hefty, by the market participants.

9.2.2.7 Value Gap

While the former deal was good with regard to growth by foraying into new segment for FHL, it did not add much value to the shareholders. Whereas in the case of P&G and Gillette, the topline growth is getting added to the bottom line which increased the EPS of the companies, thereby creating value to the shareholders.

9.2.3 Vodafone–Hutch Acquisition: "A Way to Grow......Bigger May Be Beautiful"

M&A has been extensively used as a way to grow. The growth may be in terms of geographical expansion, product line expansion, and vertical expansion in the value chain or simply the increase in market share. In February 2007, the Indian telecom industry faced transformation when Vodafone took major stake (67%) in Hutchison Essar by paying $11.1 billion in cash and assuming the debt burden of $2 billion to materialize the 22 million subscriber base of Hutchison.

With the help of this acquisition, Vodafone got an immediate access to the fastest growing mobile phone around 400 million subscribers. Cellular penetration in rural India was below 2%, Hutchison Essar was not just the number 4 player, but also one of the better run companies with higher average revenue per subscribers. 3G was set to take off in India, allowing data and video to ride on cellular networks. Vodafone was already offering 3G elsewhere in the world. India was a key to Vodafone strengthening presence in Asia, as India is a region seen as one of the biggest telecom story.

9.2.3.1 Deal Structuring & Financing & Synergies

Vodafone's comparatively stronger balance sheet with lesser debt coupled with its free cash reserves in excess of $3 billion and realization of additional $5 billion from the sale of Japanese unit, helped Vodafone bid aggressively for the deal. In addition, Vodafone had free cash reserves (for the first six months of 2006) in excess of $3 billion.

The HTIL Hong Kong had 100% stake in Mauritius-based CGP investments. CGP investments had 67% stake in Hutch-Essar India. On

Deal Between Vodafone- Hutchison

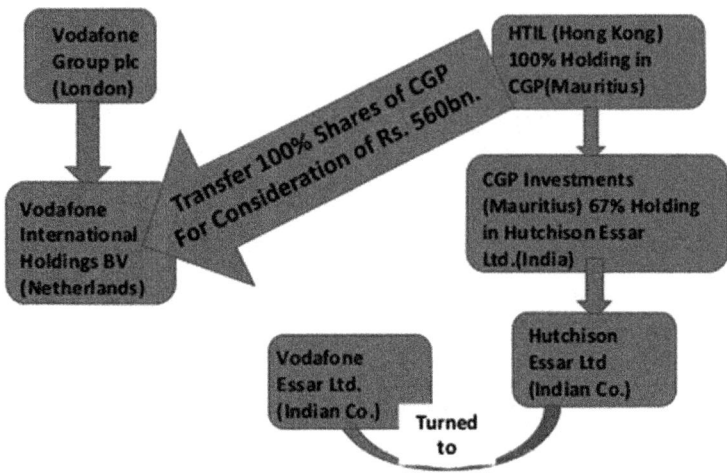

Fig. 9.3   Deal   structure   (*Source*   https://www.slideshare.net/bansal_harshit/ hutchison-vodafone-tax-case-too-much-knowledgeable)

completion of the deal, CGP investments sold its 67% stake in Hutch-Essar to Vodafone, and thereby Hutchison Essar was transformed into Vodafone Essar.

Vodafone UK was the holding company of Vodafone Netherland. For the execution of deal 67% stake of HTIL in Hutch–Essar, India was transferred to Vodafone Netherland. Thus after the deal, Vodafone Netherland got 67% stake in Vodafone–Essar India.

For the completion of deal one more transaction was done in which HTIL transferred its 100% stake in CGP Investments (Mauritius) to Vodafone Netherland removing all the claims of HTIL in the newly formed entity. The structure of deal can be understood with the help of Fig. 9.3.

9.2.3.2 Success of the Deal

Vodafone–Hutch Deal has turned out to be a great success story. Vodafone became the number two player in India in terms of revenue. The success story can be seen from the following statistics from *Business Today* (Fig. 9.4).

Revenue (Crores)

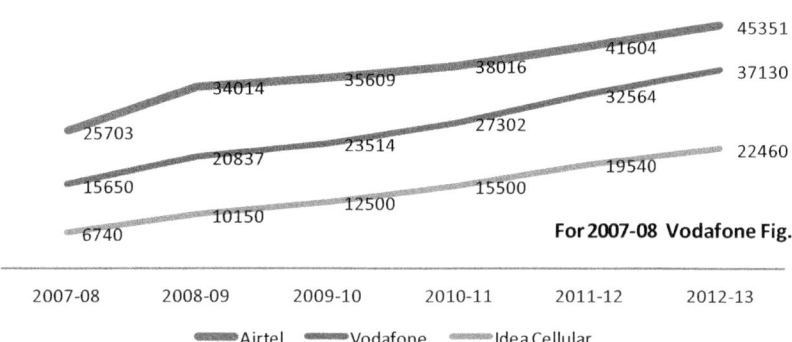

Source https://www.businesstoday.in/magazine/cover-story/vodafone-new-em-phasis-on-data-services-impact-sector-trends/story/205243.html

EBITDA (Crores)

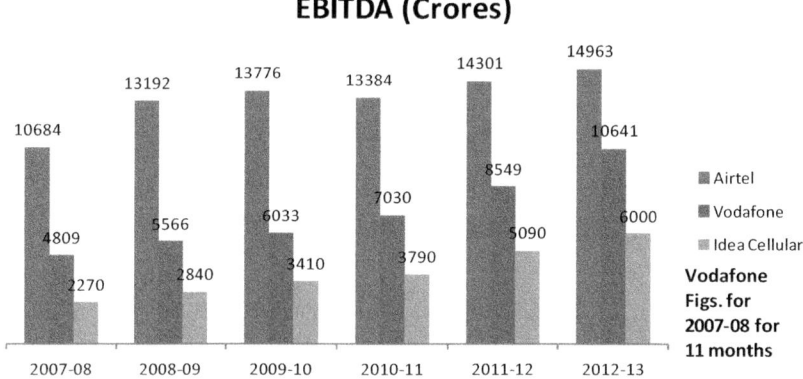

Source https://www.businesstoday.in/magazine/cover-story/vodafone-new-em-phasis-on-data-services-impact-sector-trends/story/205243.html

THE BIG OVERHAUL

Vodafone's product, customer and service mix has changed in the past three years

Scenario 2011 | **Scenario 2014**

OWNERSHIP STRUCTURE	
67% Vodafone 33% Essar Group	100% Vodafone

TOTAL SUBSCRIBERS	
134.5 million	160.4 million

3G CUSTOMER BASE	
Just Started	5.2 million

SHARE OF DATA IN TOTAL REVENUE*	
3%	10%

SHARE OF ENTERPRISE BUSINESS	
6%	11%

CUSTOMER MIX	
38% Rural 62% Urban	53% Rural 47% Urban

SPECTRUM FOR DATA BUSINESS	
3G spectrum in nine circles	Adds 1800 MHz spectrum in 11 circles. To offer 4G in five circles

RETAIL	
Salesmen selling mostly voice coupons	Salesmen trained to sell data packs and load 3G packs

ADVERTISEMENT	
Mostly on voice tariffs	Half of advertisements targeting data usage

*Rounded to units place; Source: *BT* Research

BUSINESS SNAPSHOT

Where Vodafone India stands

Investment till date*
₹64,800 crore

Contribution to exchequer (including 3G Spectrum Fee)
₹71,000 crore

Total Employment Generated
100,000 people

Prepaid Customers
150.3 million

Postpaid Customers
10.1 million

Avg Revenue Per User
₹199

Data Subscribers
45.7 million

Exclusive Retail Stores
8,000

Total Retail Points
1.67 million

Future Investments Project Spring (digitising network)
₹7,800 crore

February 2014 Spectrum Auction
₹19,600 crore

Source: Company
*Doesn't include the ₹44,000 crore spent on acquiring Hutch Essar

Source https://www.businesstoday.in/magazine/cover-story/vodafone-new-emphasis-on-data-services-impact-sector-trends/story/205243.html

DATA BUSINESS

		DECEMBER 2012	DECEMBER 2013
BHARTI AIRTEL	Data customers	41.5 million	54.4 million
	3G customers	5.2 million	9.5 million
	Average data ARPU	₹47	₹75
IDEA CELLULAR	Data customers	21.7 million	25.5 million
	3G customers*	4.1 million	8.7 million
	Average data ARPU	₹52	₹91
VODAFONE INDIA	Data customers	37.3 million	45.7 million
	3G customers	2.5 million	5.2 million
	Average data ARPU	₹53	₹67

Source: Companies   *Includes voice subscribers on 3G

Fig. 9.4 Financials with user base data (*Source* https://www.businesstoday.in/magazine/cover-story/vodafone-new-emphasis-on-data-services-impact-sector-trends/story/205243.html)

9.2.4 GlaxoSmithKline Merger: Mergers and Acquisitions— "A Way to Grow......Bigger May Not Be Better"

On July 5, 2000, GlaxoWellcome and SmithKline Beecham announced the merger of two big entities to form one of the largest pharmaceutical companies, "GlaxoSmithKline." The proposed merger had to go through the lengthy process of shareholder approval, court sanction, and several regulatory clearances. The top management of both the companies stated that merger will lead to creation of superb research and development-oriented organization with outstanding marketing capabilities and enormous cost savings. They were convinced that this merger will result into sustainable growth and fulfill the goal of shareholder's wealth maximization for the shareholders of both the entities. Jean Paul Garnier was appointed the Chief Executive of GSK.

Corporate Headquarter of GlaxoSmithKline was decided to be situated in the UK (London) while operational headquarter was planned to be in the USA. Though both the merging entities Glaxo Wellcome and SmithKline Beecham had their roots in the UK but the Chief Executive of combined entity Jean Garnier decided the USA to be as its headquar-ter as he stated that a globally leading company cannot have its head-quarter in a country which represents only 6–7% of its Global sales. The USA represented more than 45% of global pharmaceutical market.

Upon the execution of merger, the shareholders of both the entities received the shares of combined entity GlaxoSmithKline in lieu of their holdings in the merging entities in the following ratio:

- GlaxoWellcome **Shareholders received** one share of GlaxoSmithKline against holding of one share in Glaxo.
- SmithKline Beecham Shareholders received 0.4552 share of GlaxoSmithKline against holding of one share in SmithKline.
- For ADR and ADS holders, the swap ratio was as follows:
- One ADS of GlaxoSmithKline against holding of one ADS in Glaxo.
- 1.138 ADS of GlaxoSmithKline against holding of one ADS in SmithKline.

This resulted in 58.75% shares and 41.25% shares of GlaxoSmithKline being issued to Glaxo shareholders and SmithKline shareholders, respectively.

9.2.4.1 Synergies Which Were Expected from Merger

a. **Expected Cost Savings**:

The merger of Glaxo and SmithKline was expected to result into considerable cost savings of around $1.6 billion to be achieved from year 2001 to 2003. These savings were expected to occur as a result of reduction of overlapping administrative operations, Sales and Marketing activities and overlap in some Research and Development (R&D) expenditure and research activities.

Out of total $1.6 billion savings, around $1.2 billion of savings, were expected to come from reduction in the overlap in admin-istration, selling and marketing, and additional savings were expected to come from further manufacturing rationalization. A further $400 million of savings were expected to be derived from overlaps in R&D infrastructure, and these savings were planned to be reinvested in R&D. By the end of 2003, the cost savings were more than initially expected and combined entity was running at an operating margin of 35%.

b. **Enhanced Marketing Capability**:
The combined entity had huge marketing team spread globally. With marketing capability of the enterprise becoming the key drivers of growth, GSK was expected to ride a new wave of growth and profitability by capitalizing on its enhanced marketing power achieved through this merger.

A New Structure of R&D which was expected to make GSK the global leader in Pharmaceutical Research.
The merger was expected to make the combined entity a global leader in pharma research. The cost savings of $450 million were planned to be reinvested in R&D. SmithKline Beecham was an industry leader in discovery genomics and bioinformatics, with access to a large range of new drug targets originating from the human genome. GlaxoWellcome was an industry leader in discovery genetics, combinatorial chemistry, and associated drug optimization technologies. The expertise of two entities in complimentary research areas was expected to enormously benefit the merged entity.

Further, Jen Garnier announced the new structure for R&D which was combination of centralization and decentralization. They planned to give complete autonomy to the units involved in core research work and development of molecules so that they get the advantage of research focused environment available in small units and incentive to innovate. However, testing and clinical trials and marketing activities were planned to be centralized and to be handled by overall senior management team.

However, even after three to four years of merger there was little evidence on success of new R&D structure. Despite a heavy investment and combined R&D budgeting coupled with lack of introduction of significant product line, the R&D as well as the revenue stream kept on deteriorating even after 3–4 years. The management was just buying licenses in and out to try and recoup the streamlines.

9.2.4.2 Stock Price Performance
The stock price of both the entities came down on merger announcement and stock price of combined entity has underperformed the rival firm Pfizer and S&P 500. This can be seen from the interactive chart taken from morning star (Fig. 9.5):

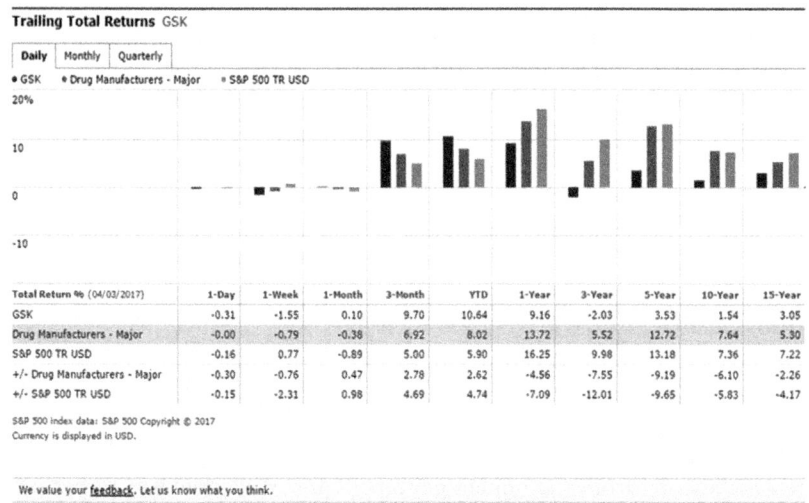

Total Return % (04/03/2017)	1-Day	1-Week	1-Month	3-Month	YTD	1-Year	3-Year	5-Year	10-Year	15-Year
GSK	-0.31	-1.55	0.10	9.70	10.64	9.16	-2.03	3.53	1.54	3.05
Drug Manufacturers - Major	-0.00	-0.79	-0.38	6.92	8.02	13.72	5.52	12.72	7.64	5.30
S&P 500 TR USD	-0.16	0.77	-0.89	5.00	5.90	16.25	9.98	13.18	7.36	7.22
+/- Drug Manufacturers - Major	-0.30	-0.76	0.47	2.78	2.62	-4.56	-7.55	-9.19	-6.10	-2.26
+/- S&P 500 TR USD	-0.15	-2.31	0.98	4.69	4.74	-7.09	-12.01	-9.65	-5.83	-4.17

Source http://performance.morningstar.com/stock/performance-return.action?
t=GSK

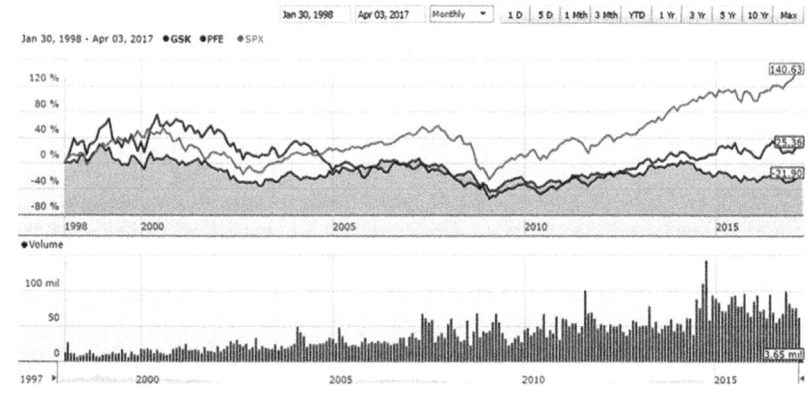

Fig. 9.5 Stock performance (*Source* http://quotes.morningstar.com/chart/stock/chart.action?t=GSK&region=usa&culture=en-US)

9.2.5   Tata-Corus Acquisition—"A Way to Grow......Bigger May Be Burden"

India's one of the largest steel companies Tata Steel with an annual production of 5.3 million tons and generating a revenue of $5 billion acquired Europe's second largest steel producer Corus during April 2007 valuing it around 6.2 billion euros. Corus was operating at a production capacity which is thrice than that of Tata Steel, where the annual production in 2005 touched 18.2 million tons and revenues being four times the revenues of Tata Steel which stood at Euro 9.2 billion in the same fiscal.

The deal took place through a series of bidding between Tata Steel and CSN, a Brazilian steel maker, where Tata Steel ended up paying 67% higher than the initial offer made by Tata's for acquisition of Corus. This helped Tata's achieve the number fifth position globally in terms of value.

The synergistic benefits were the access to European steel markets to Tata Steel, Complementary product line through its low cost production facilities on the upstream and the downstream being the high end processing by Corus. The deal was an all-cash deal financed by a combination of equity and debt, raised by Tata Steel.

9.2.5.1 Rationale of Deal

On January 31, 2007, Tata Steel's Managing Director, Muthuraman, elaborated on the implications of Corus acquisition. He observed "Firstly, it (Corus)immediately comes in with a capacity of 19 MTPA at a cost of little more than half of what a similar Greenfield venture would cost. Secondly, it (Corus) gives access to developed and mature markets of Europe where one can go downstream much more than say in India or China and where the quality of products and service is important. Thirdly, Corus has a highly developed R&D capability and although Tata Steel has better R&D than other Indian players, this is another strength Corus brings to Tata Steel. Another important factor is that the management and work culture is very similar to Tata Steel which will help in integration."

9.2.5.2 Reaction to the Deal

Stock market gave a negative reaction to the deal on account of heavy acquisition price paid by Tata Steel. Deal was seen as empire building phenomenon rather than shareholder's wealth maximization exercise. Tata Steel's share fell by INR 55 on January 31, 2007, closing 10.66%

down at INR 463.95, and wiping off INR 3215 crore in investor wealth at one go. Meanwhile, Corus shares rose 6.8% to 601.5 pence in intraday trading on the London Stock Exchange on January 31, 2007. On the same day, CSN's shares rose 5.3% to 64.96 Brazilian reals on Sao Paulo's Bovespa exchange as the news came as a relief to CNS's investors who feared a CSN-Corus deal would burden the joint company with mounting debts.

Tata's new debt amounted to $8 billion due to the acquisition, financed with Corus' cash flows, was expected to give rise to $640 million in annual interest charges (8% annual interest cost). This amount combined with Corus' existing interest debt charges of $400 million on an annual basis implied that the combined entity's interest obligation will amount to approximately $725 million after the acquisition.

Later on, fears of failure turned out to be true. Tata Steel group's operating profit declined by 30% between 2007–2008 and 2014–2015. Tata Steel Europe, meanwhile, witnessed a sharper 53% decline. In 2007–2008, a year before the global financial crisis started, the foreign subsidiary had a 50% contribution to overall EBITDA. The business never went back to that level of operating profit after that. The share in 2014–2015 stood at 33.6%. In 2015–2016 up to December, the group's consolidated EBITDA stood at Rs. 11,165 crore. Tata Steel Europe, meanwhile, reported an operating loss of Rs. 339 crore (Fig. 9.6).

Ebitda (Crores)

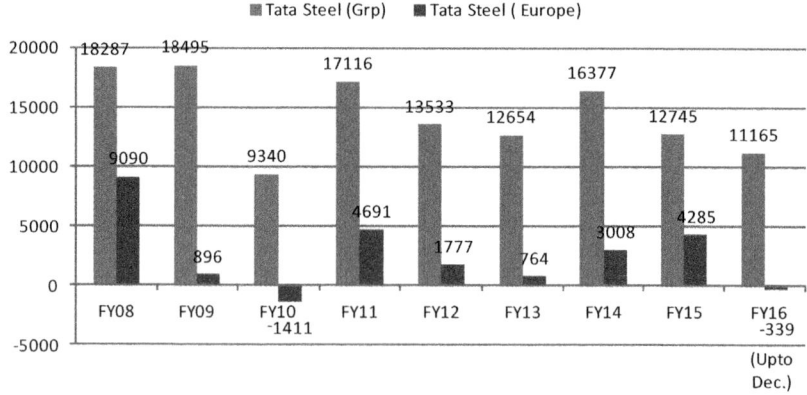

Fig. 9.6   Financial margins—Tata group/steel (*Source* http://www.firstpost. com/business/a-tale-of-2-acquisitions-in-9-charts-tata-steels-failure-with-corus-and-tata-motors-success-with-jlr-2704788.html)

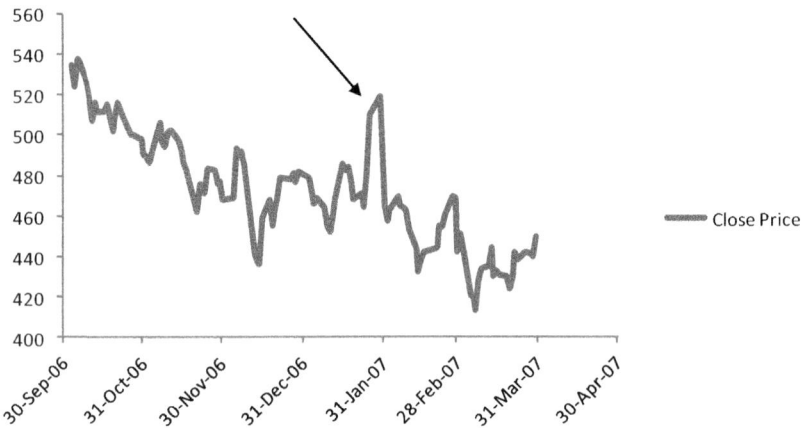

Tata steel's acquisition interest over Corus was laid openly on October 5, 2006. It is evident from the above chart that since then the stock price was falling constantly exhibiting negative sentiments in the markets by the investors as the market perceived it to be a not so good value proposition. The major fall was seen at the time of completion of auction/bidding where Tata Steel ended up bidding 34% higher than the initial offer price leading to a fall of 11% in a single day. The markets perceived it as a negative stigma.

TURNOVER (Crores)

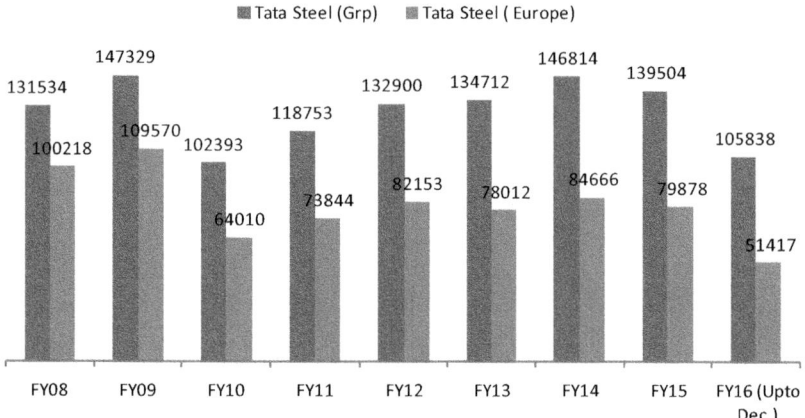

The above comparative chart (Corus being renamed as Tata Steel Europe) shows that the contribution from Corus to the overall turnover of the Tata Steel group was declining constantly over a period of time and it almost halved due to Chinese dumping of steel, lower commodity prices, global financial crisis, etc. This clearly indicates that the deal was a sheer negative badge to the feather of Tata group, in line with the perception of the investors.

Tata Steel group Net Profit (Crores)

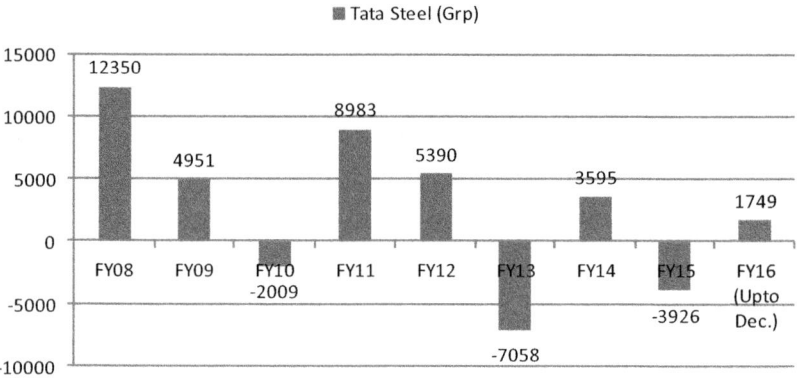

The profitability of Tata Steel post-acquisition was wavering from positive to negative territories. The immediate 3 years post-acquisition of Corus was clearly negative as the net profits declined from 12,350 crores to 4951 crores in FY 09 and to 2009 Crores in FY 10.

Ebitda (Crores)

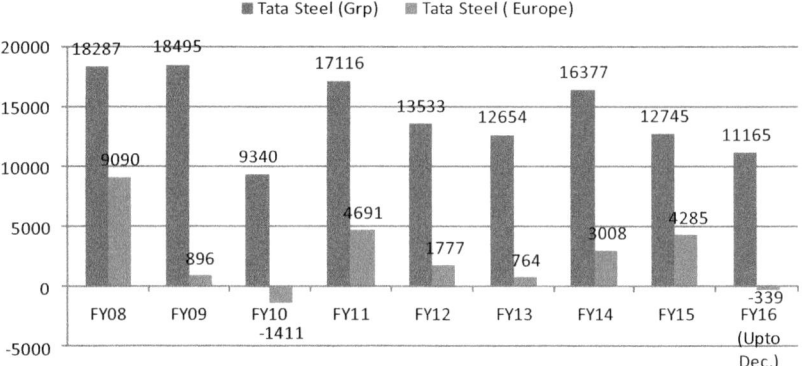

The year post-acquisition the contribution of Corus (Tata Steel Europe) to operating profit of the group was nearly 50%. That saw a constant fall over the years and the operating profitability of Corus was very much volatile which became negative twice over the past 8 years.

CHAPTER 10

Why Mergers and Acquisitions Fail?

All the companies opting the acquisition route for faster growth must know that majority of empirical studies have found that more than 50% of the acquisitions happen to be utter failures. Despite this, companies have been risking their businesses with the hope that they shall be in part of successful acquisitions. It is quite perplexing that the demoralizing data coming from most of the researchers, don't defer many corporate.

The fear of failure of a merger or acquisition has not dampened mergers and acquisitions all over the world.

Mergers and acquisitions are inherently risky, and without the adoption of a proper strategy, use of intuition and knowledge, they can be disastrous. An understanding of why most of the mergers and acquisitions fail can, therefore, help avoid some of the pitfalls for those who have M&A on their drawing board. These pitfalls can be learned by studying the failed M&A deals all over the globe including India. AOL–Time Warner, HP–Compaq, Quaker–Snapple, and eBay Skype among are some of the famous examples of M&A failures in the world, and in-depth study of their reasons can certainly help the potential acquirer to be on his guard. Mergers have failed due to varying reasons including poor planning, inadequate research, or regulatory issues.

Some of the major failures in the world are:

© The Author(s) 2019
V. Kumar and P. Sharma, *An Insight into Mergers and Acquisitions*,
https://doi.org/10.1007/978-981-13-5829-6_10

10.1   EBAY SKYPE

eBay had to eat the bullet after acquiring Skype for USD 2.6 billion and had to finally sell it back at USD 1.9 billion after four years causing it big financial loss. The acquisition failed to yield expected results and synergies due to various problems. eBay had envisaged that Skype shall become a key connecting point—between buyers and sellers. Unfortunately, this did not crystallize and the acquisition failed miserably causing huge losses.

10.2   DAIMLER CHRYSLER

Daimler Chrysler's megamerger failed because of the cultural discrepancies between the two companies and their different customer bases. This merger was thought to be an excellent route for building synergies across multiple client segments. However, it turned out to be a big failure. The merger was initially designated as the "merger of equals." However, it turned out to be a big "fiasco."

The two divisions were at war after their merger. Daimler-Benz was always considered to be relatively systematic and methodical, whereas, Chrysler had a bad reputation of risk-taking and encouraged creativity and flexibility. This culminated into a dominant German culture. Resultantly, the satisfaction level of Chrysler plummeted. By 2000, major losses and layoffs started. Finally in 2007, Daimler had to sell off Chrysler at $6 billion to Cerberus Capital Management. Again, a classic case of value destruction.

10.3   AMERICA ONLINE AND TIME WARNER

In the history of mergers, one of the most talked about mergers was that of America Online and Time Warner. America Online purchased Time Warner in 2001 for $165 billion. Both companies attempted to take advantage of the convergence of mass media and the Internet. However, the merger did not generate expected synergies, and very next year in 2002, it reported a massive loss of $99 billion. The merged company could not achieve the converged content of mass media and the Internet. It was forced in 2003 to delete the name of the "AOL" from its name, and it was simply known as Time Warner.

10.3.1   Sprint/Nextel

Sprint acquired rival Nextel for $35 billion in 2005, but within 3 years, the company had written down 80% of the value of the Nextel. The failure had been primarily on account of the cultural clash between the khaki culture of Nextel and the bureaucratic culture of Sprint. The two did not mesh together well because different cultures resulted in clashes between the two companies. The huge size of Nextel and its different culture did not result in a successful combination with Sprint.

10.4   HP AND COMPAQ

Hewlett-Packard went for acquisition of struggling competitor Compaq in 2001. The merger was again a big failure because of cultural clash. A loss of an around 13 billion dollars in market capitalization of the merged entity was the outcome of this bad merger. Some of the analysts were skeptical about the merger from the very beginning because both of the companies were struggling companies before they decided to merge.

10.4.1   Kmart and Sears

To combat Walmart, two retailers Kmart and Sears took the decision to merge. Kmart acquired Sears in 2005 for 11 billion. Kmart was expected to benefit from the synergies. Similarly, Sears was expected to benefit from Kmarts' stores' locations. However, the revenue generation dropped by more than 10% in the years following the merger. Two distinct cultures and different core competencies of the Kmart and Sears did not let the acquisition turn out to be successful.

10.5   M&A FAILURES IN INDIA

10.5.1   Sun Pharma and Taro

India's largest pharmaceutical company Sun Pharmaceuticals signed a $454 million merger deal with an Israeli company, Taro Pharmaceuticals. Since Taro was passing through the financial crisis, the offer to merge with Sun Pharma was considered as a rescue. Sun Pharmaceuticals provided a helping hand of loan of $224 million to Taro along with an interim financing of $45 million. Market reach in the US coupled with increased competencies was the major attraction for Sun Pharmaceuticals to acquire Taro. However, later on Taro withdrew itself from the deal in May stating that Sun's offer of $7.75 per share was not sufficient and no longer in the best interests of the company and its shareholders. The deal which was initiated with great fanfare collapsed miserably because of the valuation mismatch of expectations.

10.5.2   Apollo's Failed Deal

Apollo Tyres Ltd. attempted to buy Cooper Tire & Rubber Co. with great expectations for $2.5 billion. With this merger, the merged entity would have become the 7th largest tyre company in the world. Apollo's bid for Cooper was risky from the very start. Apollo relied heavily on loans to finance its ambitious attempt to take over cooper. Absence of deeper scrutiny and overenthusiasm of Apollo resulted into failure of the merger. It's an example of the insufficient due diligence culminating into a failure of a merger.

10.5.3   Tata Motors Jaguar

Tata Motors acquired Jaguar in 2008 to gain entry into European markets and improve its product position. Tata's ambition to become a global company quickly led them to purchase Jaguar. The acquisition took place at a time when markets were very bullish and valuations were very high. The deal had to be financed with borrowing because the cost of acquisition was very high. Resultantly, shares of both the companies suffered a huge blow as Tata tried to borrow to cover this huge acquisition debt. The merged entity is still struggling to generate synergistic benefits in terms of improved profitability.

10.6   Important Reasons for Failures

There are several reasons for the failure of mergers and acquisitions. Very few acquirers do the due diligence for appropriate integration process—many companies look mergers and acquisitions as a panacea to their all problems. But before going for merger and acquisition, they shun serious investigation of the target company. The parties, viz. buyer and seller, both need to do proper research and due diligence before going for mergers and acquisitions. Concrete plan with suitable involvement and control if is not prepared can lead to failure of any M&A deal.

There are many other reasons behind the failure of mergers and acquisitions.

10.6.1   Owner's Involvement

Most of the mergers and acquisitions are facilitated by appointing M&A advisors for various services. But leaving everything to the advisors and consultants just because they are charging a high fee is not wise. This neglect of the owners may become the reason for the deal's ultimate failure. Deep involvement of the owners if conspicuously absent might cause failure.

10.6.2   Exaggerated Valuation and Overpayment

The advocate for mergers generally argues that the merger or acquisition will help in reducing costs and enhance revenues by more than enough to justify the premium to be paid for acquisition. Assets that look impressive and tempting on paper may not be the real winning factor once the deal gets through. There are umpteen number of examples where the payment was an exaggerated amount. Bank of America's acquisition of Countrywide is a typical example of exaggerated price Bank of America paid for the acquisition. Similar was the case of Tata Steel paying a huge price for the acquisition of Corus. Similar was the case of Tata Motors acquiring Jaguar and Hindalco acquiring Novelis. A closer analysis of the phenomenon of failures in M&A shows majority of the undisciplined executives involved in the evaluation process fuels the prices of these deals. Consequently, they often value deals wrong. Despite the importance of accurately identifying and calculating synergistic benefits, the analysis work frequently results in an overestimated value. This, in turn, leads buyers to overpay for the acquisitions leading to the term called irrational exuberance.

The basic objective of a company in merger and acquisition is to generate benefits for its shareholders. However, in reality, most of the companies are not able to achieve this eschewed objective. Lack of due diligence is generally the cause of the overestimation of the value of the company. Two or more companies often get entangled in counter bidding to acquire the same company at a huge price.

Investment bankers and dealmakers often work on a transaction and push for a deal "just to get things done." It culminates into an exorbitant price being paid which is not commensurate with the expected benefits of the transaction. For example, in 2008, when Tata Motors acquired Jaguar, the analysts thought that it was Tata's ambition to become a global company in quick time which led them to purchase Jaguar. The expensive high-cost debts were used to finance the deal which turned out to be not meeting the expectations of the acquirer company. Resultingly, the shares of both the companies suffered a huge decline as Tata tried to raise loans to finance the high-priced deal. The company is still struggling to achieve the expected synergistic benefits.

10.6.3   Cultural Differences

The working and organization culture of every company is different. Corporate cultures of the companies getting merged are at times vastly different in terms of their cultures. The assumption that personnel issues can be easily overcome is a big mistake. For example, target company's employees might be having an easy access to top management or have flexible work schedules or even a relaxed dress code. The acquirer, on the contrary, may have tough rules and regulations. If new management does not provide the relaxed work environment, the outcome may be resentment and shrinking productivity.

The culture as to how they treat their customers, suppliers, and employees may be entirely different. How much freedom is given to the employees between two companies may be also dramatically different. The merger or acquisition between two culturally different companies eventually leads to utter failure in reaping the benefits of merger.

There are many examples including Daimler Chrysler where cultural and integration issues were the reasons for failure.

Two companies with similar work culture can be expected to have a successful merger if there are no other obstacles. For example, after a long association, the publisher CPP acquired its master distributor in Australia. There were no surprises in the deal since both the companies knew each other very well. The compatibility of the two cultures made the integration move smoothly.

10.6.4   High-Cost Debt

The acquirer many a times has to dip into excessive debts for executing merger and acquisition. Majority of the mergers and acquisitions are financed through debts carrying high-cost debts which may eventually lead to a big financial burden for the acquirer company.

10.6.5   Flawed Intentions

A booming stock market creates congenial ground for mergers or acquisitions but this can spell trouble afterward. Deals executed with highly priced shares as currency is a cakewalk, but the lack of strategic thinking behind them may cause trouble. A merger intended for glory-seeking than business strategy may turn to be a big fiasco. The executive ego, boosted by buying influenced by the investment bankers, and advisers earning big fees from clients engaged in mergers might prove expensive afterward. Many CEOs get to where they are because they want to be the biggest and the best, and many top executives get a big bonus for merger deals, no matter what happens to the company's deal or its share price later. This drive for being the CEO of a far bigger company may sometimes catapult the entity into a collapse.

10.6.6   Shareholders and Employees Interests Overlooked

Employees and shareholders of the company are two important stakeholders whose interest must be nurtured. The shareholders of the company which is being taken over may feel hostile. Mergers and acquisitions at time make the employees shift their focus from productive work to degenerative issues related to conflicts. It also puts a huge question mark in the minds of the employees regarding their job security. Proper communication should be maintained between the management and the employees so as to avoid such issues. As a result of the merger between ABB–Flakt at the global level, its branches in India also merged. However, a study conducted on this merger in India revealed that no proper due diligence was conducted as a result of which the gain on the merger was less than the capital market growth due to which the shareholders of Flakt lost heavily.

10.6.7   Lack of Common Vision

If it is not clear to the acquirer as to how the merged entity shall operate and how the divergence shall be managed, there is no point of the convergence. The organizations will never blend if the diversity of the two units is not properly managed.

Post-integration process of any deal demands clarity of the futuristic picture about integrating two organizations, and a myriad of issues need fast resolution or else the organization comes to a standstill.

10.6.8   Poor Communication

Now, manager of acquirer as well as acquiree needs to communicate properly and move together to cross the post-integration milestones step by step. The acquirer needs to be attuned to the target company's branding and the customer base. The new company or the merged entity risks losing its customers if the management is considered as divorced from the customer needs. Employees of the acquirer as well as acquiree need to be informed about why the merger is being initiated or why a merger is the last resort of action it could take. They need to be convinced as to how the company will be better off after the merger, how the merger will affect their work, and what support they will receive if they are adversely impacted. Clear communication about the purpose of a merger and the expected benefits can foster a positive attitude among employees of the two entities. An ill-constructed program of execution or insufficiently detailed implementation plans can bring the merger project to a screeching halt.

10.6.9   Weak Leadership

Integration of two organizations demands strong captain, with a close eye on the destination. Energy, enthusiasm, clarity, and clear communication capabilities are required of such a strong leader. If senior managers do not act on what they promise to act, all credibility is lost and the whole action is considered to be tall claims without execution. A strong leader only shall be able to make two distinct entities mesh together to achieve the collective goal.

10.6.10   Due Diligence

One might think that any M&A that involves big money would be a result of a good research and analysis. Thus, the company that is buying or investing in a new firm is presumed to be in know of everything about it. One of the primary reasons why M&A's falter is because of this gap analysis. Even before considering an M&A, due diligence is utmost important. Also, you must have an understanding of the brand fit once the merger is done. A lot many times, companies are impressed by the brand and its dynamics and fail to pay attention to finer details.

For instance, recently, a proposed $2.5 billion merger agreement of Cooper Tire Co. with India's Apollo Tyres terminated sooner than later because of the differences that arose over labor and pricing issues. Undertaking an extensive diligence exercise beforehand could have reduced the heartburn and litigation that followed.

10.6.11   *Irrational Exuberance: It's Always About Money*

Irrational exuberance is the root cause for companies overpaying for an M&A deal. It is the base for exaggerated valuations as valuations are based on synergy projections, and irrational exuberance leads to anticipation of growth prospects to a level which are beyond the fundamentals of the companies.

10.6.12   *Poor Integration Management*

Many a good M&A deals have been undone because of bad integration. Often, integration is poorly managed with a relatively vague set of goals, unrealistic objectives, and/or a weak framework or design. Right from managing corporate assets to managing human capital, integration must be done in a seamless manner. An important measure of the success of integration emanates from the transformation which is achieved in terms of alignment of stakeholder behavior with the new culture. One such benchmark of success is that a bulk of employees of the acquired entity feel comfortable in the new setup and continues with their jobs.

To get the integration right, a high-level team must be formed at the board level to overlook the process. There are very few instances of successful integrations, and one such is that of Mahindra & Mahindra. Several years after the take over of Eva Car (the electric car) by Mahindra & Mahindra forma, the CEO of the former company continues to be associated with the venture.

10.6.13   *Dubious Reasons*

Some mergers are entered into with the thought of manipulating the market participants, at the back of their mind. However, those mergers, if found to be manipulative, would be turned down by the regulators, be it SEBI, RBI, or any other authority for that matter.

The classic case study of GTB and UTI Bank's mergers story is one such example where UTI was supposed to merge with GTB forming "UTI-Global." However, the merger was turned down by UTI and GTB as it was questioned by various regulatory authorities like SEBI, RBI when found to be misleading the market by disrupting the prices of GTB stock early in November–December 2000.

10.7   THE INDIAN SCENARIO

Many of the M&A deals in India too did not achieve the eschewed objectives of value creation.

A decade after Indian companies ventured into the arena of mergers and acquisitions, the promise of globalization's many rewards seems to have been belied. The travails of companies such as Tata Steel Ltd., Apollo Tyres Ltd., Reliance Industries Ltd. (RIL), and Bharti Airtel Ltd. all remind us of how fragile the world of global mergers and acquisitions (M&As) can be.

Suzlon Energy Ltd. took a hit on the sale of its German subsidiary Senvion which it had acquired in 2007 for €1.4 billion. Bharti Airtel also sold its towers in Africa after demerging the business from the Zain operations it acquired in 2010 for $10.7 billion; in March, Tata Steel decided to cut its losses and divest its UK assets, which it acquired with the $12.9 billion purchase of Corus Group Plc. in 2007.

Almost every major Indian group which acquired assets abroad in 2000–2007 has been forced to sacrifice a part of the money it spent to buy those assets.

The information must flow to all internal as well as external stakeholders freely. Management must strive to understand how these groups view the deal.

Management of the merged or new entity should set standards from the very inception for cost reduction as well as growth of revenues. Majority of companies tend to focus on one or the other—but sufficient emphasis on both must be placed to see the synergetic benefits flow.

10.8   Success Mantra of Mergers and Acquisitions

Highly successful mergers that have created history provide ideas about the success mantras. In some cases, it is even difficult to remember as to when the merged entities were actually distinct. Where would Disney be without Pixar or J. P. Morgan without Chase?

In successful merger of Procter & Gamble's in 2005 with Gillette, cost synergies were realized. While Gillette dominated the men's shaving market with its Mach series of razors, P&G was strong in women's skin care marketing. The combined entity could realize the synergistic benefits by marketing deodorants, and shower gels for men, lotion, and antiperspirants.

These acquisition synergies worked wonderfully very well in this case because current offerings could be expanded in subtle but logical ways along the fuzzy demarcation between existing product definition and customer receptivity.

Many more examples of the successful mergers and acquisitions highlight some of the success mantras for effective M&A:

1. Failures and execution can be avoided provided program integration team is established well in advance. For instance, if managers at the middle level are sent to various sites for improving their skills by having the systems and practices' exposures. This can help the meshing together of the units easily.
2. A major step is to establish clear channels of communication with all the workers. They have to be informed unequivocally that they need to depend on the inherent strengths of the company rather than seeking any external help.
3. The board and management should have very clear and unbiased advice as well as the fair representations of the views of the shareholders. This shall improve the feasibility of successful execution of the merger or acquisition.
4. Clearly delineate the targets to be achieved so that their achievement is facilitated.
5. Management must have a clear vision. The cultural integration must be given utmost importance. In addition, one should have a detailed plan of action to manage the changed behavior post-integration. Interconnect the culture plan to the business goals.

6. During the merger process—from strategic planning to transaction design, utmost attention must be paid to the details. Post-merger integration does require highly dynamic leaders to lead, execute, and integrate.
7. Training to employees even before merger can go a long way in successful execution of the merger or acquisition.
8. Carefully give importance to rename, logo, color, rebranding, and the leader to the new entity.
9. Insure against possible post-merger legal tangles. Even if the merger is happening between two entities outside the country, it may invite the income tax in the domestic economy.

10.9   CONCLUSION

There are many reasons to fail but a few reasons for the success of a merged entity. Failures, however, are not springboards to success for mergers and acquisitions. If new software fails by even by 0.1%, the software fails by 100%. In a similar way, if merger is not successful by 1%, it is considered an utter failure.

Not all M&A's end up on high-notes. Corporate history is littered with instances and illustrations of how some big-ticket M&A's failed, and failed miserably. In fact, an article in the *Harvard Business Review* puts the failure rate of M&As at around 70–80%. Even the most optimistic of these assessments put M&A failures at around 50%. Namely, close to half the corporate takeovers, buyouts, acquisitions, and mergers fail to live up to the promise and deliver the value that was supposed to come.

> The reasons for such failures range from really big ones to very small ones such as improper match of the two entities. And this trend is not confined to western countries, but is also a case in Indian shores, of course to a lesser extent.

A recent study which supports this argument states that 75% of Indian companies going for outbound deals fail to enhance value in the initial years post-completion and 59% of M&A deals completely destroy value.

Now imagine that a company did all things right, namely the homework, the cultural mapping, the valuation, and even the integration. But that does not mean that it is time to relax and be laid back. One needs to continuously monitor the progress and realign their strategies. It is very important to know that mergers don't work on their own but have to be worked upon. Some years back when Kingfisher Airlines had bought out the low-cost Air Deccan, it was assumed that the two would make a winning combination. But even after the integration, where Air Deccan was rebranded as Kingfisher Red, the parent airline continued to lose traffic, and finally, the merger failed.

To sum it up, an M&A is to quite an extent like marriage where both partners need to work hard so that the relationship remains on solid ground. After all, a divorce is not all always the right way out.

CHAPTER 11

Case Discussions
of Mergers and Acquisitions

11.1   HINDALCO–NOVELIS ACQUISITION

Acquirer—Hindalco
Target—Novelis
Acquisition date: May 15, 2007
Total transaction value: $6.2 billion.

The acquisition will catapult the group into the Fortune 500 league, three years ahead of the target. The combination of Hindalco and Novelis will establish a global integrated aluminum producer.
—Kumar Mangalam Birla, Chairman of Hindalco, in February 2007

The combination of Novelis's world-class rolling assets with Hindalco's growing primary aluminum operations and its downstream fabricating assets in the rapidly growing Asian market is an exciting prospect.
—Ed Blechschmidt, Acting Chief Executive of Novelis, in February 2007

The acquisition of Novalis Inc., Aluminum producer having presence in the USA and Canada, by Hindalco, a subsidiary of Aditya Birla Group on May 2007 for an amount of $6 billion was the 2nd largest acquisition by an Indian company in terms of value.

© The Author(s) 2019
V. Kumar and P. Sharma, *An Insight into Mergers and Acquisitions*,
https://doi.org/10.1007/978-981-13-5829-6_11

The acquisition of Novelis by Hindalco not only made Hindalco a global integrated aluminum manufacturer but also helped Hindalco feature in Fortune 500 companies across the world, while for Novelis, the proposition seemed to be great given the integration of its world-class technology with cost effective and growing primary aluminum fabricating downstream activities by Hindalco, to capture the Asian Market.

11.1.1   Background of Hindalco

Hindalco is one of the largest players in aluminum and copper industry. Hindalco's plant is Asia's largest integrated plant of aluminum, and it is leading integrated producer of copper. It is one among the most cost-effective aluminum producers globally.

Hindalco is known as the world's largest aluminum rolling company. Its consolidated turnover is US$17 billion. Hindalco is Asia's biggest primary aluminum producer. Its state-of-the-art copper facility includes the world's largest custom smelters at a single location and a fertilizer plant.

The company's operations in India range from bauxite mining, alumina refining, coal mining, captive power plants, and aluminum smelting to downstream rolling, extrusions, and foils. Hindalco is known as one of the world's largest integrated producers of aluminum and has the presence in several countries across the globe.

Hindalco began its journey in 1958, and four years later, visionary late G. D. Birla established India's first fully integrated aluminum plant at Renukoot. In 1967, it was backed by a captive thermal plant at Renusagar. Under the dynamic leadership of Mr. Aditya Vikram Birla, Hindalco became the largest player in India in aluminum industry.

Under the vision and guidance of Mr. Kumar Mangalam Birla, the Group Chairman, Hindalco attained the position of non-ferrous metals powerhouse by consolidating the business segments of aluminum and copper. Hindalco became one of the top five aluminum players in the world through its acquisition of Novelis Inc., the world's largest aluminum rolling company, in 2007. Now, Hindalco is known as the largest fully integrated producer of aluminum in Asia and has a presence in various countries across the globe.

11.1.2   Background of Novelis

Novelis was incorporated in January 2005 as publicly traded company following a spin-off from Alcan Inc. Novelis commands leadership position in aluminum rolled product producer on the basis of shipment volume of 2006. With a total shipment approximated to 2960 Kilo Tones (kt). It is estimated around 19% of total production of flat-rolled aluminum in the world. It operates in 4 continents with thirty-three plants and three R&D facilities in eleven countries. It solely focused on Aluminum rolled product market and has the capability of supplying products across the globe. It masters in can, auto, foil markets, rolling technology and world leader in the recycling of used beverage cans of aluminum.

11.1.3   Rationale for the Deal

Hindalco was aspiring to attain leadership position among the players in Aluminum Industry. This acquisition made Hindalco the world's largest completely integrated aluminum giant, capable of servicing the end customers as well as clients requiring the intermediary products by having a presence at each stage of value chain.

Hindalco was majorly into the upstream aluminum business, and their operations included extracting the alumina from the bauxite and manufacturing the aluminum sheets while the Novelis was largest player in the world in downstream rolled products serving the customers in several customer industries like automobile, cans for beverage manufacturers, architecture, specialty, etc.

The business was complimentary; Hindalco was the largest player in India, and after the completion of domestic expansion in upcoming years, their end products could be used at Novelis and thereby reducing the dependence on outside suppliers. Hindalco after this acquisition became one of the largest global fully integrated players.

Increase in operating scales, entering the high-end downstream market, and increased presence in the globe were few key rationales behind the acquisition.

Apart from this, Hindalco can get access to the major clients of Novelis which includes Coca-Cola, General Motors, etc. This can help in penetrating such high-valued customers.

Above all, for both the companies it was presumed that since Hindalco is a low-cost metal manufacturer and Novelis can procure aluminum raw materials from Hindalco (since they are in same aluminum stream), it would help both the companies in their businesses as well as reducing cost. Once the integration is complete, the joint company would hedge the losses arising out of fluctuation of London Metal Exchange (LME) aluminum prices.

11.1.4   Expected Synergies from the Acquisition

Hindalco was undoubtedly the low-cost manufacturer of aluminum in the world. However, the cyclicality of LME (raw materials) prices had a thumb pressing impact on the profitability of Hindalco, and Hindalco was not able to cope up with the volatility in the commodity market.

As Novelis was the world leader of flat-rolled aluminum products (FRP) which constitutes over 40% of aluminum market in the world. With over 19% market share in FRPs by Novelis, they were able to significantly control the downstream market. This bolted the curbing of cyclicality in raw material prices for Hindalco thereby making it a perfect reason for acquiring Novelis so as to improve its profitability from its large scale revenue streams.

Novelis has the world's best technology for production of rolled aluminum products, and it would have taken at least 10 years to Hindalco to develop such technology on their own if they set up their own R&D to pursue their goal of becoming wholly integrated company and controlling the complete supply chain.

Novelis has renowned customers like Coca-Cola, General Motors, etc. Its acquisition will help the Hindalco to broad-base the clients and penetration to diverse markets.

At the time of acquisition, Hindalco didn't have excess capacity to supply the aluminum sheets to supply to Novelis and reduce the cost. Novelis used to buy its raw material from other producers. However, after the completion of aggressive expansion plan of Hindalco to increase its capacity, it can ship the economically produced sheets and reduce the overall cost by capitalizing on its end to end value chain ownership.

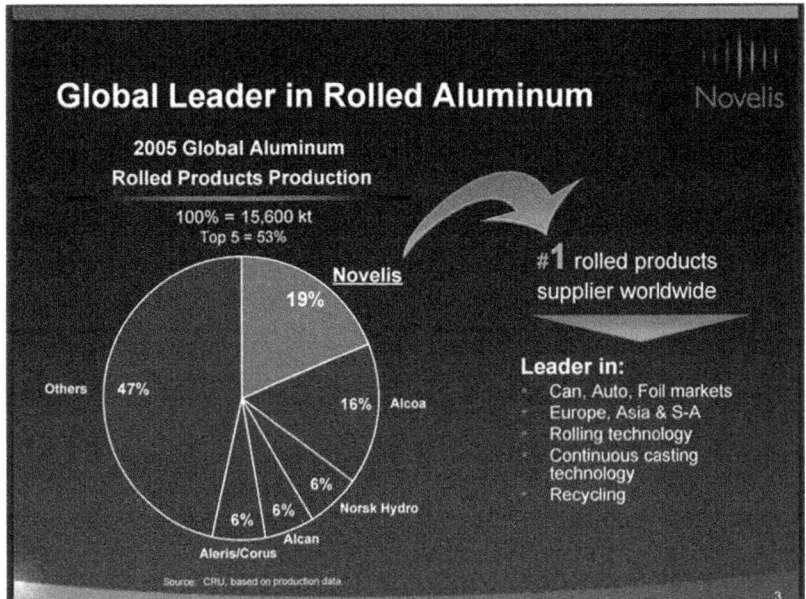

Source http://www.hindalco.com/upload/pdf/Q1_2008_analyst_presentation_novelis.pdf.

11.1.5   Problem Areas

Novelis was a loss-making entity. Though there were profits in the year 2005 as per the financial statements of year 2006, Novelis incurred net loss of $275 million which was equivalent to net loss of $(3.71) per share, the net sales were $9.8 billion. While in 2005 net income was $90 million, equivalent to net income of $1.21 per share, the net sales were $8.4 billion in 2005. Valuation was based on 2005 figures, and Hindalco was paying heavy premium above the true value of Novelis in order to pursue its dream of becoming world's largest aluminum and aluminum products producer.

Though Novelis was the largest player of aluminum rolled products with 19% share in global market place and having the customers like Coke, etc. in its customers' portfolio but their sales were majorly controlled by 5 largest buyers which contributes to 40% sales of the company. Thus, company was dominated by buyers with quantum of sales to the largest buyer amounting to 12% of company's sales.

Dominated by these large buyers, in order to secure the contracts, in the year 2005, management of the company entered into binding agreements with its customer to not to increase the prices above a specific level for next 5 years even if the raw material prices increase. In next year only, aluminum prices sky-rocketed and company had to absorb this increased cost which resulted in losses in 2006. As these contracts were for longer durations, therefore, Novelis was amenable to future losses till these contracts expire in January 2010.

Another tricky issue was that the Novelis was into losses and already had the debt of $2.4 billion on its balance sheet, on a net worth of only $322 million; this made the acquisition more challenging for Hindalco. The consideration of $3.6 billion paid to Novelis shareholders was only for their holdings, and debt was refinanced by another debt. The post-deal debt-to-equity ratio was expected to be approximately 7.2:1 which was very high.

In the light of heavy debt burden, probable losses, the deal price finalized was extremely high. They paid the heavy premium; Hindalco offered $44.93 a share, nearly a 17% premium to where Novelis' shares were trading on announcement day. The analyst considered it to be too high and only an aggressive pricing in the wake of becoming the largest global aluminum player and to be the part of Fortune 500 companies.

11.1.6   Acquisition Process—Deal Structure and Financing

Av Metals Inc., an acquisition subsidiary, created especially for the purpose of acquisition pertinent to the arrangement entered on February 10, 2007, between two parties. The approval for the subsidiary came on May 14, 2007, granted by Ontario Court of Justice. Subsequently, the acquisition subsidiary acquired all the outstanding shares of Novelis (75,415,536) @$44.93/share amounting to $3405 million (or) $3.4 billion. It was then transferred to its wholly-owned subsidiary Av Aluminum Inc. which is a direct subsidiary of Hindalco. The price of $44.93 commanded a 17% premium to the closing price on the preceding day of arrangement.

Novelis, on July 22, 2007, issued 2,044,122 additional common shares to Av Aluminum for $44.93 amounting to $92 million, though not included in the total consideration since it is related to certain costs borne by Novelis. Hindalco assumed a net debt of $2.8 billion of Novelis.

11.1.7 Funding the Deal

The bifurcation of $6 billion deal price was that $3.5 billion they paid in cash and took over $2.5 billion of its debt, including $1 billion in term loans and $1.4 billion in high-yield bonds. The entire funding happened in cash basis. Since the total consideration does not include payment of the debt of Novelis, the amount payable to shareholders of Novelis stood at around $3.5 billion. Since Novelis was carrying such a huge pile of debt amounting to near about $2.4 billion (Debt: Equity stood at nearly 7.23:1), it was next to impossible for Hindalco to opt the route of leveraged buyout. Hindalco arranged the funding for deal by selling treasury stock for $450 million and arranged $3.1 billion through recourse financing on Hindalco's own corporate guarantee. No debt was raised on the Novelis balance sheet to fund the deal. Hindalco took a temporary loan $3.1 billion repayable on November 10, 2008 from consortium of Banks, namely ABN Amro, Bank of America, and UBS. The remaining amount of $450 million was mobilized through internal funding through Hindalco's treasury. (Though some websites state Hindalco's subsidiary provided with $300 million, there are no such items in annual report stating the same.) The debt assumed by Hindalco, which was on the books of Novelis, was refinanced through Novelis' cash flows (see Excerpts).

Hindalco raised $1.25 billion through a right issue and raised term loans amounting to $1 billion from twelve global banks. With the help of these funding and some internal accruals, the 18-month bridge loan of $3.03 billion raised at the time of acquisition was paid off.

11.1.8 Valuation and Issues

Many analyst and industrialist have shared their view that Hindalco paid high price for acquiring a messy business. The company, in the nine months of 2006, posted a loss of $170 million, and the price paid was 36 times the expected earnings of Novelis in 2007. This wasn't cheap.

Other thought, was also that synergy which is anticipated, might not be that effective, if in case aluminum prices fluctuate on a larger scale. The flow of benefit is also expected on a long-term benefit. This would also pressurize the Hindalco's profitability since the debt-to-equity ratio of Hindalco will shoot to 1.8 times from 0.66 thereby increasing the interest burden.

As per SEC filings of Novelis, Morgen Stanely analyzed the valuation, and the excerpts from filing are given below:

The $44.93 per share in cash to be paid as consideration for the arrangement, which represents a 17% premium to the closing price of our common shares on February 9, 2007, and a 49% premium to the closing price of our common shares on January 25, 2007, the day before we announced that we were negotiating with potential buyers.

11.1.9   Valuation Based on Peer Company Analysis

Morgan Stanley noted trading multiple ranges for the peer group companies of $7.0\times$ to $8.0\times$ 2006 EBITDA and $6.5\times$ to $7.0\times$ 2007 EBITDA. Morgan Stanley compared these ranges to multiples for Novelis of $8.6\times$ 2006 Adjusted EBITDA and $8.3\times$ 2007 Adjusted EBITDA as implied by the consideration to be received by our shareholders in the arrangement.

11.1.10   Valuation Based on Precedent Transactions

The following table presents the high, low, and median aggregate value to LTM EBITDA for the precedent transactions:

	Aggregate value/LTM EBITDA
Low	$5.4\times$
High	$10.8\times$
Median	$6.3\times$
Arrangement Agreement Consideration	$8.6\times$

Morgan Stanley noted a multiple range of $6.5\times$ to $7.5\times$ of LTM EBITDA for selected precedent transactions and compared such range to a multiple for us of $8.6\times$ LTM Adjusted EBITDA implied by the consideration to be received by our shareholders in the Arrangement.

11.1.11   *Valuation Based on DCF Analysis*

Morgan Stanley analyzed Novelis business using three financial forecasts prepared by our management. Using a scenario that assumed consistent aluminum rolled product shipment growth and increasing profitability over the forecast period ("Case A"), the result of the discounted cash flow analysis implied a range of values for our common shares of approximately $28 to $38 per share. Using a scenario that contemplated an economic downturn occurring in 2009 ("Case B"), the result of the discounted cash flow analysis implied a range of values for our common shares of approximately $25 to $32 per share. Using a scenario that contemplated a similar economic downturn as in Case B but occurring in 2007 ("Case C"), the result of the discounted cash flow analysis implied a range of values for our common shares of approximately $21 to $28 per share.

In summary, the analyses implied the following ranges of value per share of our common shares:

	Value per share
Case A	$28–$38
Case B	$25–$32
Case C	$21–$28

Morgan Stanley compared the range of per share values observed in each of its discounted cash flow analyses with the consideration to be received by our shareholders in the arrangement of $44.93 per share.

11.1.12   *Stock Market Reaction to the Deal*

After the announcement day, Hindalco stock plunged by approximately 14% as the market considered the deal price to be too high in the light of losses and heavy debt on the balance sheet of target and uncertain synergy. While the Novelis stock gained heavily as the news was extremely good for the shareholders of loss-making giant entity and premium was high in comparison with fair value of Novelis. Following charts depicts the stock price movement of both the entities around the acquisition event in February 2007.

11.1.13   Hindalco: (for the Year 2007)

Source https://economictimes.indiatimes.com/markets/technical-charts?symbol=HINDALCOEQ&exchange=NSE&entity=company&periodicity=day.

11.1.14   Novelis Stock Performance

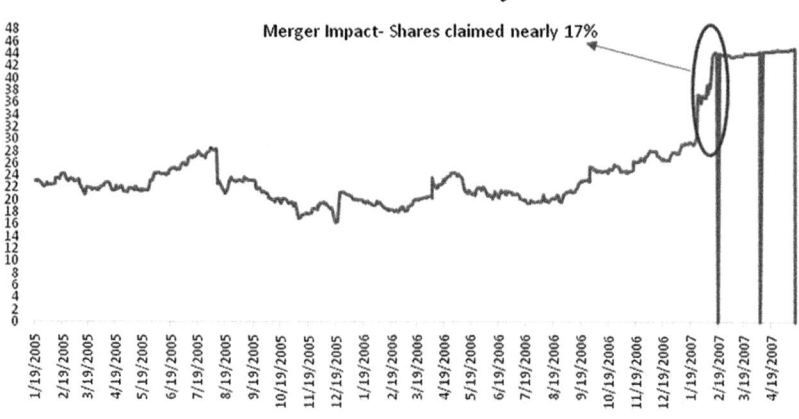

11.1.15   Post-Deal Outcomes

11.1.15.1 Year Ended 2008

Hindalco consolidated statements reported a flat profit of Rs. 2387 Cr in 2008 (2007 profits stood at Rs. 2686 Cr) despite posting a revenue growth of 211% (approx.) in 2008 (Rs. 60,013 Cr) in comparison with

2007 (Rs. 19,316 Cr) sales. The main reason of almost no growth in profits was increased interest cost caused by the debt-funded acquisition of Novelis. Interest cost increased by approximately 488%.

Novelis also posted a significant improvement in their financials driven by lower operating cost, reduced exposure to price ceiling contracts. Normalized EBITDA of Novelis increased from $303 million in 2007 to $491 million in 2008 indicating a growth of 62%. Free cash flows also improved by $164 million on the back of better working capital management, volume improvements, refinancing of senior secured credit, etc.

11.1.15.2 Year Ended 2009

In 2009, the performance of consolidated entity declined, depicted by decline in net profit (after Minority Interest and Share in Associates) from Rs. 2193 Cr in 2008 to Rs. 485 Cr in 2009 depicting a decline of around 78% in earnings. Net worth eroded from Rs. 17,286 Cr to Rs. 15,798 Cr.

During the year 2009, Novelis has posted a loss of $1.9 billion, which was primarily because of the goodwill impairment. Free cash flows got worsened on the back of same to reach negative $353 million.

Meanwhile, Hindalco's net profit also declined by 22% to Rs. 2230 Cr because of the decline of commodity markets lead by subprime crisis.

However, Hindalco repaid the bridge loan by using the remaining amount of 1500 Cr (approx.) of the previous rights issue and freshly issued rights stocks amounting to 4500 Cr. The remaining money was arranged through liquidating the treasury investments.

11.1.15.3 Year 2010

Year 2010 was excellent for Novelis. It posted a net income of $405 million where EBITDA increased by 55%. Free cash flow also improved strongly to $355 million.

The key reason for the increase was the integration of the merger. Despite a sales drop of 15%, Novelis was able to post tremendous result because of the cost reduction exercise, favorable contracts, and efficiency improvements. Novelis also announced its expansion in Brazil to meet the increasing demand. This was supposed to directly result in capacity maximization.

Though Novelis saw an increased profitability and margins, the cash was trapped in company as there were restrictive debt covenants curbing the access to cash by Hindalco. On the other hand, Hindalco was requiring Rs. 23,000 Cr in order to fund its growth plans by means of Capex.

To make the cash fungible, Hindalco came up with a strategy called Project Nalanda, where the objective was to integrate the two companies financially. As accord to the strategy, Hindalco refinanced the debt of Novelis by imparting $4.8 billion fresh debt wherein $4 billion would be the term loans with 7–10 year maturities and $800 million serving as a working capital loan. The earlier restriction of deployment of capital was eased down, as the fresh inflow of funds was agreed upon by the bond-holders as the net debt to EBITDA was only three times. This made Novelis access cash to enhance its operations on further scales which would help in repayment of the debt infused by Hindalco. Thereby, this was icing the cake in helping Novelis improve its financial performance and also helped Hindalco with continued remittances.

11.1.16   Stock Performance

11.1.16.1 Since the Date of Acquisition

Source https://www.valueresearchonline.com/stocks/snapshot.asp?code=1549 &utm_source=direct-click&utm_medium=stocks&utm_term=&utm_content=Hindalco+Inds.&utm_campaign=vro-search.

11.1.17   Some Facts

- Hindalco M.Cap before announcement of acquisition: Rs. 20,084.28 Cr.
- M.cap after the announcement of acquisition: Rs. 17,325.28 Cr.
- Demand for automotive sheet exceeded 1 million tons in 2015 and is expected to touch 1.7 million by 2020.

- Worldwide Aluminum capacity in the year 2007—38,132 kt.
- Worldwide Aluminum capacity in the year 2016 (till September)—38,061 kt.
- Hindalco Aluminium caters automotive and transportation, building and construction, pharmaceuticals, electricals and electronics, industrial applications, white goods, defence, and packaging.

Hindalco Production Capacity 2007
1. Primary Metal—477,723 mt
2. Wire Rods—71,798 mt
3. Flat-Rolled Products—215,198 mt
4. Extructions—43,315 mt
5. Wheels—174,069 mt
6. Foils—27,756 mt

- Novelis top customers include Agfa-Gevaert N.V., Can-Pack S.A., Anheuser-Busch Companies, Inc., affiliates of Ball Corporation, various bottlers of the Coca-Cola system, Ford Motor Company, Alcan's packaging business group, Crown Cork & Seal Company, Inc., Lotte Aluminum Co. Ltd., Kodak Polychrome Graphics GmbH, Rexam Plc, Ryerson Tull, Inc., Tetra Pak Ltd., Pactiv Corporation, Daching Holdings Limited, and ThyssenKrupp AG.
- In 2006, approximately 43% of the net sales of Novelis were for its top 10 large customers whom they were supplying for more than 20 years. Rolled Products Shipments: 2006—1229 kt, 2016—3123 kt.
- Till now Novelis hasn't been merged with Hindalco. It stays as the indirect subsidiary of Hindalco. Novelis registered a record sale of $11.1 billion in the year 2015.

11.1.18 *Questions for Discussion*

1. Based on post-merger financial and stock price performance of Hindalco, comment upon the ability of Hindalco to turnaround the Novelis?
2. Ignoring the post-merger outcome, do you think Novelis acquisition by Hindalco was a right move in 2007?
3. What were the major challenges in front of Hindalco as an aggressive acquirer? What would have been the fate of this deal, if 2008 Global Crisis wouldn't have been there?

4. Do you think that expanding to downstream business, in which Hindalco had a very little presence, was a wrong move? Do you think, if they would have expanded only in their core competencies (upstream products) then shareholder's wealth would have multiplied?

Exhibit I

CONSOLIDATED STATEMENTS OF OPERATIONS
(In millions, except per share amounts)

	Year Ended March 31, 2010 *Successor*	Year Ended March 31, 2009 *Successor*	May 16, 2007 Through March 31, 2008 *Successor*	April 1, 2007 Through May 15, 2007 *Predecessor*
Net sales	$ 8,673	$ 10,177	$ 9,965	$ 1,281
Cost of goods sold (exclusive of depreciation and amortization shown below)	7,190	9,251	9,042	1,205
Selling, general and administrative expenses	360	319	319	95
Depreciation and amortization	384	439	375	28
Research and development expenses	38	41	46	6
Interest expense and amortization of debt issuance costs	175	182	191	27
Interest income	(11)	(14)	(18)	(1)
(Gain) loss on change in fair value of derivative instruments, net	(194)	556	(22)	(20)
Impairment of goodwill	—	1,340	—	—
Gain on extinguishment of debt	—	(122)	—	—
Restructuring charges, net	14	95	6	1
Equity in net (income) loss of non-consolidated affiliates	15	172	(25)	(1)
Other (income) expenses, net	(25)	86	(6)	35
	7,946	12,345	9,908	1,375
Income (loss) before income taxes	727	(2,168)	57	(94)
Income tax provision (benefit)	262	(246)	73	4
Net income (loss)	465	(1,922)	(16)	(98)
Net income (loss) attributable to noncontrolling interests	60	(12)	4	(1)
Net income (loss) attributable to our common shareholder	$ 405	$ (1,910)	$ (20)	$ (97)

Source http://app.quotemedia.com/data/downloadFiling?webmasterId=101533 &ref=6981661&type=HTML&symbol=1304280&companyName=Novelis%2C+Inc.+&formType=10-K&dateFiled=2010-05-27&cik=1304280, page 70.

11.1.18.1 Hindalco Plant Locations

46 Operations in 13 countries

Industry Structure (Globally)

11.1.19   Domestic Market Share

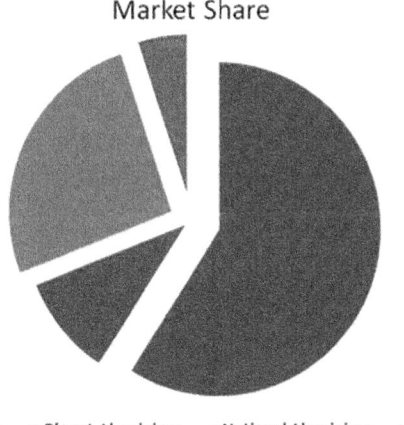

Market Share

■ Hindalco   ■ Bharat Aluminium   ■ National Aluminium   ■ Others

Excerpts:

Table 7.1   Production capacity: Hindalco vis-à-vis Novelis

	2005 (in tonnes)	2006 (in tonnes)
Hindalco	190,581*	211,088*
Novelis	2,873,000**	2,960,000**

Notes: * Actual production of rolled products against installed capacity of 200,000.
** Shipments of rolled products.
Source: Hindalco Industries Ltd., Annual Report 2007, p. 100; and Novelis Inc., 10-K, 1 March 2007, p. 51.

Table 7.3   Major sources of funding

Sl. No.	Source	US $million
1	ABN AMRO	384.64
2	Bank of America	280.63
3	UBS (Singapore Branch)	280.00
4	Bank of India	185.53
5	ICICI Bank	180.26
6	Mizuho Corporate Bank	180.26
7	Deutsche Bank (Singapore Branch)	178.16
8	Citibank (Bahrain Branch)	175.00
9	Standard Chartered Bank	175.00
10	Sumitomo Mitsui Banking Corp	175.00
11	State Bank of India	170.00
12	Bank of Tokyo-Mitsubishi UFJ	150.00
13	BNP Paribas	135.53
14	HSBC	125.00
15	Rabobank	105.26
16	Calyon	100.00
17	Commonwealth Bank of Australia (Singapore Branch)	50.00
	Total	3,030.27

11.2   Hewlett-Packard Company (HP) and Compaq Computer Corporation (Compaq)

The case gives an overview of the merger between two leading players in the global computer industry—Hewlett-Packard Company (HP) and Compaq Computer Corporation (Compaq). The case explores the reasons for HP's failure to realize the synergies identified prior to the merger. It highlights that the leadership, legacy, and cultural issues play an important role in mergers. The case describes in detail the rationale for HP–Compaq merger, problems faced in integrating the merged entities and whether the merger made business and economic sense. It also describes the product profile of the merged entity and how the new HP compares with its major competitors, IBM and Dell Computers.

Finally, the case presents the challenges faced by the new CEO of HP, Mark Hurd, in mid-2005. The case is designed to help students critically analyze a merger deal and understand the various issues involved such as product synergies, cost savings, and technological compatibility. The case also provides an insight into the possible hurdles that might crop up while implementing a megamerger.

"The HP-Compaq merger was a big bet that didn't pay off, that didn't even come close to attaining what Fiorina and HP's board said was in store. At bottom, they made a huge error in asserting that the merger of two losing computer operations, HP's and Compaq's, would produce a financially fit computer business."

11.2.1   A Megamerger

On September 4, 2001, two leading players in the global computer industry—Hewlett-Packard Company (HP) and Compaq Computer Corporation (Compaq)—announced their merger. HP was to buy Compaq for US$24 billion in stock in the biggest ever deal in the history of the computer industry. The merged entity would have operations in more than 160 countries with over 145,000 employees and would offer the industry's most complete set of products and services. However, the stock markets reacted negatively to the merger announcement with shares of both companies collapsing—in just two days, HP and Compaq share prices declined by 21.5% and 15.7% respectively. Together, the pair lost US$13 billion in market capitalization in a couple of days. In the next two weeks, HP's stock went down by another 17%, amidst a lot of negative comments about the merger from analysts and the company's competitors. Industry analysts wondered what benefits HP, a global market leader in the high-margin printers business, would reap in acquiring a personal computer (PC) manufacturer like Compaq at a time when PCs were fast emerging as low-margin commodity products. Though the merger helped HP in achieving economies of scale in the PC business, it faced fierce competition from Dell Computers (Dell),[1] a low-cost, direct-marketer of PCs. The merger also did not help HP to compete with IBM, which not only sold PCs[2] but was also a market leader in the high-margin consulting and service businesses. In June 2005, HP's shares hovered around US$23 per share, below the price just before the merger was announced. This indicated that the merger had failed to create shareholder value. In contrast, the share price of US-based Lexmark, HP's major competitor and the second largest company in the printers business, rose by 60%, while Dell's share price moved up by 90% in the same period. With the PC and other hardware businesses of HP making minuscule profits, analysts opined that the company's printer business should be spun off into a standalone company. Commenting on the dilemma faced by HP, George Day (Day), Professor of Marketing at Wharton School of Business, University of Pennsylvania, said, "HP is trying to be cost competitive with Dell and be the same kind of integrated-solutions provider that IBM has become. If that doesn't work—if it's clear IBM has too big a lead—then HP, which has this hugely profitable printer business, has to think about breaking up."

11.2.2   Background Note

11.2.2.1 HP
Stanford engineers Bill Hewlett and David Packard started HP in California in 1938 as an electronic instruments company. Its first product was a resistance-capacity audio oscillator, an electronic instrument used to test sound equipment. During the 1940s, HP's products rapidly gained acceptance among engineers and scientists. HP's growth was

---

[1] http://www.icmrindia.org/casestudies/catalogue/Business%20Strategy/HP-Compaq%20-%20A%20Failed%20Merger.htm#bot2.

[2] http://www.icmrindia.org/casestudies/catalogue/Business%20Strategy/HP-Compaq%20-%20A%20Failed%20Merger.htm#bot3.

aided by heavy purchases made by the US government during World War II. During the 1950s, HP developed strong technological capabilities in the rapidly evolving electronics business. HP came out with its first public issue in 1957. HP entered the medical field in 1961 by purchasing Sanborn Company.

In 1963, HP entered into a joint venture agreement with Yokogawa Electric Works of Japan to form Yokogawa-Hewlett-Packard. In 1966, the company established HP Laboratories, to conduct research activities relating to new technologies and products. During the same year, HP designed its first computer for controlling some of its test-and-measurement instruments.

During the 1970s, HP continued its tradition of innovation. In 1974, HP launched its first minicomputer that was based on 4K dynamic random access semiconductors (DRAMs) instead of magnetic cores. In 1977, John Young was named HP president, marking a transition from the era of the founders to a new generation of professional managers. During the 1980s, HP emerged as a major player in the computer industry, offering a full range of computers from desktop machines to powerful minicomputers. This decade also saw the development of successful products like the inkjet and laserjet printers. HP introduced its first PC in 1981, followed by an electronic mail system in 1982…

11.2.3   The Rationale for the Merger

In the late 1990s, the PC industry slipped into its worst-ever recessionary phase, resulting in losses of US$1.2 billion and 31,000 layoffs by September 2001. According to analysts, with the computer industry commoditizing and consolidating very fast, mergers had become inevitable. The HP-Compaq merger thus did not come as a major surprise to industry observers. The details of the merger were revealed in an HP press release issued soon after the merger was announced. The new company was to retain the HP name and would have revenues of US$87.4 billion—almost equivalent to the industry leader IBM (US$88.396 billion in 2000).

Under the terms of the deal, Compaq shareholders would receive 0.6325 shares of the new company for each share of Compaq. HP shareholders would own approximately 64% and Compaq shareholders 36% of the merged company. Fiorina was to remain Chairman and CEO of the new company while Capellas was to become the President...

11.2.4   The Merger Integration

The new HP developed a white paper giving complete details of its post-merger product strategy. The HP and Compaq brand names were retained for desktop PCs and notebooks for both consumers and commercial segments. The merged entity supported Compaq's brand name for its servers while it continued with HP for workstations. The electronic shopping sites of both the companies were also integrated. To make the merger work, the new HP initially focused on two areas—avoiding culture clashes internally and reducing any problems to the customers. The company devoted a significant amount of time in planning to minimize any instance of culture clashes that usually happened in such megamergers. The task of ensuring this was given to Susan Bowick, HP's senior VP of HR. She put all employees through a training workshop named as "**Fast Start**," designed to explain the merged entity's new organizational structure and allow employees to overcome concerns about their new coworkers. HP also made efforts to strengthen its image as a single unified company...

11.2.5   Does the Merger Make Business Sense

Soon after the HP-Compaq merger deal was approved by the HP's board and its shareholders in March 2002, industry analysts termed the deal as a strategic blunder. Critics ridiculed Fiorina by saying that one bad PC business merged with another bad PC business does not make a good PC company.

Many analysts felt that the synergies HP foresaw would not materialize easily. They said that the merged company would have to cut costs drastically in order to beat Dell in PCs, while constantly investing money in research and development and consulting to compete with IBM and Sun Microsystems.

In the high-end server markets, IBM and Sun Microsystems were constantly introducing new products. Since more than half of the new HP's sales came from low-margin PCs, analysts expressed concerns that it would not have enough cash to invest in R&D in order to compete in the high-end market.

11.2.6   Does the Merger Make Economic Sense

A few HP divisions that were big revenue earners were not able to contribute correspondingly to profits. An analysis of the company's business segment revenues in the fiscal 2004 revealed that the Enterprise Storage andServers and the Personal Systems divisions, the erstwhile Compaq strongholds brought in revenues of US$39.774 billion, comprising approximately 50% of HP's total revenues (refer Exhibit II for HP's business segment information for the fiscal 2002–2004).

However, the operating profits from both these divisions combined were US$383 million, less than 1% of the divisions' revenues. Moreover, the total contribution of these two divisions in the overall operating profits of HP of US$5.473 billion was just 7%. Another major business of the erstwhile Compaq, HP services which generated revenues of US$13.778 billion, witnessed a fall in operating profits from US$1.362 billion in fiscal 2003 to US$1.263 billion in fiscal 2004. HP's own imaging and printing was the only business division that posted respectable operating profits of US$3.847 billion...The Challenges Ahead.

Due to inability to revive the performance of hardware businesses, HP's board asked Fiorina to step down as the company's Chairman and CEO on February 9, 2005. The day Fiorina resigned, the shares of HP increased by 6.9% on the New York Stock Exchange. Commenting on this, Robert Cihra, an analyst with Fulcrum Global Partners said, "The stock is up a bit on the fact that nobody liked Carly's leadership all that much. The Street had lost all faith in her and the market's hope is that anyone will be better…

Exhibit II

HEWLETT-PACKARD COMPANY AND SUBSIDIARIES
SEGMENT INFORMATION
(Unaudited)
(In millions)

Net revenue (which includes intersegment revenue) and earnings from operations for each segment are provided in the tables below, which includes a reconciliation to our consolidated condensed statement of earnings:

	Twelve months ended October 31,	
	2004	2003 [a]
Net revenue:		
Enterprise Storage and Servers	$ 15,152	$ 14,593
Software	922	774
HP Services	13,778	12,357
Technology Solutions Group	29,852	27,724
Imaging and Printing Group	24,199	22,569
Personal Systems Group	24,622	21,210
Financing	1,895	1,921
Corporate Investments	449	344
Total segments	81,017	73,768
Eliminations of inter-segment net revenue and other	(1,112)	(707)
Total HP Consolidated	$ 79,905	$ 73,061
Earnings from operations:		
Enterprise Storage and Servers	$ 173	$ 142
Software	(145)	(190)
HP Services	1,263	1,362
Technology Solutions Group	1,291	1,314
Imaging and Printing Group	3,847	3,596
Personal Systems Group	210	22
Financing	125	79
Corporate Investments	(178)	(161)
Total segments	5,295	4,850
Corporate and unallocated costs, and eliminations	(260)	(310)
Restructuring charges	(114)	(800)
Amortization of purchased intangible assets	(603)	(563)
Acquisition-related charges	(54)	(280)
In-process research and development charges	(37)	(1)
Interest and other, net	35	21
Gains (losses) on investments	4	(29)
Litigation settlement	(70)	-
Total HP Consolidated Earnings Before Taxes	$ 4,196	$ 2,888

(a) Certain reclassifications have been made to prior year amounts in order to conform to the current year presentation.

HEWLETT-PACKARD COMPANY AND SUBSIDIARIES
SEGMENT INFORMATION
(Unaudited)
(In millions)

Net revenue (which includes intersegment revenue) and earnings from operations for each segment are provided in the tables below, which includes a reconciliation to our consolidated condensed statement of earnings:

	Twelve months ended October 31,	
	2003	2002 [a], [b] (Combined Company)
Net revenue:		
Imaging and Printing Group	$ 22,623	$ 20,447
Personal Systems Group	21,228	21,895
Enterprise Systems Group	15,379	16,194
HP Services	12,305	12,326
Financing	1,921	2,088
Corporate Investments	345	284
Total segments	73,801	73,234
Eliminations of intersegment net revenue and other	(740)	(888)
Total HP Consolidated	$ 73,061	$ 72,346
Earnings (loss) from operations:		
Imaging and Printing Group	$ 3,570	$ 3,345
Personal Systems Group	19	(372)
Enterprise Systems Group	(54)	(664)
HP Services	1,372	1,369
Financing	79	(128)
Corporate Investments	(161)	(232)
Total segments	4,825	3,318
Acquisition-related inventory write-downs	-	(147)
Corporate and unallocated costs, and eliminations	(285)	(180)
Restructuring charges	(800)	(1,780)
Amortization of goodwill and purchased intangible assets	(563)	(664)
Acquisition-related charges	(280)	(772)
In-process research and development charges	(1)	(793)
Interest and other, net	21	20
Net Investment losses and other, net	(29)	(56)
Total HP Consolidated Earnings Before Taxes	$ 2,888	$ (1,054)

(a) Certain reclassifications have been made to prior year amounts in order to conform to the current year presentation.

(b) The combined company results of each of HP's segments for the twelve months ended October 31, 2002 include the results of Compaq as if the merger had taken place as of the beginning of the period presented. Due to different fiscal period ends for HP and Compaq, the results for the twelve months ended October 31, 2002 combine the results of HP for the twelve months ended October 31, 2002 and the historical quarterly results of Compaq for the six-month period ended March 31, 2002 and for the period May 3, 2002 (the acquisition date) to October 31, 2002.

REFERENCES

http://www.hindalco.com/about-us.

http://novelis.mediaroom.com/index.php?s=127.

http://www.hindalco.com/investor-centre/reports-and-presentations.

https://www.valueresearchonline.com/stocks/snapshot.asp?code=1549&utm_source=direct-click&utm_medium=stocks&utm_term=hindalco&utm_content=Hindalco+Inds.&utm_campaign=vro-search.

http://www.business-standard.com/article/companies/novelis-shot-in-the-arm-for-hindalco-112120100074_1.html.

Printed by Printforce, the Netherlands